THE COMPLETE
Afghan Hound

by CONSTANCE O. MILLER
and EDWARD M. GILBERT, JR.

ILLUSTRATED
including special drawings
by Lois Gossner

Third Edition
1977 — 3rd Printing

HOWELL BOOK HOUSE INC.

730 FIFTH AVENUE

NEW YORK, N.Y.   10019

Her Majesty, Queen Homaira of Afghanistan, being greeted
by Charlotte Gilbert and Khanjee's Rondeau on September
15, 1963.

*To our families who sacrificed countless
hours of companionship that this book
should become possible*

*This book is also dedicated to the
dignified and aloof "King of Dogs"—the Afghan Hound*

Contents

Cover: Original oil painting from Constance O. Miller's collection by artist Lois Gossmer of Ch. Crown Crest Topaz (Ch. Ophaal of Crown Crest Tae-Joan), black-mask red dog, bred by Kay Finch, owned by Gordon W. and Constance O. Miller.

Foreword
to Third Edition

WHEN it originally appeared in 1965 this was the first and only Afghan Hound "breed book" to be published in the United States. Indeed, except for Hubbard's excellent but slender British "Handbook" some 15 years earlier, it was the first in the world.

As such it required a tremendous amount of work by the authors in research, writing and organizing. During the then 39 years that the Afghan Hound had been in the United States little had been done to compile accurate basic records on the breed. Each first-hand account of the breed in Afghanistan seemed to contradict all others. And beneath the surface of the commonly accepted "ancient history" of the Afghan Hound lurked an almost impossible tangle of slender threads. Obviously, this was a project requiring an extraordinary range of talents and knowledge and an appalling amount of time and energy.

Perhaps the best evidence of how well the authors succeeded in their formidable task lies in the fact that, although other books on the Afghan Hound have since been written and published, each with its merits, this volume remains the most complete and definitive work on the breed. Its subsequent printings and editions have required little in the way of corrections; as in this latest edition, the changes have been largely a matter of updating to include more recent dogs and history.

The major reason for the success which this book has had lies, of course, in having found the right authors and publisher. Conni Miller brought to the task years of practical experience in breeding and raising Afghan Hounds, plus a lively and perceptive interest in every other aspect of the breed and its history. Together, she and Ed Gilbert possessed an unusually appropriate background in scholarship and a strong determination to get at the facts and to assemble them in a clear and balanced presentation. All told, they spent two years of virtually full-time work researching, writing, compiling records and collecting illustrations. The result was one for which the entire Afghan Hound fancy will long be grateful.

In Howell Book House this volume was also fortunate in finding the right publisher—one able and willing to produce a relatively large and handsome volume on a breed which then had a relatively small circle of fanciers.

That circle, however, began to expand greatly and rapidly as the book was being written and published. At the start of the project in 1963, annual AKC Afghan Hound registrations meandered up to the 1,000 mark after some 15 years of hovering in the mid-100s. At that point, however, registrations began to skyrocket, increasing more than six-fold in the next eight years, with corresponding rises in the number of fanciers and in the amount of breeding and exhibiting activity.

This boom, of course, was good for the book, but the book may have been even more beneficial to the boom. Prior to its appearance, virtually the only sources of information on the breed were magazine articles, correspondence and word-of-mouth. These sources were hardly adequate to meet the needs when newcomers to the breed were few and far between; when they started numbering in the thousands, the information gap would have been abysmal without a reference such as this.

Here, in one place, are solid facts and sound advice on every aspect of the Afghan Hound. For the novice it provides answers for all the basic questions. For the veteran fancier, it serves as a storehouse of more information and data than any one head could possibly hold.

For anyone living with an Afghan Hound, this is not only a volume of fascinating reading, but a book with which you will also find yourself living long after the first reading.

DONALD A. SMITH

Mr. Smith served as Secretary-Treasurer of the Afghan Hound Club of America, Inc., from 1951 to 1955 and as President from 1955 to 1960 and from 1961 to 1967.

Preface

WHERE can I find information on the Afghan Hound? How many times has the breeder and exhibitor of the Afghan Hound asked or heard this question? For years, the only available work was Hubbard's *The Afghan Hound* which was printed in England. This book, as Hubbard states, is "merely a small handbook on the breed for those who are interested in it. . . ."

The authors undertook the task of writing *The Complete Afghan Hound* in order to supply the urgent need for a standard reference book on the breed. This book is an attempt to compile a comprehensive story in regard to the Afghan Hound's history, conformation, breeding, feeding, grooming, training and exhibiting. This is not a rehash of old cliches; it is the product of painstaking research into the past in order to compile an accurate story of the Afghan Hound.

No attempt has been made to cover general information pertaining to all breeds in regard to feeding and breeding, but rather to discuss these topics as they relate to the Afghan Hound. In other words, the general subject of dog nutrition can be found in books on feeding dogs, but the peculiar problem of the finicky-eating Afghan Hound is covered herein. Some of the more general books are the *Howell Book of Dog Care and Training* and *The New Standard Book of Dog Care and Training*.

This book has been copiously illustrated to inform the newcomer to the breed and to show the old timer where we have been. The drawings in Chapters 3 and 6 were made specifically for this book by Lois Gossner. All the illustrations will enable us to know better where we are going.

The authors received the help and aid of many people throughout the world. This group included dog fanciers, non-dog fanciers, and Afghan Hound breeders and exhibitors. Their help is greatly appreciated. In particular, the officers and members, both past and present, of the Afghan Hound Club of America provided individual aid and encouragement. Mrs. Waldron S. Macdonald, Secretary of AHCA, was particularly helpful in providing both references and leads to material.

One of the purposes of this book is to promote the Afghan Hound as a breed for those people lucky enough to appreciate his traits. This is also one of the purposes of the parent club and the various regional Afghan Hound clubs. In order to obtain the address of the Afghan Hound club nearest to you, write to the current secretary of the AHCA. The name and address of the current secretary is listed in each issue of *Pure-Bred Dogs—American Kennel Gazette* under The American Kennel Club—Members.

To those who answered our letters, often providing a link in the chain, and the various helpers and contributors to this effort, the thanks of the authors are hereby extended. The authors also thank the librarians, museum curators, and the various scholarly research organizations. In particular, the authors wish to thank Mr. Elsworth Howell, the publisher, for helping and encouraging our efforts, and Mrs. Betty Garrison who so ably typed and retyped the manuscript. Finally, thanks are due to the breeders: without their interest nothing could have been written. But most of all, thanks go to the Afghan Hound—King of Dogs.

1

What Is an Afghan Hound?

THE official breed standard (approved by the American Kennel Club, September 14, 1948) of the Afghan Hound Club of America opens with the following preamble:

> "The Afghan Hound is an aristocrat, his whole appearance one of dignity and aloofness with no trace of plainness or coarseness. He has a straight front, proudly carried head, eyes gazing into the distance as if in memory of ages past. The striking characteristics of the breed—exotic or "eastern" expression, long silky topknot, peculiar coat pattern, very prominent hip bones, large feet, and impression of a somewhat exaggerated bend in the stifle due to profuse trouserings—stand out clearly, giving the Afghan Hound the appearance of what he is, a king of dogs, that has held true to tradition throughout the ages."

This short essence of the "hound" as he should be at maturity means much to the dedicated breeder and knowledgeable judge. But to the passerby who glimpses his first Afghan Hound, the dog presents a bizarre and strange effect, even prompting children to occasionally ask, "Is it a dog?" When told it is an Afghan Hound, there is probably no retort as common or as irritating as the oftheard, "An African what?" With his haughty air and unusual coat pattern, the hound makes a pronounced impact and rarely goes unnoticed in any surroundings. Response to the sight of the hound is instantaneous; viewers are either strongly and immediately attracted to the dog's elegance and "different" beauty, or just as strongly repelled by its strangeness and "comical" aspect. The dog itself is quite apt to reply in kind, being determined to pick his own friends. His reactions to strangers can be most unpredictable.

The Afghan Hound puppy is quite a different matter as no dog goes through such marked transitions during one lifetime, both in temperament and in physical appearance. Born flat-nosed, wrinkly-faced, short-haired, and rat-like, it would take an expert to pick an Afghan Hound puppy from a nest of mongrels of similar size. The breed pattern takes form very slowly. By three months of age, the legs have lengthened to approximately the same length as the body, and the sheen of short hair has been replaced by a dense puppy fluff. The coat begins to lengthen, blurring the outline of the dog's form from toes to tail. "Monkey whiskers" frequently sprout from the sides of a still short and broad muzzle. Accompanying this outlandish appearance is a similarly outlandish puppy personality often thoroughly abandoned in wild, carefree play and knockdown exuberant demonstrations of affection to owners and litter-mates.

The prospective buyer who expects to find more than a faint hint of the flowing-coated, sedate and elegant hound in a pup is certain to be not only disappointed, but fairly skeptical of the parentage of these bewhiskered apparitions. The puppyhood state is an integral part of the hound's unique development. As the frame lengthens and the coating bursts forth, the yearling who has not yet broken "saddle," nor gained firm control of his limbs, is apt to be more reminiscent of a misbegotten sheep dog than of any Afghan Hound-to-be. With the shedding of much facial hair and the development of a natural short-haired saddle running from withers to tip of tail, comes the emergence of an inscrutable "Oriental" attitude and restrained dignity. In maturity, the "foolish Prince" becomes a responsible King.

Many pure-bred dog fanciers in America have read the following description of "The Dog of the Mystic East" by Miss Jean C. Manson in the *American Kennel Gazette* of June 1929:

> "From about three months of age, the Afghan puppy is a most wonderful youngster, all legs and the most lovely soft fur. More like down, and all eyes, just like Teddy Bears. From babyhood, they are most wonderfully gentle, never snatching food and in every way they are most lovable. They make charming pets and are so distinguished looking, stately and graceful that the most fastidious fancier would consider them an ornamental asset. There is something so foreign about his appearance—something perhaps a little outlandish—that the dog brings to mind the splendor of the mysterious East. Instinctively, one associates him with Eastern magnificence, stately palaces, gardens, and courtyards . . . and native attendants to grant their wishes. . . . In spite of this aristocratic appearance and look of reserve, these dogs are the very reverse of unapproachable and are, indeed, most docile and affectionate. A kind word and pat are never forgotten. A rebuff will be taken to heart with great distress."

Modern use of the hounds in fashion illustrations and current emphasis on coat beauty lead outsiders to think of the dog as purely ornamental. Intimate knowledge of these dogs gives clear lie to this concept, and evidences of his amazing mental and physical versatility are astonishing and plentiful. A rare combination of fierce hunting abilities and conversely, gentle herding instincts, endeared him to tribesmen and royalty in turn. His marked physical adaptability to extremes of climatic conditions provided him with the endurance to thrive where other dogs would have perished. His natural wit and independence of thought enabled him to survive with or without the guidance of man as successive civilizations rose and fell. He was as much at home in a tent as in a palace.

Legends place the Afghan Hound in a fantastic variety of situations. Widely quoted claims by the Afghan people place him on the Ark with Noah, as the only representative of the *Canidae*. Archaeological devotees stress his resemblance to some of the ancient Greyhound-type dogs appearing on Egyptian tombs dating back to 3000 B.C. Another student of the lore of antiquity insists the Afghan is the "monkey-faced dog" mentioned in papyrus documents of 4000 B.C. found on the Sinai Peninsula. More recent interpretations of

Chinese manuscripts place the hound in the company of Genghiz Khan and before that time as one of the most primitive of all dogs running with the earliest nomadic tribes that roamed the Steppes of Asia. One of the first Westerners to export the hounds from Afghanistan lays claim for the breed's pre-Christian history on the basis of some ancient and colossal rock carvings from the Balkh area of Afghanistan.

Tales, reeking with the incense and romantic mystery of the Bagdadian Mid East, infer that the Afghan Hound jealously guarded harems of beautiful concubines, and was the pampered pet of Kings' daughters. The Afghan peoples, in rare reference to the breed in native writings, referred to the hound as having been a zealous herder of flocks of sheep, a courier, guard and mascot for war-lords of the tenth century A.D.; and as an animal that primarily made his reputation as a hunting dog *extraordinaire* in the company of tribal chieftains and kings. From India comes an amazing eye-witness account of the hounds functioning as independent, unbidden garrison sentries.

Some of the earliest claims of the versatility and value of the hound are not supported by example. To write a breed book, one might expect that all that is required is a practical knowledge of the breed and an aggregation of articles containing references to the breed and its history. Close scrutiny of the many scattered writings on the Afghan Hound of today and yesteryear, however, brings disappointing evidence that a large part of the literature from books and magazines is nothing but repetition or plagiarism, with amazing embellishments, of a few statements. Many of these statements are of dubious authenticity but accompanied the hounds as they left Afghanistan in the late 1800s and became an inseparable part of the breed's history. When all has been considered in light of present-day knowledge, a distinctly uneasy feeling remains that the basic questions asked most often by the fancy are yet to be solved to the satisfaction of anyone. Such questions are: Where and when did the Afghan Hound originate? What are the differences and the relationship of the Afghan Hound to other sight-hound breeds? What "type" hound is typical of the best of the native Afghan Hound?

In answering such questions, probably the simplest reply is the old Eastern statement on the breed, "No man knoweth whence they came, but there they are and there they stay." In California, the

13

Kato Indians have a story about creation that states: "Negaicho, the creator, the Great Traveler, was walking around creating, and he took along a dog." Many Afghan Hound owners are content with a similar thought: God had a dog, and it was an Afghan Hound. But, as the nature of human beings is to look for explanations, we will attempt to explore what is and what is not known of our breed's colorful past in a concerted effort to discover what an Afghan Hound is.

Original oil painting by F. T. Daws (English artist) of Westmill Omar, Ch. Badshah of Ainsdart, Ch. Asri-Havid of Shazni, and Ch. Sirdar of Ghazni in the Khyber Pass. From collection of Kay Finch, Crown Crest Kennels. Kay has generously willed this historical painting to the American Kennel Club, to be hung in its New York City office.

14

2

Famed Hunting Hounds of Afghanistan

ARCHAEOLOGISTS tell us that dogs were man's first domesticated animals, with signs of the relationship dating back to the beginning of recorded history. Unfortunately the structural details that separate wild dogs from domesticated dogs are extremely subtle, and the true story of where or when man sought the services of dogs remains conjecture. We know only that in antiquity, the dog had become practically universal, roaming the globe in a wide variety of shapes and sizes.

Kennel club grouping and common sense place the Afghan Hound with the "Greyhounds," a generic term for a family of unusually long-limbed, long-muzzled, swift dogs that overtake and quickly dispatch game by means of sharp eyesight as opposed to trailing a ground scent. The Afghan Hound fits the group easily but can also follow a spoor with considerable talent.

Gazehounds (those which hunt by sight), ranging from the stately 36-inch Irish Wolfhound to the terrier-sized Whippet, are known for their lean, oval-shaped bodies and "tucked up" narrow loins within a range of lighter to heavier frames. In structure the Afghan is intermediate, possessing larger feet, more breadth of body, and less streamlining than other Greyhounds of comparable size. Among the coursing breeds the Afghan is not, nor was he meant to be, the leader in sheer straightaway speed. But, as a jumper and broken field runner, he is without peer, being built for the rigors of actual prolonged field combat with a wide variety of game under difficult ground conditions. His ability to wheel, dodge, and leap obstacles must be seen to be believed.

There is conclusive proof that a greyhound type, long-jawed and long-limbed, was among the very earliest of the recorded domestic dogs. At Tepe Garwa, a few miles northeast of Mosul in north Iraq, an ancient stamp seal considered to be over 5,000 years old was excavated with the likeness of just such a hound on it. A pre-Sumerian skull from the same site was shown to be remarkably similar to that of the Salukis that inhabit the area today. But archaeologists rarely find the soft fleshy parts that are needed for meaningful precise breed identification. Aside from the sheer size, it is primarily the differences seen in ears, tails and coats that clearly distinguish the various greyhound breeds.

The majority of today's greyhounds carry an intermediate or "rose ear," small in size, that folds back against the side of the head. Only the rare Ibizan Hound of the Balaeric Islands off Spain still exhibits a large archaic upright hound ear. Among the gazehounds, the Afghan Hound and the closely related hounds of Persia and Arabia alone have retained the pendent "lop" ear so common in short-legged scent hounds and other canine groups.

Sighthound coats range from the smooth velvet of the Greyhound proper through the harsh roughness of the English Deerhounds and Wolfhounds to the soft wavy coat of the Borzoi. The Arabian Saluki is basically a smooth-coated hound, but there is a highly prized "fringed" variety characterized by its exquisite, heavily plumed tail and thick furnishings on ears and toes. Despite the extreme and deliberate development of long, thick coats on modern Afghan Hounds, a study of the breed in Afghanistan indicated that in coating the hounds begin where the Saluki leaves off, and the Afghan's hunting dog is casually accepted in a wide variety of coat types from smooth-haired to shaggy or corded.

In searching for valid breed differences between the Saluki and

16

the Afghan Hound, one finds himself on loose ground. While the Afghan is said to have lower-set ears, a shorter, higher-held tail and more prominent hipbones, in actuality there is great overlapping of these characteristics in the two breeds. With such muddy breed boundaries, most early writers preferred to lump the Saluki and the Afghan together as Oriental greyhounds. Yet a fair amount is known of the history of the Saluki, and it is a question of just how much of this history can be rightly claimed by the Afghan Hound that remains unanswered. A newspaper clipping from Kabul, Afghanistan, dated 8 August 1962, written by Gulbaz, clearly illustrates the overlapping coat characteristics.

> "The greyhound or 'Tazi' as it is called all over Afghanistan . . . There are three popular breeds of this dog. One is called 'Bakhmull' meaning 'velvet' because it has a long silky coat which covers the whole body including the ears. Another is called 'Luchak' or smoothcoated, and the third one is 'Kalagh' (rhyming with 'blast') which has long silky hairs on its ears and legs, but the rest of the body is smoothcoated."

This same article depicts the Afghan shepherd's dog as somewhat similar in the range of size, colors, and coat varieties to the native greyhounds. But the massive-headed "sheepdogs" are decidedly different in build, showing a marked affinity to the powerful and brutish Tibetan Mastiff.

The Afghan Hound as a breed is reputed to be heavier-boned and less delicate than the Saluki, but the breeds vary greatly within themselves. Such diversity is definitely not random, but to a marked extent follows geographical patterns. The lowland Afghans of south and west Afghanistan, towards Iran or Baluchistan, lean towards the sparse coat and the lean and racy build of the adjacent Saluki types. But the Afghan Hounds of the rugged mountain country of the formidable Hindu Kush range tend to be shorter, more powerfully built, and often considerably shaggier-coated. As a matter of fact, only in these mountain areas surrounding the ancient city of Kabul has our modern concept of full-coated hounds with flying topknots been reported in considerable numbers. It is the mysterious development of the "mountain type" of hound that remains historically perplexing. The discovery of these great shaggy dogs has touched off a never-ending controversy as to which is the senior sight hound, the coated Afghan Hound or the short-haired Saluki type.

In the absence of paleontological evidence, it is necessary to turn to ancient art renderings for clues to superficial breed differences. Dog types, including greyhounds, are found in Egyptian dynastic art tracing back to the third millenium before Christ. This does not mean that such dogs were necessarily indigenous to Egypt as the bulk of osteological evidence points to prior importation from other areas, but we are greatly indebted to Pharaonic scribes for their picturesque renderings of animals known to them. Tomb paintings include greyhounds adorned with elaborate jeweled collars, framed with falcons, gazelle, and other symbols of the chase. These leggy, pointed-jawed Egyptian greyhounds were in contrast to pendulous-lipped, heavy-bodied, huge mastiffs and short-legged hounds of Dachshund proportions. The Pharaoh's greyhounds varied in details of ears and tails, with the very earliest representations illustrating the upright ear. Strangely enough, no "rose-eared" hounds are to be seen, but the "lop" ear becomes increasingly evident in succeeding dynasties. The tails of these greyhounds vary from the short, tight screw tails of today's Basenji through the high curled loops typical of the Afghan Hound to unimpressive limp ropes.

In the tomb of Rekh-mi-Rē of the 18th dynasty (ca. 1450 B.C.), there is a panel depicting a pack of hounds, all lop-eared, with short hair lines on the tails. Most of the tails hang limp, but at least one waves high and fairly well curled. The tomb writings tell that these hounds were a tribute gift from Upper Nubia. The giving of gift dogs was common practice then as it is today. In this manner, ancient dog types quickly spread throughout the world. It is stretching things to connect the long-coated Afghan Hound directly with the dogs of ancient Egypt for, excluding a few short hair lines on the tails, the latter were completely smooth.

Many centuries later in the sixth century B.C., evidence of hounds with some featherings occurs, on a hydria of Athenian fabric and a Hellenistic amphora of the same era. Once into the Christian era, a magnificent feather-tailed dog called a "Persian Greyhound" caught the imagination of European and Oriental artisans. In the 16th century A.D., a marvelous bronze medallion of a graceful beauty was done by Benvenuto Cellini, and similar hounds are to be found

18

Athenian amphora of the 6th century B.C., illustrating a type of Greyhound with a feathered
tail not featured in Egyptian works of the time.

British Museum

A Pack of Hounds: copy in tempera of an Egyptian wall painting dated in the
XVIII Dynasty from the tomb of Rekh-mi-Rē in Thebes.

The Metropolitan Museum of Art

in the delicate brushwork of the Chinese, dating to well over a thousand years ago.

The terms Persian Greyhound or Persian Gazellehound appear rather frequently in canine literature, usually with reference to a fringe-tailed Saluki, but also to a passable light-coated Afghan Hound. Note the prominent hipbones and sturdy bone structure so obvious in the photograph of the Cellini bronze on page 21. The Persian Greyhound is pivotal in the two breeds, being basically smoothcoated, but trimmed with handsome ear fringes and a gracefully ringed plume tail. Featherings to a greater or lesser degree are found on legs, chest, feet, and tail and sometimes shoulders in the pattern seen on today's Setters. The plume-tailed hounds are known to have ranged with man from Arabia, north through Iraq, from Iran into Turkestan, and to whatever far-away fields the trade routes would carry them, even into China.

There is little doubt that the Persian Greyhound is a sub-species of the Saluki, for in all recorded time Persians have called this hound *sag-i Tazi* which translates, "dog from Arabia." There is also little doubt that there are connections between these dogs and Afghan Hounds, if for no other reason than that the Afghan name for their own hunting hound is also *Tazi*.

Artistic representations of the smooth Saluki or the plume-tailed Persian hound are found in many sources. Unfortunately to date absolutely no authenticated representation of an even passably coated Afghan Hound has been found, dating prior to 1800 A.D. To make matters worse, one of the distinguishing characteristics of the Afghan Hound is the fact that his tail is not supposed to be bushy.

The absence of pictorial evidence, however, to support the claim that a long-coated Afghan Hound existed in antiquity, could be due to the historical circumstances surrounding the country of the breed's major development. It is helpful to study Afghanistan with map in hand. Since the beginning of man's migrations for food, wealth and power, the land-locked country now known as Afghanistan has been in the middle of the major overland routes from Greece and Persia to India and China. These routes were formed by ancient tribes of hungry nomads who came from the great Asiatic steppes following the seasonal grasses with huge flocks of sheep and goats, living a transitory existence in tent-camps. The northern region of Afghanistan was once a part of ancient Bactria and came under the

A Meenah of Jajurh with Afghan Hound (1813) from "Letters Written in a Mahratta Camp during the Year 1809" by Thomas D. Broughton. *Courtesy Gerald Massey*

Persian Greyhound: bas relief in bronze by Cellini (1500–72). *Alinari photo, courtesy Fratelli Alinari*

swords of Alexander the Great, Darius, Genghiz Khan and Tamerlane, whose powerful armies cut wide swaths from Persia to India, both coming and going. Residues of the armies remained to occupy the regions of miscellaneous tribes, thereby planting foreign cultures into the ancient soils. In consequence, Afghanistan grew as a loose-knit nation of multiple, highly confusing, and often mobile, layers of changing ethnic groups, desperately clinging to their own identity. Such tribesmen often cannot tell you the names of their grandparents, yet seriously claim direct descent from Timur (Tamerlane). Wandering nomads rarely left tangible messages to posterity, and neither did warring armies. Some accounts of these periods of conquest do appear in ancient Persian and Chinese literature, but rarely mention dogs.

In the seventh century A.D., the overwhelming Islamic religion flooded Afghanistan from the west. Mohammed, determined to strengthen the "one God only" thesis, waged holy wars and dictated grave penalties against the raising of heathen images. Simple drawings of animals concocted idol worship. The dog, which had been revered in previous Zoroastrian times, was suddenly regarded as an unclean object of loathing. The priceless Saluki and Tazi escaped a large part of this stigma, but such religious barriers prevented the preservation of any clear picture of the dogs in Moslem countries. Older evidences may well have been destroyed at this time in Mohammedan idol-breaking frenzies.

The development of the independent country of Afghanistan was marked by constant skirmishes with the neighboring countries and bloody internal tribal power struggles. In recent centuries, the country has been considered "out of bounds" for strangers and a hostile land of mystery. From 1839 to 1921 England established a "protectorate" which was strongly resented by the tribal chiefs. Today the tiny country fights valiantly to remain utterly independent against constantly encroaching political powers.

With scant information available from Afghanistan, the arguments over "which came first, the Saluki or the Afghan Hound?" resolve into two points of view with seemingly logical hypotheses on both sides. Proponents of the coated hounds point to evidence which says the original domestication of herd animals took place in the extensive steppe region of central Asia which includes Mongolia, the Black Sea area, south Russia, north Afghanistan, Iran and Iraq.

Due to the severity of the steppe winters, they contend, it would have been essential for these sheep, goats, cattle and horses to have thick woolly coats for protection against freezing. When these animals were transported to the warmer climates of Egypt and Arabia, their heavy coats would have been useful in cloth-making and thus would have been preserved.

According to this reasoning, it is plausible to assume that the hunting dogs of the most primitive inhabitants of the steppe region would have had similarly long and heavy coats, but that unlike their bovine, ovine and equine neighbors, these hounds would have found no use for their thick hair in the valley of the Nile. Thus a new breed with a short and sleek coat would have been developed for comfort in warmer temperatures.

This argument is hardly congenial to those who credit the Saluki as being the most primitive canine type. Their contention is that the smooth-coated hound could have been carried through Afghanistan and traded in China where evidence exists of Saluki types dating back to the tenth century A.D. Supporters of this theory claim that a blending of one of the "royal hounds" with any one of a number of native types could have supplied the ingredients that differentiate the mountain hound from the Saluki. The similarities between the massive Tibetan Mastiff which is thick and long-coated with a fair length of bushy tail curled over its back and the brutish Afghan shepherd's dog are mentioned. The inference is that a bit of this type of influence could well have drastically changed a poor shivering Saluki into a dog better suited to the terrain. Other debaters point to the better-tempered woolly shepherd's dog of south Russia as a possible relation of the Afghan Hound. Some of these shepherd's dogs are quite graceful and agile and are known to have played a part in the development of the Borzoi. And so the argument runs on . . .

The herding instinct, whether primeval or acquired through blood blending, is not to be glossed over. Verified reports of the regal hound being used with sheep come directly from Afghanistan. Modern fanciers have noticed some Afghan Hounds' tendency to be heel biters and follow round-up procedures at play. Dr. Betsy Porter in England was quite struck by a spontaneous demonstration of herding by one of her champion Afghan Hounds during the Second World War. She was in the habit of taking the dog with her on hospital duties, and then allowed him to run home alongside of the car for the last five miles. One day, when going past a dairy yard with about 30 cows in it, her hound suddenly jumped the fence and herded the cows. He worked them into a small circle and then ran down the field to retrieve a stray. After working it back to the herd, the dog moved the bunch to the corner of the pasture. When satisfied with his work, he jumped back across the fence and continued on his way home.

We seriously doubt that the "which came first" arguments can ever be resolved. The very concept of "breed" is man made for his own purposes. Only through physical restraint and human selection, or through absolute geographical isolation, can any breed be kept pure. There is, however, one valid reason for contemplating the origin of the coated Afghan Hound. Only if the Afghan Hound is actually the primeval type believed by some, are we correct in accepting the various different types of hounds in Afghanistan as being true varieties of one ancient breed. But, if the opponents of the theory are correct and the breed is a more recent mixture of two or more ancient dog types, we must accept the fact that only the precarious mixture seen in the best hounds constitutes the true desired modern "breed," with all other types being degenerates pointing back to the delicate Saluki or the stocky peasant herd-and-guard dog types. As such borderline specimens frequently occur in modern litters, it might be wise not to rely too heavily on the concept of the "ancient Afghan Hound" until one can be located. Instead, we might better work to carefully preserve the best of the hounds described and seen in the 19th and 20th centuries.

Early written accounts of hounds that could conceivably be true coated Afghan Hounds are extremely scarce. A few were found by the amazingly diligent searching of Jackson Sanford who published the results of his studies in the *"Afghan Hound Club of America Bulletin"* of March 1942. In the article entitled, "Are Afghans the Oldest Breed?," Mr. Sanford attempted to trace a logical history of the hound back to the oldest known *Canidae*, or pre-dog forms. While some of his conclusions such as ". . . the Afghan or its immediate ancestor inhabited the steppes of central Asia no less than 100,000 years ago," do seem premature on the basis of available evidence, he did unearth a reference that could just possibly refer to very early Afghan Hounds. Sanford postulated that the Yucchi

24

peoples brought the dog from Central Asia into northern Afghanistan about 126 B.C., basing this on a quotation from a Chinese manuscript of the era describing the Yucchi as follows:

"They are of the race that inhabits the Land of the Frozen Earth. They are keepers of herds, breeders of horses, and drinkers of mare's milk. Their sheep and horses are herded together . . . At night . . . their dogs stand watch by the common herd . . . These dogs are as large as the foals in the herd, black and exceedingly fierce; the hair on them is long and, on the ear, is of such texture that the women shear them as sheep, and make from the ear-wool a felt, which is the material of their finest headgear . . . When they hunt no animal stands before the ferocity of the dogs, and the mounted huntsmen are hard pressed to keep in view of the pack."

While such passages can be applied almost as easily to the fierce Tibetan Mastiffs of Mongolia, nevertheless, black is a known color of the Afghan Hound. The shaggy Asiatic horses of that era were scarcely larger than a good-sized pony, therefore the size of a "foal" (new born colt) is well within the size range of the hound.

A more specific description from the time of Tamerlane, in the 14th century A.D., is found in *Zafar-nama*, Sarafu 'd-Din, Calcutta, 1887, as follows:

"Now you should be informed that the people of this land beyond the river (Oxus) have a race of hounds as large as young colts, which excited the interest of the Tartars to no small degree . . . When we first saw them in no case could we come up with any. They looked down at us from the strongholds of their mountain master, a thousand feet above and eluded us. They amazed us by the (three words undecipherable) with which they eluded the arrows we sped at them . . . At night they would come in silence, like great cats, and (having been trained in this art by their roguish masters), they would loose the horses' tethers and lead them away. One such fell victim to Dojhur's arrow, and we examined the beast with amazement. Except on the foreface, the hair on these dogs . . . is long and tangled. The ears are abundantly hairy and drooping, as are none of other beasts. The Chinese surgeons examined the dog; they say that its stomach is under the

25

great-rib. The captives from Herat had seen such dogs in the hills to the Westward. The mountain chieftains, they say, are wont to hunt with these hounds, and to this end, they train them leopards and falcons, as do the Franks, to work with the dogs . . . When these dogs run, no man nor beast can come abreast; or so it is said . . ."

While Sanford logically looked to the steppes of Asia for the birthplace of the breed, others have cited different opinions. The cornerstone of the very widely read breed write-up in the American Kennel Club's *Complete Dog Book* reads as follows:

"It was near Jebel Musa, or the Mountain of Moses, on that small peninsula called Sinai, between the Gulf of Suez and the Gulf of Aqaba, that the breed now known as the Afghan Hound first became a recognizable type of dog."

The basis for this statement falls directly on a translation of a certain papyrus document, attributed to 3,000 B.C. The connection between the document and the Afghan Hound stems from the translation of the word *cynocephalus* into "monkey-faced hound" by one Major H. Blackstone. Illustrations on nearby tombs of associated age depicted a dog-like form with a head suggestive of a baboon. However, later experts generally agree that while the Afghan Hound could possibly have been known in the area, the word *cynocephalus* should be more accurately translated as "dog-faced monkey" and rightly refers to the gelada monkey, or baboon. Such monkey remains have been found in mummified form within the tombs, and were sacred pets in the time of the New Kingdom of Egypt. Evidence of *cynocephali* as being other than dog-faced baboons is lacking in scientific circles.

Written clues to the breed that actually come from Afghanistan are the rarest of all. After acquiring an Afghan Hound of his own in 1956, a Lt. Col. Kullmar of the American Embassy in Kabul, made an attempt to attach local history to the breed. He sought out a native Afghan General who was willing to search the historical archives. The General supplied the following notes:

"The Tazi Dog . . . According to Afghan history, the Tazi dog first became popular and well known in the time of Sultan Mahmud Ghaznawe (note: Mahmud is known as a particularly able and energetic ruler. He deposed his younger brother, Ismail, and ascended the throne in 988. He invaded India no less than twelve times before his death in 1030. In addition to his military campaigns, he was known as a patron of learning). Mahmud admired the Tazi and always carried a pack of them with his army, using them as couriers, guards and hunters. He considered them to be symbols of luck and victory. Following one of his Indian campaigns, he named a location in eastern Afghanistan (between Ghazni and Kandahar) for the breed and this area is still known today as Tazi."

The General added, "There are two types of Tazi found in Afghanistan; the long-haired (called the most pure and the most valued) and the short-haired. The long-haired Tazi lives in the north and northwestern parts of Afghanistan. The short-haired Tazi lives principally in the eastern, southern and western parts of the country."

As a name for these long-coated hounds, "tazi" only compounds confusion in attempting to unravel the origin of the breed. In all parts of Afghanistan "tazi" clearly differentiates the respected greyhound from the despised common dogs. Various reputable sources within Afghanistan have translated *"tazi"* into "fast," "sprinter" and even "white" on one occasion with reference to the hounds.

The various Afghan dialects are basically of Persian derivative but often stray far from classical Persian counterparts. In modern Iran, as well as in Persian literature dating back at least as far as Firdausi's Ghaznavid tenth century epic poem, Shah Nama, "tazi" has been accepted as meaning "from Arabia." Middle Eastern historians have been unable to suggest any faintly similar Persian words that can be tied to either "speed" or "white," but sources in Afghanistan continue to ignore any possible connection between their canine "tazi" and Arabia. When queried on this inconsistency, official Afghan correspondence re-affirmed the translation of "tazi" as "sprinter" despite the fact that Persian greyhounds of Iran, up to and certainly including the huge white, heavily-feathered Kirghiz greyhounds of Turkestan, are all known as "tazi" with reference to Arabian background, within their respective borders.

Dr. Van Beek, of the Smithsonian Institute, considers the word "tazi" to have come from the ancient seacoast city of Taiz, in

Yemen, Arabia. Sailors and traders of bygone eras plied the entire Far and Middle East with trade along oceans and through the tributary networks of rivers and lakes. One such passage was the Indus River in today's Pakistan with northern tributaries flowing directly into northeast Afghanistan. Men from the port of Taiz, and, their wares, including the distinctive Arabian horses and hounds, became *taiz-i* (from Taiz) which easily shortened to "tazi." The word Tazi is also bound in the *Tadjiks* (pronounced "taziks"), a widespread tribal population in north Afghanistan and south Russia, who were originally said to have emigrated from Arabia during the Moslem conquest era.

We would seem to have a definite source link between the Arabian Saluki and the Afghan Hound in the word "tazi," but care must be taken before running too far with this assumption. In studying the ethnic hodge-podge of north Afghanistan and its migratory tribes, Dr. Schurmann, University of California, with other ethnologists, stumbled onto tribes of obvious Mongol features who had completely abandoned their ancient Mongol mother tongue in favor of local Persian or Tadjik dialects. Such "lost" tribes could well have unwittingly picked up the word "tazi" believing it to mean "fast," and pinned it onto long-haired hounds that they had possessed for previous centuries. Following such lines of conjecture, it is as possible that early Oriental migratory groups with rugged, rough-coated dogs adopted not only dialects from the west but also incorporated qualities from native hounds as well, gradually forming new breeds well-suited to the prevailing terrain.

A mention of the hounds is found in *An Account of the Kingdom of Caubul, and Its Dependencies,* published in 1815 by the Hon. Mountstuart Elphinstone. This tome is heavy with descriptions of the countryside, the peoples, customs, and history of Afghanistan. The author writes: "The dogs of Afghanistan deserve to be mentioned. The Greyhounds are excellent; they are bred in great numbers, particularly among the pastoral tribes, who are much attached to hunting . . ." Elphinstone gave these hounds no name other than "greyhounds," but of more than passing interest is his mention of "tauzee" horses seen in the Balkh region, quite unlike the common rough Afghan horses and obviously related to more elegant Arab breeds. Regarding the *Dooraunee* peoples, tent-living nomads following flocks of sheep and goats, Elphinstone remarked

28

that, "Almost every man has a horse and a great number of them keep greyhounds." At no time does he mention any other type of herding dog.

Modern fanciers prefer to think of the Afghan Hound, not as the property of crude, tent-living herdsmen, but as the prized sporting possession of ruling chieftains. Elphinstone does not disappoint them: "They were received by the chief's brother, who had just come in from hunting. He was a fair good-looking young man, with a rude but becoming dress, a bow and quiver at his back, a hare's scut in his turban and two fine greyhounds following him." Elphinstone frequently dwells on the great passion of the Afghans from all stations of life for hunting and hawking. It would have been most helpful had he donated an extra sentence or two to his greyhounds rather than to the table-settings. His lack of words leaves one with the suspicion that the dogs he saw might not have been greatly different from the greyhounds of England.

Before the 20th century, compilers of all-breed books were vaguely aware of the "eastern greyhounds" and made rudimentary, but often confused, attempts to catalogue them. Richardson, in *Dogs: Their Origin and Varieties,* published in 1857, writes of two distinct varieties of Persian Greyhounds. The latter one sounds suspiciously like a coated Afghan Hound. The first variety, with the usual tail and ear featherings, is described as being tan in color and a "most powerful creature frequently exceeding thirty inches in height at the shoulder, (but) the other variety is furnished all over the body with long silky hair of the length of five to eight inches, according to the purity of the blood, and the ears are feathered like those of a Spaniel. The latter dog seldom exceeds twenty-eight inches in height, and is far less powerful than the preceding. His color is usually black relieved with tan."

With decided opinions on the temperaments of the varieties, he continues: "The Persian greyhound differs from all the varieties of rough greyhounds in his hair, it being soft silky texture like a Spaniel. In dispositions the varieties present a striking difference—the black (bicolor) variety being very docile and gentle as a Spaniel, and the tan fierce and untouchable . . . the tan variety is a match for the caracul or Persian lynx and can kill that very formidable animal single-handedly. The black is fit only for hare coursing."

Sir Harry Lumsden, who was with the English Army in Kandahar during the Indian Mutiny of 1857, was not greatly impressed by these hounds as he wrote in his biography, "The dogs of Afghanistan used for sporting purposes are three sorts: the greyhound (Afghan Hound), Pomer and Khundi. The first are not formed for speed and would have little chance on a course with a second-rate English dog, but they are said to have some endurance and, when trained, are used to assist charughs (hawks) in catching deer, to mob wild hog, and to course hare, fox, etc. . ."

A Frenchman, Count Henry de Bylandt, wrote a monumental but seldom seen work, *Les Races de Chiens,* in 1894. By the third edition, published in 1904 in four languages, de Bylandt included a chapter jointly titled "Afghan Greyhound—Persian Greyhound" with illustrations and a standard of sorts, based primarily on the Persian type. A head portrait of an "Ideal Afghan Greyhound," sketched by Mr. L. Beckman, shows a hound with profuse ear coating, no topknot, and a white blaze from nostrils to eye level. A few of the interesting points from this description follow:

General appearance—A rather big dog, but delicate and elegant.
Eyes—Mild, intelligent, dark brown, like a gazelle.
Legs—Fine, straight, clean and nervous.
Tail—Of medium length, carried hanging like a sabre, slightly feathered.
Coat—Smooth and very soft; on the ears and tail much longer, covered with wavy, silky hair; sometimes entirely smoothcoated.
Color—Self-colored black and the different shades of fawn, sometimes dirty white.
Height at shoulder—Between 23½ and 29½ inches.
Weight—60 and 70 pounds.

During the Indian wars that opened Afghanistan to foreign influences, several Englishmen on duty with the attachments found themselves completely captivated by the unusual hounds seen hunting with the native horsemen or disappearing into the forbidden native encampments. A Major Mackenzie was able to procure several such hounds and took them to Switzerland where he set up residence. Two of his hounds were used to illustrate *British Dogs,* written by W. D. Drury in 1903, under the "Barukhzy and Allied Eastern Greyhounds" chapter. The plate shows "Muckmul and Mooroo II." One hound is lying down with the other standing alongside. They are just passable Afghan Hounds. There is some coat on body and legs, with a suggestion of feathering on the toes, but absolutely no top-knot at all. The tails are a proper length with a good ring on the end. It is unwise to gauge heights of dogs from pictures devoid of objects for comparison, but these appear to be leggy animals of Saluki proportions. Major Mackenzie's letters to author Drury inspired the breed chapter and just happened to include some of the best known and most abused quotations ever circulated within the breed. Major Mackenzie writes in part:

"The sporting dog of Afghanistan, sometimes called the Cabul dog, has been named the Barukhzy Hound from being chiefly used by sporting sirdars of the royal Barukhzy family. It comes from Balkh, the northeastern province of Afghanistan, where it is believed that dogs of this variety entered the Ark with Noah. That it is an old variety (probably the oldest domesticated breed in existence) is proved by very ancient rock-carvings within the caves of Balkh of dogs exactly like the Barukhzy Hound of today. On some of these carvings, of colossal size, are inscriptions of much later date that were written by invaders under Alexander the Great."

The breed is strongly indebted to Major Mackenzie for much of the information that later writers repeated and embellished, occasionally with credit to Mackenzie, but more often as "new finds." Mackenzie's now famous mention of "rock-carvings" at Balkh has a rather substantial ring to it, but the subsequent and fantastic development of this story, with dates receding further into the past with each telling, leads one to question even the original statement in light of the fact that absolutely no trace of these carvings has been scientifically authenticated.

In search of evidence of early Afghan Hounds in the country of their development, extensive correspondence has been exchanged between the authors and the Afghan Government, including the Minister of Culture and various Museum Directors, as well as with the French Embassy in Afghanistan and a wide array of authorities from several countries who have explored the Middle and Near East. Without exception they have expressed disbelief in Mackenzie's "rock-carvings," stating that the Balkh area is without caves of any sort.

Most archaeological work in Afghanistan has been directed by the French *Delegation Archaeologique Française en Afghanistan* (D.A.F.A.). All finds, no matter how small, have been completely photographed, cataloged, and described in multiple D.A.F.A. volumes. Senior living members of the D.A.F.A. maintain that the only possible representation of a "levrier Afghan" (Afghan greyhound) that has ever been reported in Afghanistan was found and photographed in 1928 by Monsignor J. Hackin of the D.A.F.A., and appeared in Tome III on an illustration entitled "Le Roi Chasseur" or "The King's Hunter." Mrs. W. S. Macdonald (secretary of the AHCA) has graciously translated the accompanying text from the French as follows:

"A Princely Personage, shown full face (long description of costume follows). Beneath the throne appears, turned in profile to the left, the mouth open and his outstretched muzzle slightly lifted, a dog rendered in grey blue, in whom we do not hesitate to recognize as an authentic Afghan Hound. Two arrows are affixed between the dog and the column that supports to the right the broken pediment . . ." (Note: The area at the right that looks suspiciously like a dog's hind leg, is merely flaked off plaster.)

This painting with its peculiar little dog is dated between 450 and 700 A.D. and located in Kakrak, well to the south of Balkh and northeast of Kabul. Mackenzie's mention of superimposed Hellenistic inscriptions on his cave-renderings completely negates any connection between them and the younger Kakrak paintings, should one be able to overlook the other apparent discrepancies.

Mackenzie also makes the earliest known reference to these dogs as having been on the Ark with Noah. There seems little doubt that this story is told in good faith by the Afghan peoples. With the acceptance of the Islamic beliefs came the teaching of the Koran. Many of the writings of the Koran are based on the more ancient Jewish Pentateuch or Books of Moses. The story of the Flood is one of these. There are modern tribes in Afghanistan which firmly claim to be direct descendants of Noah and his sons. Perhaps, in regard to the hound, it would be wisest to interpret the story to mean that the Afghan Hound, in some form or other, has been indigenous to that country for as long as can be remembered. This belief is also

The writings at the top and bottom of this Afghan stamp have the same meaning. Under "1962" is the Mohammedan year 1341, and the left hand side reads "Tazi Hound."

Le Roi Chasseur: copy of the Kakrak original.
J. Hackin photo, courtesy D.A.F.A.

useful in furnishing religious grounds for lifting the hound well above the level of the common dog.

Major Mackenzie also relates the famous leopard-killer story of how Koosh singlehandedly killed a nearly full-grown leopard attempting to carry away the bitch Mooroo II. He used this story to illustrate his contention that while these hounds may appear timid, they are actually very courageous. He ascribes their seeming timidity to the fact that the bitches are kept in seclusion by the women of the tribes except when required to hunt. He does not explain how this would affect the temperament of the males. His description of the dogs, which pre-dates any Standard, is informative:

> "They usually hunt in couples, bitch and dog. The bitch attacks the hinder parts; while the quarry is thus distracted, the dog, which has great power of jaw and neck, seizes and tears the throat. Their scent, speed and endurance are remarkable; they track or run to sight equally well. Their long toes, being carefully protected with tufts of hair, are serviceable on both sand and rock. Their height varies from 24 to 30 inches; their weight from 45 to 70 lbs. Usually they are of a fawn or bluish-mouse color, but always of a darker shade on the back, which is smooth and velvety."

Major Mackenzie's own hounds would seem to be the best representatives of the breed in his day, principally because there are so few pictures for comparison. In his excellent *Afghan Handbook,* however, Clifford Hubbard managed to obtain and include a rare plate called, "A Meenah of Jajurh with His Afghan Hound," dated 1813, and taken from Broughton's "Letters Written in a Mahratta Camp during the Year 1809." This small dark hound, about 24 inches at the withers according to Hubbard's guess, with lighter-colored underparts, is really quite heavily coated, with good top-knot and long coat except for a tapering at the pasterns, over very large furred feet. The existence of such a fine picture from the early 1800s relieves us of the necessity of accepting Major Mackenzie's rather scraggly, smooth-skulled hounds as being the best specimens known to date. Visitors to Afghanistan constantly repeat that the natives will rarely part with really good stock, and it is quite possible that Major Mackenzie knew of far handsomer hounds than he was able to take out of the country.

The now rare *Hutchinson's Dog Encyclopedia* furnished another famous tale of dogs said to be Afghan Hounds which were located with the Army at the Indian Frontier. These dogs were grotesquely described as being, "large extraordinary-looking creatures . . . in size and shape they somewhat resemble a large Greyhound, but such slight resemblance is dispelled by the tufts with which they are all adorned; some having tufted ears, others tufted feet and others again possessing tufted tails." The author of the tale, writing under the name of "Mali" calls them "Baluchi Hounds" and marveled at the sight of these dogs patrolling the fort in pairs, seemingly without human direction: "Between a deep ditch and wall of the fort is a narrow path. Throughout the night, this path is patrolled by successive couples of dogs. Immediately one couple has completed the circuit of the walls and arrived back at the main gate, another couple starts out. When it is remembered that these extraordinary hounds have never had any training whatsoever, that their duties are absolutely self-imposed—for no human being has the slightest control over them—the perfection of their organization and the smoothness with which they carry out their tasks makes man gasp."

Modern history of the breed took on new significance during the time a Major Amps from England was stationed in the Kabul area shortly after the Afghan War of 1919. He and his wife, Mary, developed a lasting interest in the breed and became influential in the future of these hounds with their "Ghazni" Kennels, established in the hill country of Afghanistan at an elevation of 6,000 feet. Their Sirdar and Khan of Ghazni left lasting lineage effects to be found in the pedigrees of most American hounds. Much of our current knowledge about the hounds has been left by Mrs. Amps, a prolific writer on behalf of her beloved breed. Her many letters to editors of newspapers, magazines and books furnish the basis of the Afghan Hound chapters in most of the English books on dogs in the 20th century. When occasionally challenged by other importers on her concept of the "correct type" of hound, she spared no words in spearing her opponents to the wall with facts and quotes, establishing herself very shortly as *the* authority on the breed. It is possible that her words went a bit further than her actual knowledge, but her sincerity and genuine admiration for the breed cannot be questioned.

Mrs. Amps wrote of the great difficulties in acquiring these hounds after becoming intrigued by their unusual appearance as they accompanied native hunting groups. She found it absolutely necessary to enlist the aid of influential Afghan officials before gaining access to the hostile Afghan villages, and even then the natives were reluctant to admit to having such hounds. It was not unusual to have the dogs, recently purchased from the natives, stealthily re-stolen by their original owners who relished having the price of a good hound despite the risk involved in retrieving it from the 10-foot high walled compound. Good bitches, said Mrs. Amps, were the most difficult to come by.

She took great relish in blasting some of the myths surrounding the breed. She saw the legend of bitches being used to guard the harems as nonsense: "The hounds of Afghanistan were all hard-working hunters, regardless of sex." She also concluded that the hounds were fed very rarely by their native owners, for at sundown each new acquisition would become resistive and try to get out of the compound gates, presumably in search of food. Once used to regular feedings inside the fort, however, they settled down quietly after the evening meal. The even temper of the dogs surprised and certainly pleased the Ampses, who often had 20 to 30 hounds in the same enclosure with very little fighting or resentment of any newcomers by the group. A high appreciation of the breed's temperament pervades all of Mrs. Amps's writings, as she repeatedly cautions against turning these sensitive and affectionate hounds into kennel dwellers.

In A. Croxton Smith's *Hounds and Dogs* (1932), Mrs. Amps gives a fascinating detailed description of Afghan Hounds trained to work with hawks:

"One of the oldest forms of hunting, which is often portrayed in old Persian and Moghul manuscripts, is still being carried on in the remoter parts of Afghanistan. The quarry, a small very swift deer called Ahu Dashti, is hunted by Afghan Hound with the aid of hawks. . . . The young birds and Afghan puppies are kept together, the young hounds being fed on the flesh of deer whenever possible. The food of the young hawks is placed each day between the horns of a stuffed deer; later a string is attached to the head and it is drawn across the floor, the young bird flapping after it. As soon as they are able to fly, they are released and called to this

36

lure. As the training progresses, they are flown at a young kid, and when they seize it, the animal is killed and they are fed on the flesh. When fully-grown the hounds are loosed after a fawn and the hawks flown at it. The training completed, hawks and hounds are taken to the hills. Immediately when the deer is spotted, the birds are unhooded and released, and they descend above the head of the unfortunate beast and, by flapping about it, impede its progress sufficiently to enable the hounds to overtake it and pull it down. The Ahu Dashti or chinkara, as it is known in Indian, is so swift that it is said that, 'The day a chinkara is born, a man may catch it; the second day a swift hound; but the third, no one but Allah.' "

Major Amps spread proof of these hounds' remarkable hunting abilities when he took four of them along with him to visit the Maharajah of Patiala in India. Greyhound coursing events were in progress and the Maharajah asked that the Afghan Hounds be allowed to participate. Major Amps agreed, although well aware that the flat grassy parade grounds where the coursing meet was held was a far cry from the rough stony country his hounds were accustomed to. He was dubious about their performance in comparison to the Greyhounds, but his shaggy mountain hounds acquitted themselves surprisingly well. While somewhat slower on the straightaway, they proved extraordinarily quick on the turns, and illustrated unbridled enthusiasm for the sport that astonished some of the jaded spectators. Major Amps had no doubt that if the test had taken place over rougher country, his hounds being built for the maximum staying power under the most arduous of hunting conditions, the Afghans would have had the distinct advantage over the Greyhounds. The Maharajah was enough impressed to purchase a number of the mountain hounds from Major Amps for his royal kennel.

A provocative note from Major Amps brought out his opinion that the tribesmen living in the plains near India often crossed the Afghan Hound with the Saluki to reduce the coat so that the dogs could better withstand the intense heat of the flat summer plains. This brings up the question as to whether the lesser-coated hounds found in Afghanistan, especially those that most strongly resembled Salukis, were, in fact, a fair percentage of Saluki crossed with coated Afghan Hound stock. The truth of this hypothesis is not

37

and probably will not be known, but several such lesser coated dogs have played important parts in modern Afghan Hound pedigrees.

During the 1920s and 1930s, a fair number of these hounds slipped through the borders of Afghanistan. Evidence from descriptive notes and from the few available pictures indicate that the exports were a diverse crew with respect to size, leg-to-body ratio, coat pattern, texture, quantity and color, and attitude and temperament. The tendency was for various exporters to claim that their own hounds were, according to native standards, the only correct type.

The bulk of early Afghan Hounds that arrived on American shores came by way of a generation or two in Great Britain, or in a few cases, from India. But in 1934 "Saki of Paghman" and "Tazi of Beg Tute" were exported to America directly from Afghanistan with foreign correspondent Laurance Peters of Seattle, Washington. They were registered with the American Kennel Club in the days when such direct imports from the East were acceptable. This is no longer true; any hounds coming directly from Afghanistan to America today function only as fascinating curiosities, ineligible for registration. Fearing that it is being looted of one of its national treasures, Afghanistan now prohibits the exportation of these hounds except under very special circumstances.

In 1950, Walter Fairservis, Jr. led an American archaeological group into Baluchistan and Afghanistan. While in Kabul he fell heir to an Afghan puppy whose parents had been given to the Persian Ambassador's wife by the King of Afghanistan. The puppy, named "Besyar Hob" (meaning "very good" in Persian), was brought by the Fairservis family to the United States and, in 1952, was exhibited unregistered at the Afghan Hound Club of America Specialty Show. In a letter to the then AHCA President, Charlotte Coffey, Mrs. Fairservis told what she knew of these precious hounds:

"Afghan Hounds are privileged (unlike the despised dogs) and sleep in a kennel. Their masters provide them with crude coats of felt or goat skin to protect their short-haired backs in the cold mountain winters. They are led on light chains or leather thongs. Though they have been prized and cared for above other dogs for untold generations, we never saw any signs of warm friendship between the dogs and their masters.

38

5000-year-old Stamp Seals from Tepe Gawra illustrating Greyhound type dogs.

Chota, black-masked silver, Mid-east import to Dutch V.D.O.M. kennels of Eta Pauptit; unknown pedigree.

"They are not bred for any particular traits, lest it be speed and general vigor.

"The diet of Afghan Hounds over there is largely 'nan,' an unleavened whole wheat bread, and meat. Their appetites are not as unlimited as the carrion eating pie-dogs, but they could not possibly be called fussy eaters. There is little clean food left for dogs in the East; consequently, only those with the strongest constitutions can survive."

Besyar Hob was coated in the chaps-and-bolero pattern of feathering rather than in long pants. Mrs. Fairservis wrote that they never saw any really long-coated hounds but had heard of a few. They were gratified to find that the sullen temperament of the Eastern hounds they knew was not innate, as their own puppy grew up gay, gentle, and highly intelligent, sharing a home with loving owners.

An interesting note on native hounds appeared in the Canadian *Our Dogs* in 1947 wherein Juliette de Baïracli-Levy, noted hound fancier and author of *The Herbal Book for the Dog,* told of a conversation with a Mr. R. Dalby, recently returned from Afghanistan:

"The best time (according to Mr. Dalby) to see Afghan Hounds in any numbers in their native land is at the feast of the goats. At this time, vast numbers of goats are brought down from the mountains to the plains, and most of the herding is done by Afghan Hounds. The hounds are decorated for the occasion, with necklaces of beads, especially the native blue stone lapis lazuli which is held to bring good fortune—or with garlands of flowers."

Mr. Dalby also states that many of the Afghan Hounds in the interior had cropped ears as a precaution against dog-fights. As regards the hound's diet, Mr. Dalby mentioned that when meat was in short supply, the hunting hounds were fed large quantities of figs and dates.

Despite stringent regulations against the exportation of hounds from Afghanistan, specimens do continue to cross the border and find their way west in one manner or another. Most of these hounds are said to have come from the "King's Kennel" for the kings of Afghanistan have for many generations kept large packs of these hounds for sportive hunts. At times, these hounds are given as gifts to foreigners in residence, such as ambassadors who have found royal favor. Most of these hounds do not leave the country but are handed from consul to consul or from friend to friend in the turn-over of officials coming to and going from the country.

A royal pair of bitches was brought to California from Afghanistan in 1960 by Melvin Gade who obtained them from a resident Army officer. The mother and daughter were of a black-and-tan color pattern, but with bright silver-colored feet and trim. Mr. Gade managed to get his beloved pair of hounds out of the country by means of official intervention. Hoping to circumvent some of the shipping expense of heavy wooden or metal dog crates, he had large leather crates made especially for the hounds. The plan back-fired when guards decided to make export charges on the huge crate according to the square inch rather than to the usual pound weight. On the ocean liner the hounds, unaccustomed to dog food, were kept alive with galley scraps and hamburgers, buns and all. On their arrival in California, the hounds were thin and unapproachable by strangers. They were inclined to scream in panic when left alone in the family car but were very affectionate with their owners. These two bitches, moreover, conform to our visions of the beautiful Afghan Hound, having lovely full-length coats which hang in rich silken waves. They were both small, about 24 inches in height, and weighed barely 40 pounds apiece, but had elegant carriage, long refined muzzles, and dark, exotic, almond-shaped eyes under pro-fuse silken topknots. Within six months, however, whether due to a drastic change of climate, diet, or to the onset of the troublesome female seasons, both bitches had lost much of their luxuriant coats. The Gades were most disappointed at not being able to register their lovely pets with the AKC.

We suspect that the only point we have made in this chapter is that what is actually known about these intriguing hounds of Afghanistan is quite limited, both here and in the Middle East. As one Afghan exchange student who owned a pair of these hounds in Afghanistan commented when attending a regional Afghan Hound club meeting, "There is very little I can tell you, for not only have you people bothered to find out more about these hounds than we would ever do, but you see a good many more of them right within your own club group than I could hope to show you in Afghanistan."

3

Early Afghan Hounds in England

PRIOR to 1907 there were no important Afghan Hounds in England. A few "hounds from Afghanistan" had been entered in the Foreign Dog Class, but none caught the fancy of either the judges or the public. In truth, these hounds were far below the modern sub-standard of a bad Afghan Hound. They ranged from "Khelat," who resembled an Old English Sheepdog to the point that sheepdog fanciers seriously considered using him for stud, to "Afghan Bob" who could have easily passed for a third rate Irish Setter, right to his tail.

The Foreign Dog Class perked up smartly in 1907 with the sudden appearance of Mrs. M. C. Barff's Zardin, who immediately astonished the English dog world with his arresting and haughty demeanor, combined with an impressive size and a unique profusion and pattern of coat. Mr. A. Croxton Smith, noted canine authority of the times, wrote of Zardin in *Sporting Dogs,* ". . . All of us who looked on him realized that we were in the presence of a very fine animal, whether he embodied the correct type or not." Other experts pronounced him the "finest Oriental Greyhound ever seen in England." Zardin was never defeated in the Foreign Dog Class, and was later presented to Queen Alexandra.

Originally from Seistan, Afghanistan, Zardin had been exhibited in India while en route to England. In October of 1906, an *Indian Kennel Gazette* article described him in minute detail (*Kennel Review* 8/48): "Zardin is a light-coloured hound, almost white, with a black muzzle. He has a very long, punishing jaw of peculiar power and level mouth; his head resembles that of a Deerhound, but with skull oval and prominent occiput, surmounted by a top-knot; ears fairly large, well feathered, and hanging to the side of the head rather than carried to front. He has a keen, dark eye, and little or no stop. A long, strong, clean neck, fairly well arched, running in a nice curve to shoulder, which is long and sloping and well laid back; his back is strong, loin powerful and slightly arched. He, as well as all this class of hound, falls away towards the stern, which is set on low, almost destitute of hair, and usually carried low. He is well ribbed, tucked up under loin; forelegs straight and strong and covered with hair; great length between elbow (which is straight) and ankle. The forefeet are long, fairly broad and covered with long hair. Not too narrow in brisket, which is deep, with good girth of chest. Hind quarters very powerful, furnished with plenty of muscle; great length between hip and hock, which is low and strong, a fair bend of stifle, hind feet not so long as forefeet, but fairly wide and well protected with hair. The hind quarters, flanks, ribs and forequarters are well clothed with protective hair, thick and fine in texture, showing some undercoat. The coat on the back is shorter."

This observing note quoted Zardin's height as being "about 28 inches, or nearly so." A 1907 English newspaper account of him stated that Mrs. Barff thought him to be about five years old, and that he stood at least 26 inches at the shoulder. Unfortunately weight figures are not given.

We have one small quarrel with the Indian article which says that Zardin's tail (stern) was "usually carried low." Most pictures of Zardin show a rather short, loosely curved tail, carried well above the back level, and feathered on the under side. To illustrate Zardin we selected a copy of the portrait by Arthur Wardle, done in 1907 shortly after the dog's arrival in England. This picture shows a hound of the true working sort with torn coat under chest and lower legs, but jagged fur thick enough to promise the good length of coat that materialized after a year of good British care. Beneath the torn coat Wardle faithfully portrayed the hound's strong leg bones, huge feet and powerful frame, which cannot be seen in later photographs due to his profuse coat.

The term "Afghan Hound" gained sudden meaning with Zardin, and when talk of forming a breed standard arose, he automatically became the model. In 1912 such a standard was written, but at that time standards were private ventures as the British Kennel Club did not take on the responsibility of approving and filing breed standards until 1948. During the First World War, all copies of the 1912 standard simply vanished. For that reason we included the lengthy Indian description of Zardin as clues to the lost Standard's wording. Two tag ends of the 1912 standard turned up in *The New Book of the Dog*, by E. C. Ash, in the form of parenthetical additions to a later standard which is also obsolete: "1912 standard—colour: silver fawn and golden. Height: 24 to 30 inches—weight 50 to 60 lbs." Zardin's name remains basic in the breed, but unfortunately it has never been located on any old pedigrees. He touches the breed as a shadowy and lost ideal and as a model for a vanished standard.

The difficult years of the First World War brought a necessary pause in breed activity. In 1921 when Miss Jean Manson arrived in England, together with Maj. Bell-Murray and a select group of 12 Afghan Hounds from the border of Baluchistan and Afghanistan, the next breed chapter opens.

Miss Manson glimpsed her first Afghan Hound when out riding near Quetta (Baluchistan) and was enchanted by the sight of the distant graceful hound loping alongside her mounted master. Miss Manson caught up with the native and after firm dickering managed to purchase the hound. She named her Begum, meaning "queen," because of the bitch's courtly house manners. According to Jean Manson, Begum was "white in color, with large brown eyes and a perfect body and carriage." The hound and woman were inseparable. Once when riding through a native bazaar, Begum caught scent of her original owner of more than two years past. She dashed from Miss Manson's side, through the thick crowd of faces to greet him with frantic whines of joy. Jean Manson was thoroughly impressed with her dog's beauty, manners and uncanny intelligence.

44

Miss Jean Manson and Eng. Ch. Ranee, cream, and Kanee, fawn with a black mask, both bitches, taken at Crufts in 1924 (daughters of Rajah and Begum). Courtesy, Charlotte Coffey.

Zardin
1907

From a photograph of the original painting by A. Wardle.

For four long years Miss Manson searched for a suitable mate for Begum, finally locating a handsome male she christened "Rajah." This male came with a hunter's reputation and was therefore coveted by the natives. He was repeatedly stolen, once returning after an absence of two months, thoroughly disguised in red paint, dragging broken ropes behind him. With the aid of Maj. Bell-Murray, Miss Manson was able to send Rajah, Begum, their offspring, and a few additionally procured hounds to Cove Kennels in Scotland. Once in Britain these 12 imports became known as the "Bell-Murray hounds."

Dissimilarities between the "Bell-Murray hounds" and the earlier Zardin must be mentioned. The new imports for the most part were racy in build, with some males reaching a full 32″ at the shoulder. Their coats, so impressive to Miss Manson, who actually had seen very few specimens of the breed, were scarcely more than exaggerations of a Persian Greyhound's coat. Typical hounds from Begum and Rajah were frilly on shoulder, thighs and sometimes on ribs, with feather between toes and on ears. Top-knots were vestigial. These Bell-Murray hounds, however, play supporting roles in subsequent breed chapters.

In 1925 various owners of these hounds formed the Afghan Hound Club under a standard reading remarkably like the Indian description of Zardin, found in *Pedigree Dogs,* edited by C. C. Sanderson in 1927 with a breed chapter by Evelyn Denyer, then Hon. Sec. of the Afghan Hound Club. The "Denyer standard" was quite short-lived in England, but happened to be around long enough to serve as a basis for the early American standard that held until 1948.

Standard (*obsolete*) of the Afghan Hound Club of Britain (*inactive*)

Head—Skull oval with prominent occiput. Jaw long and punishing, mouth level, ears long, eyes dark, little or no stop.

Neck—Long, strong, arched and running in a curve to shoulder.

Shoulder—Long and sloping—well laid-back.

Back—Strong, loin powerful and slightly arched, falling away towards stern.

Forelegs—Straight and strong—great length between elbow (which is straight) and ankle.

46

Forefeet—Very large, both in length and breadth, toes well arched and the feet covered with long thick hair, fine in texture.

Brisket—Deep and not too narrow.

Hindquarters—Powerful, well muscled, great length between hip and hock, which is low and strong. Fair bend in stifle.

Body—Well ribbed and tucked up under loins.

Coat—Hindquarters, flanks, ribs and forequarters well covered with long thick hair, very fine in texture. Ears and all four feet well feathered. Head surmounted with top-knot of long silky hair.

General appearance—Strong and active looking, a combination of speed and power with a graceful outline.

Height (to shoulder)—Dogs about 28 inches; bitches 25–26 inches.

High in Kabul, Afghanistan, a counterpoint to the Bell-Murray theme was shaping as Maj. and Mrs. Amps, stationed in the mountain country, discovered hounds of a rather different sort. Late in 1925 Mary Amps brought a small group of her "Ghazni hounds" to England, immediately proclaiming them to be the first "true Afghan Hounds since Zardin." She used the press effectively in side-by-side layouts emphasizing the general resemblance in coat and outline between Zardin and her favorite, Sirdar of Ghazni. Pictures did not tell the whole story, however, as Sirdar was a mere 24 inches at the shoulder. Mrs. Amps insisted that he might have grown taller had his legs not been broken in puppyhood and badly set, but this hardly seems reasonable as Sirdar was famed for his grand gait, showing no trace of foreshortened or uneven legs. The great Sirdar was certainly not a large hound, but he was a mighty one, carrying more hair than had been dreamed of since Zardin. His esteemed kennel mate, the powerful, leopard-killing Khan of Ghazni, was of an even sturdier build and similarly coated.

A head-on clash between Mary Amps and Maj. Bell-Murray was inevitable, and it appeared publicly in the *Letters to the Editor* pages of the canine journals. Both called each other's dogs "imposters." Maj. Bell-Murray remarked that he had not been enough impressed by the "Ghazni hounds" to bother buying one when he saw them in Peshawar. He claimed that his hounds had lost much of their coating in the damp British climate. Mrs. Amps rejoined that none of her hounds had been for sale, and furthermore, that they were growing better coats in England than they had before. A nasty battle opened with Maj. Bell-Murray wielding the weapon

47

Eng. Ch. Sirdar of Ghazni, red with a black mask, earned his title in 1927 and was owned by Mr. and Mrs. Amps. This drawing was made from photographs.

of size against Mrs. Amps's shield of coat. Mrs. Amps admitted that Sirdar was "a bit on the small side" but otherwise excellent, and that she had seen but one quality Afghan hound in Afghanistan that measured over 28 inches.

Mrs. Amps won the early skirmishes, convincing the "authorities" that she had the superior hounds and better background and knowledge of both the breed and the country of Afghanistan. Judge A. Croxton Smith in *Sporting Dogs* wrote with a noticeable trace of awe: ". . . Mrs. Amps . . . brought over the counterpart (of Zardin) except for size in Sirdar of Ghazni, a dog that came as a revelation. In structure and movement and all the attributes that we expect from a really good dog he excelled. . . . It is no wonder that this dog carried everything before him and that he made a great impression on the breed."

In 1962 an English judge, Ursula Rees, revitalized faded interest in clear definition of "Bell-Murray" and "Ghazni" types in a published critique. She intimated that while she had no special preference for either of the two original types and enjoyed a well-balanced blend of the two, what disturbed her was seeing entirely too many hounds which were not harmonious and displayed distinct clashes of type. She averred, furthermore, that due to inherent differences in structure, the two types called for very different handling in the ring. This startling opinion brought frantic agitation from older fanciers, as novices, quite reasonably, wanted to know just what Judge Rees was talking about.

Studies of old photographs and clippings abetted by consultation with various senior English and Continental breeders have inspired the composite illustrations of the so-called "desert" and "mountain" types of pioneer Afghan Hounds. Major structural differences between the two types lie in variation in bone length, substance and in the outline of the dog's carriage. The desert hounds, like Begum, were of the long fine-bone type, distinctly racy and Saluki-like. Their heads were very long, practically without stop, with sharp, slanted eyes. In outline, these racy dogs stood over a lot of ground. Despite well laid-back shoulders, forequarters were set to the front of the dog rather than well beneath him. This facilitated an effortless, prancing action, seen so frequently in the Saluki and often accompanied by rather upright pasterns and tight feet. Rear legs, also very long, placed well behind the hound. Loins were long and very mobile. At their best, these desert hounds were magnificently noble, elegant and graceful, and extremely fast.

As is the case with slim-line breeds, the lesser specimens fell heir to one or more faults in a predictable pattern. Overfine heads turned weak and "snipey-jawed." Bodies too often were extremely narrow, completely lacking in adequate forechest, with such poorly developed front ribs that elbows practically came together, forcing the feet to turn outward for sufficient base of balance. Such skimpy bodies were accompanied by thin loins and, not infrequently, by weak hindquarters to match. These dogs were far more attractive when viewed in profile than from the front or the rear. One breeder recalls that these fine-boned hounds, unfortunately, had a bad tendency to rickets.

The "mountain hounds," as exemplified by Sirdar and Khan of Ghazni, were sturdily built, well-boned hounds, packing a fair amount of weight to the inch, and showing considerably less of the greyhound-look of being poised for flight. Their heavier bone and foreign type was evident from topknot to stern. Heads were long, but broader and deeper of skull than the Bell-Murray hounds with more noticeable stop and eyes set rather level. Their firm, broad forebreasts carried fuller briskets and heavy ribbing that curved upward to meet short tight loins and wide hindquarters. In body silhouette, the mountain hound stood with his legs well beneath his body, poised to spring in any direction. Front legs, set well under the shoulders, accompanied sloping pasterns and large feet. Rear legs, bent at stifle, placed more under the body than behind it. Such leg positioning gave a look of special compactness to the frame. At their best, these sturdy little mountain hounds carried unusually erect necks and tails and radiated power and remarkable agility. The heavier construction of these hounds, however, produced the more common weaknesses of the mountain type. When built to excess, headpieces turned gross, and stops became more pronounced. Necks tended to be short and thick. Bodies were apt to barrel and interfere with elbow action, sometimes to the point where the feet were forced to toe-in.

In coating, the scantily-clad Bell-Murrays boasted of lovely silken textures. The heavier-clad mountain hounds, with good topknots and fair to good leg and side coats, tended to a thick stand-off type

Above: "Desert" type; below: "Mountain" type, composite drawings by Lois Gossner, based on photographs.

of cotton texture. These mountain hounds had excellent definition of saddles, but were inclined to frilly tails.

Aside from structural differences, from the mountain hounds, the desert hounds were more skittish, headstrong and aloof, quite inclined to resent advances from·strangers. The mountain hounds, with their milder expression, were more tolerant of human beings, with Sirdar showing definite signs of amiability on short acquaintance. In subsequent imports, a possible link between the heavy-coated mountain type and more docile tempers is seen, as noted by Miss Drinkwater who deeply valued the sweet disposition of her very heavily coated import, Lakki Marwat, in days when dangerously temperamental Afghans were no rarity.

Now that we have carefully placed "Bell-Murray" and "Ghazni" Afghans into their respective boxes, we shall open the lids and let them right out again. It is neither true nor fair to infer that all the Bell-Murray imports, or that all the Ghazni hounds, fitted snugly into separate colonies. Maj. Bell-Murray and Mrs. Amps preferred to perpetuate a concept of two distinct Afghan Hound types, with one supposedly "right" and the other "wrong," and each feared having his stock contaminated by the other's. Yet, in a public letter to Maj. Bell-Murray, Mrs. Amps strongly hinted that her Khan could supply precisely what other Afghans in England lacked. Khan was considered, even by Mrs. Amps, to be a bit on the heavy side, and not of Sirdar's exquisite quality, but of a sturdy type desirable in the Oxus area of Afghanistan where Khan was born.

Jean Manson's Rajah, Begum, and offspring fit the frame of typical "Bell-Murray," but the Major had also procured other Afghan Hounds from the East in Peshawar and elsewhere. At least two of these additions, appearing in old photos of the Major, were several steps towards the mountain type by virtue of their breadth of brisket, coarser bone and more profuse coats. We have not been able to identify one type, a clear cream, and cannot guess its pedigree influence. The representative of another type, "Pushum," was a brindle bitch of great note, if only because her brindled ancestors are around today. Only when Pushum is in the background of the Bell-Murrays do even fair coats appear, and her name is in most all Bell-Murray pedigrees of any consequence. When bred to Ooty (Zorawar ex Dil), Pushum produced three offspring of note. Her son, Ch. Buckmal, a 32 inch, remarkably intelligent, faintly brindled

Pushum, bitch: foundation brindle for present-day Afghans in America.

Maj. and Mrs. Bell-Murray with foundation stock. L. to r.: Ooty (dog), pale fawn with a black mask; Begum (bitch), cream; Pushum; Baluch (dog); Kanee; Straker; and Eng. Ch. Ranee.

and well-coated hound, was England's first male champion Afghan. Pushum's dark brindle daughter, Daghai, was the dam of Ch. Taj Mahip of Kaf, the grandsire of the famous English and American Ch. Badshah of Ainsdart. Her other daughter, Oolu, produced Ch. Shadi. As a matter of record, these three English champions coming down from Pushum, plus the very first English bitch champion, Ranee (Rajah ex Begum) make up the entire roster of undiluted Bell-Murray champions. They also constitute four out of five of the first English champion Afghans, the fifth being Ch. Sirdar of Ghazni.

On the other side of the fence, we see that while Sirdar and Khan were each of one type, the Ghazni *bitches* were of a mixed lot. Roshni of Ghazni (Jack ex Jane) was a fawn of statuesque proportions, being lengthy in neck, tail and legs, very deep in chest and practically devoid of coat. Mrs. Amps explained these features by claiming that the mountain bitches characteristically carried far less coat than did the males. This claim is open to speculation, as we recall that the heaviest coated of the Bell-Murrays was a bitch and see what happened when light-coated Ghazni bitches were bred to Sirdar. From such a breeding Roshni of Ghazni produced the well-known Ch. Asri-Havid of Ghazni. "Rif," as he was known to his owner, Phyllis Robson, was notable as England's first Best-in-Show Afghan and first black-and-tan champion in the breed. His photo, seen in Hubbard's *Afghan Hound Handbook,* proves him to have had an extremely long, refined head, keen Oriental eye, and a startling lack of coat on his lower legs and feet. His overall appearance seemed to reflect a blend of types rather than direct inheritance of the Sirdar strain.

Ghazni, as an uncluttered strain, came to a close just a few short years after the demise of pure Bell-Murrays. Sirdar achieved long-lasting fame and his title in 1927. Taking the sceptre from him in 1929 was the previously mentioned Ch. Asri-Havid of Ghazni, then another son, Ch. Ashna of Ghazni, whose dam was Shireen of Ghazni, and in 1931, a very lovely, coated daughter came to the fore, Ch. Marika of Baberbagh whose dam was Sada of Ghazni, a daughter of Khan of Ghazni. The dynasty concluded with Ch. Westmill Ben Havid (Ch. Asri-Havid of Ghazni ex Elsa of Ghazni) in 1934. These names are important in the background of later English and American breedings.

Just before the close of the 1920s, a few fanciers with elegant Bell-

54

Murray bitches cast envious glances at the Sirdar coat, character and accumulating fame, and chanced a quicker route to a more Zardin-like Afghan by breeding their bitches directly to Sirdar. Within a few short years most of the English championships fell to progeny from blendings of Sirdar, or of one of his sons, to a Bell-Murray type bitch. Judge Rees certainly would have had reason to be critical of the lack of harmony of many of the structurally mixed-up results, and of the wild extremes created by this breeding combination. Only the name "from Afghanistan" held the breed together; judges could rarely agree on a standard of quality. As the supremacy of the pioneer strains was ended, some breeders chose to establish new types from the various local stocks. Others, unsatisfied with the available possibilities, imported fresh blood.

Mrs. Olive Couper's Ardmore Anthony, a small white hound from India, was mated to her Ch. Garrymhor Souriya (Ch. Ashna of Ghazni ex Ch. Alfreda) to produce Garrymhor hounds frequently appearing on later English and American pedigrees. Souriya's dam, Ch. Alfreda, classifies as an import of sorts, being out of the eastern-born Shahzada and Afroz.

At Mrs. Drinkwater's Geufron kennels, Ch. Alfreda's daughter, Ch. Sirfreda, combined well with Lakki Marwat, an extremely heavily-coated, dark-eyed, ginger colored hound of the compact type, imported from the Orient by Col. Marriott. When combined with Geufron bitches of Bell-Murray and Ghazni backgrounds, Lakki Marwat produced some of the most fantastically coated hounds of the era in Ch. Kisagotami of Geufron and the American Ch. Lakshmi of Geufron-Cawtaba, both bitches.

Such breeders, well aware of the questionable backgrounds and breeding potentiality of these hounds, tended to use them sparingly for immediate flashes of stock improvement, with long-range breeding plans for recovering any lost type. These very heavy coats were more often than not of inferior, coarse and woolly textures. The appearance of heavy coats in conjunction with coarse bone structure and short, thick heads was no less prevalent in new Eastern imports. Later breedings were constant struggles to blend the two types into a single form approaching the illusive balance found in the great Zardin. Unfortunately, one generation of happy success was frequently followed by disappointing reversions to extreme types.

By 1933, the Afghan Hound Association was formed and had its

Head study of Ranee (Rajah ex Begum), first champion bitch in England, 1927.

Mrs. E. E. Drinkwater's early Afghans in England; l. to r., Eng. Ch. Sirfreda (bitch), golden; Aswakarna of Geufron (dog); Eng. Ch. Kisagotami of Geufron (bitch), cream; Eng. Ch. Agha Lala of Geufron (dog), red with black points; Eng. Ch. Mahaprajapati of Geufron (bitch), fawn with black points; and Karnikara of Geufron (bitch).

own standard, a document decidedly more extensive and detailed than the early, terse description of Zardin. The first A.H.A. president was Mrs. Mary Amps and the Chairman was Mrs. Phyllis Robson. The standard emerged as a compromise attempt to include the best of both types of hounds and yet point towards the ideal of the early Zardin. Mrs. Amps's insistence that the compact, close-coupled dog was the only correct type was accepted, but the size stipulation was in favor of the larger Bell-Murrays. This standard covered the breed until 1946.

Standard of Points—obsolete

Head—Skull long and not too narrow, prominent occiput. Foreface long, punishing jaws, and little stop, mouth level. Nose usually black, liver no disqualification in lighter colored dogs. Eyes, dark preferred; golden colour no disqualification. Ears long, heavily feathered and carried close to the head, which is surmounted by a long top-knot of hair.

Neck—Long, strong, with proud carriage of the head.

Shoulders—Long and sloping, well set back, well muscled and strong.

Back—Well muscled the whole length, falling slightly away to the stern. Loin straight, broad, and rather short. Hip joints rather prominent and wide; a fair spring of ribs and good depth of chest.

Forelegs—Straight, well-boned, elbows rather straight.

Feet—Large. Toes very long, well-arched, and heavily feathered.

Hindquarters—Powerful and long, with plenty of bend to hock and stifle, and well under the dog.

Tail—Set on low and carried "gaily," with a ring at the end; sparsely feathered.

Coat—Long, of very fine texture on the ribs, fore and hindquarters and flanks. From the shoulders backward along the top of the back, the hair is short and close. Hair long from the eyes backward, with a distinct silky top-knot; on foreface hair is short as on the back. Ears and legs well feathered.

Any color.

Height—Dogs 27 to 29 inches. Bitches 2 to 3 inches smaller.

The whole appearance of the dog should give the impression of strength and activity, combining speed with power.

The object of the dog is to hunt its quarry over very rough and mountainous ground, in a country of crags and ravines. For this, a compact and well-coupled dog is necessary rather than a long-loined racing dog whose first quality is speed.

Expression—Dignified, aloof and intelligent. In motion his head and tail are carried high; springy gait.

From the time The Kennel Club awarded the breed individual status in 1927 until the curtailment of shows during WWII, 38 Afghan Hounds became champions. This number may seem small to Americans, unfamiliar with the British system, wherein a dog must defeat even champions in attendance to win the necessary three Challenge Certificates, under different judges, to qualify for its title. One reigning champion may, and often does, accumulate many such certificates, shutting out the young class winners. The C.C.s are awarded only at a few large entry shows. Small English dog shows are frequent, taken seriously by entrants, but champions are not permitted to enter, and wins do not count towards championships. These shows are comparable to American all-breed "matches," and as a result of their system, there is a smaller percentage of champions among the total number of shown Afghans in England than there is in the United States.

Readers might like to know something of the colors of the early hounds. The great majority from all camps were some shade of red or cream, with or without masks. The Bell-Murrays, excepting Pushum, tended to very faded coloration. The three pre-WWII brindle champions (a legacy of Pushum) included Ch. Badshah of Ainsdart, later sold to America. During the breeding lull of WWII, these brindle genes were completely lost on the Isle and had to be re-introduced from the United States in the 1960s. Black-and-tan genes arrived with the Ghazni hounds, Sirdar and "Roshni," both red themselves, but carrying the factor. Mrs. Amps brought back a few black Afghans directly from Afghanistan, but the black Afghan made no appearance on the championship roster until after the war in 1948 with Ch. Netheroyd Turkuman Camelthorn. There were no blue or gray champions up to 1959, but Mrs. Amps wrote that her red-fawn Khan of Ghazni and his son, Mustavfi of Ghazni, sired a few rare, gray pups. Khan was said to have come from a tribe near the Oxus that coveted the gray coloration, and when hounds other than gray were born, they were tossed out into the greedy arms of less finicky natives.

58

Newspaper clippings from the 1930s illustrate Afghan Hounds at the shows with peculiar half-coats, like sheep sheared half-way up and half-way down with thick wool patches sticking out from thighs to hocks and from shoulders to mid-lower legs. These hounds appear tiny-footed and flat-headed from lack of foot fur and topknots. Such pictures have bred the false assumption that the handsome full-coated Afghan is a modern item, but Sirdar and Khan were fair coated, as were some of their offspring. Ch. Westmill Tamasar, born in 1932 of about equal Ghazni and Bell-Murray stock including Pushum, and illustrated in Brian Vesey-Fitzgerald's *The Book of the Dog,* is a gray-brindle hound which has an adequate coat, huge hairy paws, and a good length of mandarin whiskers. His coat, his long, lean muzzle and his exquisite structural balance would place him favorably in today's competition. The factors for full coat and all-over breed quality were there, but the selection and the retention of the desired characteristics from such a background served a mighty challenge to the breeders.

The next world war hit England in 1939 and brought a halt to dog shows and breeding activities. The staunch British carried on as best they could, mindful of the Kennel Club edict that "No bitch should be mated unless it is for the express purpose of keeping in existence a line of blood of great use to the future of the breed." The warning was well taken. Women who did not bear arms for Britain did volunteer work and fought on the homefront to keep themselves and a few beloved hounds from starvation. Dogs were not allowed in the Public Air Raid Shelters, and England's quickly formed Canine Defense League devised a system whereby dog lovers made their homes available refuge to strangers with dogs. Red-white-and-blue tags on fenceposts and in windows indicated such homes.

Gas masks were designed for dogs, but without success, for the "average dog takes no more kindly to a mask than he does to a discarded salmon can wedged on his muzzle." Luminous leads and collars were designed by the "League" to allow dogs to exercise and still be seen by motorists and pedestrians in the nightly blackouts.

Many beloved hounds were reluctantly sold or "lent" to friends in countries that were not under air bombardment. America was indebted to the war years for dogs like Ch. Rana of Chaman of Royal Irish and Ch. Sardar Khan el Kabal, which might never have left England under normal circumstances. In 1941 a "refugee" on the

59

S.S. Ville D'Anvers was Tajana Glamour Girl of Chaman, bound for Marion Florsheim's kennel where her valuable bloodlines could be protected. Ties of sympathy between American and British fanciers were tightened during this period.

In 1946 a small group of fanciers regrouped with their aging breeding stock in hopes of rebuilding the breed. Dissatisfaction was voiced with the pre-war Standard, and several dedicated people set about working on revisions. They included Dr. Betsy Porter (Kabul Kennel), Mrs. E. E. Drinkwater (Geufron Kennel), Mrs. Barbara Rothwell-Fielding (Kuranda Kennel), Mrs. Howard Gibson (Ackam Kennel), Miss Marjorie Matthews (Westover Kennel), and Phyllis Robson the columnist. That year a new official standard was recognized by the British Kennel Club, one not greatly different from its predecessor, but attempting to delineate details in clearer order. There was a new stress on the "Oriental" character of the hound's triangular eye; the tail was to be carried as if "raised in action," instead of "gaily," and ears and legs that had merely to be "feathered" in the past, were now to be "coated," except for the pastern joints.

With the shortage of litters from the year 1939 on, the post-war Afghan population of 1946 was a mixture of immature youngsters and aging, war-raised adult dogs. The first post-war champion was the eight-year-old Mitzou of Acklam. With a fresh Standard, plentiful supplies of meat and dog food, and a nucleus of persistent fanciers, England planted and harvested an impressive crop of Afghan Hounds. Names such as Khorrassan, Bletchingly, Netheroyd, Turkuman, Carloway and others rose to share the bounty. In a few short years, through the cooperative efforts of the fanciers, much of the globe was again being supplied with quality Afghan Hounds from England.

Current British Afghan Hound Standard

(Adopted in 1946, accepted by the British Kennel Club in 1948)

Characteristics—The Afghan Hound should be dignified and aloof with a certain keen fierceness. The Eastern or Oriental expression is typical of the breed. The Afghan looks at and through one.

General appearance—The gait of the Afghan Hound should be smooth and springy with a style of high order. The whole appearance of the dog should give the impression of strength and dignity combining speed and power. The head must be held proudly.

Head and skull—Skull long, not too narrow, with prominent occiput. Foreface long with punishing jaws and slight stop. The skull well balanced and surmounted by a long topknot. Nose preferably black but liver is no fault in light-coloured dogs.

Eyes—Should be dark but golden colour is not debarred. Nearly triangular, slanting slightly upwards from the inner corner to the outer.

Ears—Set low and well back, carried close to the head. Covered with long silky hair.

Mouth—Level.

Neck—Long and strong with proud carriage of the head.

Forequarters—Shoulders long and sloping, well set back, well muscled and strong without being loaded. Forelegs straight and well boned, straight with shoulders, elbows held in.

Body—Back level, of moderate length, well muscled and falling slightly away to the tail. Loins straight, broad and rather short. A fair spring of ribs and good depth of chest.

Hindquarters—Powerful, with well bent and well turned stifles. Hipbones rather prominent and wide apart. Great length between hips and hocks and a comparatively short distance between hocks and feet. The dew-claws may be removed or allowed to remain at the discretion of the breeder.

Feet—Forefeet strong and very large both in length and breadth, and covered with long thick hair, toes arched. Pasterns long and springy, especially in front, and the pads well down on the ground. Hind feet long, but not quite so broad as the forefeet, and covered with long thick hair.

Tail—Not too short. Set on low with a ring at the end. Raised in action. Sparsely feathered.

Coat—Long and very fine texture on ribs, fore and hindquarters and flanks. From the shoulders backwards and along the saddle the hair should be short and close in mature dogs. Hair long from the forehead backward on the head, with a distinct silky topknot; on the foreface the hair is short, as on the back. Ears and legs well coated. Pasterns can be bare. Coat must be allowed to develop naturally.

Colour—All colours are acceptable.

Weight and size—Ideal height; dogs 27–29 inches, bitches 2–3 inches smaller.

Faults—Any appearance of coarseness. Skull too wide and foreface too short. Weak underjaw. Large round or full eyes. Neck should never be too short or thick. Back too long or too short.

Ch. Makarabi's Joniboi—"Korla"—(El Khani Sahm-Ba ex Dakar's Fiesta Parade), black mask red dog, bred by Betty McCargar, owned by Edward M. and Trudie Gilbert. Korla appeared in the movie "The Maltese Bippy" with Rowan and Martin, in an episode of the "Here's Lucy" TV show with Lucille Ball, and in various magazine advertising displays.

4

The Afghan Hound
Comes to America

"To own one is to love one! The Afghan Hound gains daily in popularity. The oldest known breed of domestic dog. Wonderful companions and house dogs. Charming dispositions, gentle, equally amiable to children and other dogs. Easily trained for any sport. Immune to either intense heat or cold. Prices range from $150 to $1000."

In June, 1929, the ad above first appeared in the *American Kennel Gazette* at a time when there was a scarce handful of Afghan Hounds in the whole United States. Fully 99 and 44/100% of American dog fanciers had not the vaguest notion that an "Afghan" was anything other than a remote Asiatic native or an inanimate knitted coverlet.

The Afghan Hound had definitely made its noble presence felt in England well before this, though, and by 1926, a few of Miss Manson's hounds had arrived on the Eastern seaboard, creating little attention and leaving no lasting pedigree effects. This advertisement referred to "de Flandre" hounds of "Sirdar" lineage imported by Edward Abrams and seen occasionally at Eastern shows during 1930 and 1931. The fortunate but few fanciers who were aware of this exciting breed were sublimely optimistic about its potential, but judges and the general public considered the dogs freakish and only paused to smirk at them. What the breed needed was a good Madison Avenue type of press agent, and some really outstanding specimens to point up the virtues of the somewhat bizarre breed to a curious American public.

Pertinent American history of the breed begins in 1931 with a Hollywood story starring Zeppo, the youngest of the zany Marx brothers. When in England on film location, Zeppo and his wife were completely fascinated by a fleeting sight of these hounds and agreed that they should take a pair for breeding back to California. Fortunately they approached Phyllis Robson, then Editor of the English *Dog World,* who also owned the famous Eng. Ch. Asri-Havid of Ghazni. Mr. and Mrs. Marx left the selection in her hands, stipulating only that they preferred a pair of light-colored hounds with good coats. Asra of Ghazni (litter sister of Ch. Ashna of Ghazni) sired by the great Sirdar ex Shireen of Ghazni, was the first selection. The search for a suitable male ended at the Westmill kennel where Mr. and Mrs. Marx were both delighted by young Westmill Omar, a dark cream male by Danenda of Ghazni ex Surkh of Ghazni. By today's standards Omar was barely fair coated, and the solid cream-colored Asra was considerably less so, but both had the lively character and wonderful upstanding carriage, finely chiseled head and keen dark eyes that characterized so many of their finest get.

Zeppo Marx brought Omar and Asra to California in the Spring of 1931, but by the close of that year the Marx family had again been forced to leave Hollywood for an extended movie tour and thought it kindest to turn their charming pets over to George Thomas, respected judge and dealer in valuable dogs. Fully aware of their value, Thomas determined to keep them himself until he could find someone who would properly appreciate the unique hounds. In his care Omar and Asra mated and awaited their first litter. Shortly before the pups arrived, George Thomas and his two Afghans returned to Massachusetts. On impulse he called a friend, the highly respected breeder of Wire Fox Terriers, Q. A. Shaw McKean, suggesting that he have a look at his new "prizes." McKean was instantly captivated by Omar and Asra, begging to buy them on

64

Asra of Ghazni (Eng. Ch. Sirdar of Ghazni ex Shireen of Ghazni), cream bitch imported from England and the foundation of Prides Hill Kennel.

the spot. Thomas finally agreed, but only under the condition that he be able to remain breeder and owner of the unborn litter.

McKean took Omar and Asra to the spacious Prides Hill kennels in Prides Crossing, Mass., gave them the run of his home and was amazed at their droll and lively outdoor antics contrasted with their marvelous unobtrusiveness in the house. In Q. A. Shaw McKean the Afghan Hound had found the energetic, wise and experienced press agent the breed so badly needed! The astute McKean concocted long range plans for his exciting new acquisitions, worried that the single pair had limited breeding possibilities: another stud of a different, but not too different, bloodline was needed. As George Thomas was soon to leave for Europe on a judging and dog-buying trip McKean requested that he look out for a suitable second stud. Eventually George Thomas cabled that he had found *the* right dog, and confident of his friend's educated judgment, McKean said "Buy." Thus in 1934 the acclaimed young English Champion Badshah of Ainsdart arrived on American shores. For good measure Thomas also bought Badshah's litter brother, Tufan of Ainsdart. It is a rare American pedigree that does not trace directly back to one or both of these pioneer sires.

Badshah, familiarly known as "Loppie," leaped into McKean's heart and stayed there. A good-sized, pale brindle Afghan, the color of smoke, Loppie's unquenchable spirit shone from his fierce Oriental eyes and showed in his proudly carried head and highly curved tail. A direct son of Sirdar of Ghazni, Badshah's dam was Ku Mari of Kaf, a typical Bell-Murray bitch, giving McKean his desired bit of outcross blood while protecting the Sirdar legacy. Badshah was quite sparsely coated, especially on the legs, but this was easily ignored in sight of his remarkable free-floating stride and energetic breed character.

Shaw McKean first exhibited his fine English Champion at the North Shore Kennel Club in Hamilton, Mass. on Aug. 25th, 1934, where "Loppie" startled the canine world into sharp awareness of the Afghan by shooting straight through to become America's first Best in Show Afghan Hound. Badshah, one of those wily hounds who knew the secret of opening latches and vaulting fences, had the run of the McKean estate, but he was most happy to be within adoring distance of his new American master. On Badshah's death in 1940 McKean fondly recalled the hound's superb expression and

Ch. Tufan of Ainsdart (Badshah's bro.), imported dog owned by Amelia White.

Eng. & Am. Ch. Badshah of Ainsdart (Eng. Ch. Sirdar of Ghazni ex Ku-Mari of Kaf), pale brindle dog, America's first Best-in-Show Afghan; owned by Q. A. Shaw McKean.

his rare combination of great substance and refinement. Said McKean, "In head points he was a class above any Afghan that I have ever seen. He was a beautiful moving animal, with tremendous speed and spring, and could take a six-foot jump without breaking stride." The great smoky-brindle sire was buried in the orchard where he best loved to run, at the close of his tenth year.

After acquiring Badshah, McKean set about educating in earnest the dog owning public about Afghans. Articles authored by him appeared in dog journals. Special Prides Hill folders were freely circulated. In this manner the older breed stories told in England, plus a few new ones, became part of the American breed image. Other writers spun fresh yarns from the basic substance of McKean's loom. There was no time to back up and check to see what was made of true cloth and what was synthetic. Once the public became better acquainted with the breed and its glamorous background the enchanting hounds could sell themselves at close contact.

Part of McKean's strategy was to show his hounds *enmasse* at the New England shows, and as Omar and Asra had two litters before Badshah arrived, the classes were sizeable. There are those who scoff at dogs who win championships by defeating only their own kennel-mates, but in a newly introduced breed there is much to be said for this scheme. A gathering of several lively Afghan Hounds is considerably more impressive than a single specimen. This device also forced the judges to really inspect and familiarize themselves with the unique hounds in order to make reasonable merit judgments. From a practical view, the tactics gave McKean young champions who might never have "finished" without the home kennel competition. With young champions on hand McKean was able to make "package deals" with a champion and a selected mate to serve as foundation stock for fanciers with awakening interest in the exotic new breed.

Despite the fact that the Afghan Hound was revered as a sporting dog extraordinary in Afghanistan and India, from the moment that Omar and Badshah reached America, the breed received its billing as a show dog extraordinary capable of winning Best in Shows and great glory for proud owners. Certainly his fascinating history and reputed hunting prowess added to the breed's stature, but one is hard put to find hunting Afghans that left strong marks on the American branch of the breed. There has always been an unusually large percentage of the total Afghan Hound population under exhibition at the shows with marked and enviable success in winning top honors.

The American Kennel Club had accepted Afghan Hound registrations from 1926 under a Standard that was said to have been furnished by The Afghan Hound Club of England. The breed was placed in the Sporting Group as the Hound Group was not given separate status until 1937.

Original American Standard
Superseded in 1948 by the current Standard

Head—Narrow, conforming to that of a greyhound but more powerful; skull oval, with prominent occiput; jaws long and punishing; mouth level, not overshot nor undershot; ears long; eyes dark; little or no stop.

Neck—Long, strong, arched and running in a curve to the shoulder, which should be long and sloping and well laid back.

Body—Strong powerful loin, and slightly arched, falling away towards the stern, well ribbed and tucked up under loins; should be that of a hound and have ample length; the tail set not too high on body, similar to greyhound, having a curve at the end, but on no account a bushy tail.

Legs—Forelegs straight and strong, great length between elbow and ankle, elbows well tucked in; forefeet very large both in length and breadth, toes well arched and the feet covered with long thick hair, fine in texture; pasterns long and pads well down on ground.

Brisket—Deep and not too narrow.

Hindquarters—Powerful, well muscled, great length between hip and hock, this is one of the main features of the hound; fair bend of stifle.

Hind feet—Broad but not as long as forefeet; toes arched; feet covered in long, thick hair.

Coat—Hindquarters, flanks, ribs and forequarters well covered with silky, thick hair, very fine in texture; ears and all four feet well feathered; head surmounted with top-knot of long silky hair.

General appearance—Strong, alert, and active; looking a combination of speed and power, with a graceful outline.

Height—Dogs about 27 inches, bitches 25 inches.
Weight—About 60 pounds.

Despite the marked similarity between this terse standard and the contemporaneous but short-lived "Denyer Standard" based on the Indian description of Zardin, there are curious features in the American document not easily attributed to any known source. Differences in the criteria for head shape, coat and size are superficial, but where the American Standard requests a body that "should be that of a hound and have ample length" was inconsistent with the English ideal that the Afghan Hound was more compact than the other Greyhound types. This loose American Standard did hold court, however, often quite uncomfortably, until 1948.

Ch. Kabul of Prides Hill, from the second Omar-Asra litter, became the first Afghan Hound champion in America in October of 1934. From George Thomas's first Omar and Asra litter, a bitch, Barberryhill Illusive, had been sold directly to the Sealyham breeder, Bayard Warren, a close neighbor of Shaw McKean. On early maturity Mr. Warren bred this bitch to Badshah of Ainsdart, precisely in line with what McKean planned for his own Omar-Asra daughters. At the 1935 Westminster show several "Barberryhill" Afghans issued a friendly challenge to a large McKean entry. Badshah took the breed, and his young daughter, Barberryhill Dolly, captured the bitch points as a quiet forecast to the great future ahead of her.

By 1935 Afghans were spreading to other states. In New Mexico, Miss Amelia White, encouraged by a wise kennel manager, Alex Scott, sensed greatness and climatic suitability in the furry hounds. She obtained Badshah's brother, the cream Tufan of Ainsdart, a bitch, Kali of Prides Hill, and a promising young puppy sired by Badshah ex Zahera of Prides Hill (an Omar-Asra daughter) named Amanullah of Kandahar. This singular young puppy soon put "Kandahar" Afghans on the list of immortals.

Without intending to slight "Tufan" we must emphasize the Omar-Asra-Badshah triple play. These dogs were mated together repeatedly, forming a cornerstone of American breeding. Asra of Ghazni produced some 76 puppies with various studs, including three breedings to Omar, according to McKean's own words. Known affectionately as "Bibbles," Asra left Prides Hill to live with Muriel Boger (Doreborn) where she produced her later litters, dying at the age of 14, the Grande Dame of Afghans. The Badshah-Zahera of

Prides Hill combination produced over thirty pups for Shaw McKean, Margaret Nison, and later for Dr. and Mrs. Combs (Arthea).

With this much early breeding of a hound of limited demand it is fortunate that these experienced dog fanciers did not panic at the threat of over population and were able to keep surplus hounds from the hands of unscrupulous dog merchants. McKean calmly advertised having over 50 hounds at Prides Hill—with over 40 of them for sale. There were good entries at the prestige New England shows courtesy of McKean and Warren. The southwest classes were patronized by Miss White's Kandahar hounds and the Kingway dogs of Mrs. Porter of Colorado. By the close of 1936 and following Kabul of Prides Hill, Badshah of Ainsdart, ' Barberryhill Dolly, Kundah of Prides Hill and Barberryhill Charlie were Eastern champions, and in the Southwest Amanullah of Kandahar and Tufan of Ainsdart had completed their title requirements.

Undoubtedly the most successful show Afghan of the 1930s was Ch. Amanullah of Kandahar who picked off groups and Best in Shows like bones from a plate. Not only in the Southwest did he reign supreme, but as breed winner at Westminster he bested all Eastern competition. By 1940 Amanullah had amassed a record of nine Best in Shows. Part of Amanullah's success was directly attributed to his superlative handling and conditioning by Alex Scott, who intimately understood the hound character. A large, spectacular, well-trained, cream hound with a long impressive head, Amanullah had that show-spark that induced him to "perform" with great animation the moment he sensed human eyes turned his way.

Word of the graceful beauty of the first bitch champion, Barberryhill Dolly, raced cross-country to character actor, Charlie Ruggles, in Hollywood, also a noted dog fancier. As quick as transportation could be arranged Dolly was installed in the Ruggles's ultra-luxurious kennel of canine stars.

At this point, letting Dolly sit in Charlie Ruggles's kennel, which is just what she did do, we might digress to the influx of other imports found on the West Coast. Undoubtedly the most exciting, but least known, were Tazi of Beg Tute and Saki of Paghman, transported directly from Afghanistan to Port Blakely, Washington, by Laurance Peters, foreign news correspondent. Having stepped over an animated Afghan Hound "rug" in Kabul in the French Consul's

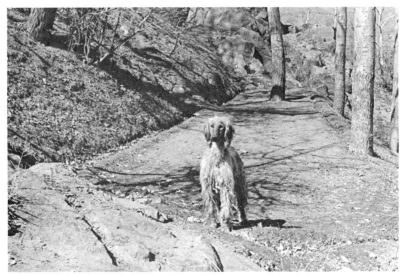

Tazi of Beg Tute, fawn dog, imported from Afghanistan in 1934 by Mr. & Mrs. L. Peters. Picture taken in Afghanistan. Courtesy Mrs. L. Peters.

Ch. Amanullah of Kandahar (Ch. Badshah of Ainsdart ex Zahera of Prides Hill), cream dog owned by Amelia White.

office in 1932, Peters determined to own such a dog someday. In 1934, again in Afghanistan, and with Mrs. Peters, he made a family project of acquiring a brace of the memorable hounds. While certain that there were many fine hounds hidden away in the native villages, he had a time locating them. The natives preferred not to part with their hounds and rather than antagonize the foreign visitors by outright refusal they politely insisted, "Yesterday we had many fine hounds, but last night they all died." The Peters were also frustrated by their Moslem guide and interpreter who disapproved of all dogs and, with an interpreter's advantage, encouraged the natives to deny having hounds. When Peters realized the conspiracy, he enlisted the aid of a friendly Afghan soldier who smoothed relations for a hound purchase. But even to their countrymen the natives maintained that "The females all died the night before." At the village of Beg Tute, Mr. Peters was allowed to select a male hound. He was immediately attracted to a small wild-eyed, fawn colored dog, who stood out by alienating himself from the friendly pack to sulk suspiciously in the background. Peters selected the independent young male, and then spent two hours with the natives chasing the panicky hound. Once captured, Tazi of Beg Tute lived in terror under the Peters's bed, completely unapproachable. When they finally decided that they might have to give him up or trade him for a real Oriental rug, he suddenly calmed down, became obedient, affectionate and eventually Americanized, although he always preferred the sound of Persian words. In disgust, the Moslem servant vanished when the dog moved into the hotel.

Procuring a female was a real task. Almost ready to give up the search, one day they pessimistically asked about Tazi bitches at the small village of Paghman. A wily native offered them a tattered and forlorn looking tiny gray female. Knowing that the native was trying to put something over on them, but under her sad haunting gaze and the fear that they might never find another, they made the purchase. In spite of the fact that her coat was always poor and she had no desire to be a show girl, Saki of Paghman developed great charm and proved to have brood bitch potential when mated to Tazi. Among their offspring was the handsome black Ch. Jac-A-Leen's Shab and the slate gray Blue Mist of Egypt which transferred the exotic Maltese Blue coloration from Saki to the later famous Ch. Felt's Thief of Bagdad.

73

In Southern California Mrs. Caroline Hall Richmond was the owner of an imported bitch, Fatima, born in India in 1928. In 1936 a litter was registered from Fatima, sired by Ch. Tufan of Ainsdart. From this union, Fatima's Daughter Peri, Fatima's Daughter Kushdil and Fatima's Son Tufan Khan won championships in 1937. Despite great acknowledged quality these hounds were not further campaigned by Mrs. Richmond, who apparently was not really bitten by the Show Bug. Ch. Fatima's Daughter Peri is behind the maternal side of the exotic, nearly-white Ch. Felt's Allah Baba, acclaimed by some breeder-judges as one of the most nearly perfect Afghan Hounds ever seen. Ch. Fatima's Son Tufan Khan, bred to Ch. Dura of Prides Hill, sired some of Dr. Marxmiller's "Dellire" champions in the late 1930s.

R. W. Samson of Redwood City, California, was exhibiting as contemporaries of the Fatima-get his English imports, Ch. Garrymhor Kishtwar and bitches, Garrymhor Khasa (who became a champion) and Jalalabad Kara, as his basic "Kuhsan" Afghans. He later imported the lovely English Mounha of Kuhsan, and when her championship was made, sold her to Mrs. Porter's Kingway kennels where she blended well with Ch. Niliyo of Prides Hill.

The remainder of the West Coast competition was made up of Prides Hill and related stock. Venita Vardon Oakie, beauteous wife of comedian Jack Oakie, developed a rapport with the Arabian Nights hounds and in 1936 was showing a Tufan daughter, Morgiana of Kandahar, in the classes with the Samson and Richmond entries. At this time Ch. Barberryhill Dolly arrived in the West. She won a few honors under the Ruggles banner, but as a sensitive girl not always in an outgoing mood, she was considered unreliable and left in the kennel temporarily forgotten.

Samson's Kishtwar was the Special of the day, above fighting in the class preliminaries, ready to battle the Hound groups, which he topped frequently. With his thick, short, all-over coat Kishtwar looked like a saddled puppy. His head was unlike the typical Prides Hill muzzle, being deeper and more blunt in profile, but with good length.

Suddenly Athos Nilson hit California with Ch. Barberryhill Charlie, Dolly's litter brother. At his first appearance in the west Charlie topped the Hound Group and became the first Best in Show Afghan in California at the Los Angeles Kennel Club in 1937.

74

Venita Vardon Oakie and some puppies from her Oakvardon Kennel. *Ludwig photo*

Ch. Barberryhill Dolly (bitch) and Ch. Umberto (dog), imported from India for Oakvardon.

Charlie rolled up a quick record of western wins at the expense of Kishtwar, and in friendly rivalry Mr. Samson sent for the third champion of the Badshah-Barberryhill Illusive litter, Ch. Barberryhill Phillip, who did not equal Charlie's show career but did leave a definite mark on Kushan pedigrees through an intermix with the English bitches.

Late in 1937 Ch. Barberryhill Dolly, shamefully wasted in the vast Ruggles kennels, went to Venita Vardon Oakie, who lavished understanding care on the lovely hound. In return, with great devotion for Venita, Dolly gained self-assurance and found new favor with the judges, who had always appreciated her graceful femininity and excellent gait. Handled by Russell Zimmerman, with Venita standing close by, Dolly began to collect groups regularly. At home, Dolly was Mrs. Oakie's beloved companion and inspiration for the great Oakvardon Afghan kennel that was to rival Prides Hill in size.

Umberto was imported from India for Oakvardon, winning his championship in 1938 and adding distinction to the Oakvardon stud force. From Ireland came Hanuman of Enriallic. Dolly began to hit her best stride and under the guidance of Phyllis Ranier, at the Del Monte Kennel Club show in 1940, became the first Best in Show bitch in California and the second in the United States at the age of six years old. Rather than retiring on the honor, Dolly again stood alone in the charmed circle twice the following year.

Oakvardon was enriched by two English hounds, Westmill Razuran and the English Champion bitch, Westmill Natanz. The black-masked, light red Natanz was then six years old and carried a full and decidedly wavy coat. She was a granddaughter of Ch. Tufan of Ainsdart through a breeding made before he was exported to the United States, and also of the famous heavy-coated import Lakki Marwat. Natanz had a wonderfully sweet personality and a lovely gait, like a purposeful feather. The judges liked her immediately. When shown at Fresno and Ventura with no class competition, she won her needed points by taking both Best in Shows. With Ch. Umberto also hitting the top all-breed honors in 1941, Oakvardon boasted of three Best in Show hounds that year and the broadest base of quality bloodlines in America. Venita Vardon Oakie became a highly respected judge, and a totally devoted friend of the breed until her untimely death in 1948.

In the Ohio area during 1938, Frank Andrews, Dr. Combs and

Frank Weithoff (Kerrin Kennels) and a few others with Prides Hill stock formed the nucleus of a breed club. The previous year the Afghan Hound Club of America had its embryo formation, but became noted only for its complete inactivity. Midwestern fanciers agreed to form a splinter group of greater vigor. On October 9, 1938, the enthusiastic Midwest Afghan Hound Club held America's first Afghan Hound Specialty in conjunction with the Detroit Specialties group. Out of an entry of 12 hounds, Best of Breed went to Garrymhor Pearie, an imported English bitch owned by Miss Nancy Andrews.

In a mild sort of a way, by 1939 the Afghan Hound had arrived in America. There was little danger of the breed rivaling the German Shepherd in popularity, but registrations had climbed to 148 in that year. Afghan Hound devotees were determined, experienced, and could be found throughout the country. As a prestige item the breed was getting good space in fashion magazines and Hollywood publicity shots.

From the beginning, the number of types of the breed which existed in Afghanistan had served as a natural obstacle to producing uniformity of character, and the early English outcrossings did little to help this situation. In America, however, selective line breeding of Omar, Asra, Badshah and Tufan had produced a certain degree of uniformity which was mainly threatened by the arrival of the new imports. Prides Hill hounds were certainly not all identical, nor did they lack room for improvement, but the assets of a long chiseled head and the agile, purposeful action of the original group had been retained in the best specimens of this kennel.

At this time in America, coats were moderate to poor, but especially in comparison to the lushness of contemporary English winners. George Thomas had told McKean to "show your dogs fit and strong and forget about too many ruffles." This became the Prides Hill creed, and the kennel produced hounds that were marvels of structural soundness. As spokesman for the breed, McKean emphasized breed character and action over physical embellishments.

As cream hounds, totally devoid of black hairs, Omar and Asra had poor skin pigment with light noseleathers and eye rims. Among their offspring and those of Badshah and Tufan were colored pups with large white facial blazes and high white stockings, frequently studded with freckles of color.

The Standard was beautifully unspecific on surface details. Criticisms and penalties were weakly advanced on the grounds of general unattractiveness. Blazed champions and those with practically no coat at all from elbow to the ground were not unusual, as some judges felt that the graces of showmanship and an impressive gait could be better appreciated when not hidden by an excessive coat. Surprisingly enough, through the stockpiling of Sirdar genes, some pretty fair coats with lovely, silken textures appeared from time to time as they did on Dolly and on Ch. Rudiki of Prides Hill.

Each import tended to be a surprise and sometimes a bit of a shocker. In 1939 Mrs. Austin of Catawba Pekingeses brought out her fantastically coated English import, the lovely cream Ch. Lakshmi of Geufron-Catawba, which startled the breeders and judges on the East Coast. That year Lakshmi became the first Best in Show bitch in America. To some, she was a drippy-coated freak, but others realized that she was a sample of things to come in the breed.

The heavier-coated English dogs continued to seep into America, always being mixed with the existing Yankee stock. A race for physical superiority was begun as the newer imports advanced coat potential, bringing leg coat and rich topknots, as well as deeper pigment in skin and fur. Such aims had the effect of softening the set type of Omar and Badshah, and some dogs, valued greatly for their impressive coats and rich coloring, were penalized only slightly for less than elegant muzzles, crooked legs, puny bodies and unsound gaits.

By 1940 the practically defunct Afghan Hound Club of America had pulled its inactive shreds together and applied for membership with the American Kennel Club. Q. A. Shaw McKean was elected President, Mrs. Robert Boger, secretary, and Dr. Beck the first delegate to the A.K.C. Mrs. Boger opened a column in the American Kennel Gazette and remained the breed correspondent for the next nine years. The subject of standard revision came up immediately as the existing one was under fire for its omissions. Judges and breeders complained that it gave no guidance on the finer points of the breed. The obvious need for a more detailed standard was

Ch. Lakshmi of Geufron-Catawba, a cream imported from England and America's first Best-in-Show Afghan bitch, owned by Mrs. James Austin.

quickly acknowledged, but talk of any specific changes was followed by immediate bickering.

The characteristic American Afghan Hound head, with the slight Roman rise and piercing Oriental almond eye was not detailed in the standard, but had gained acceptance as a model of strength and Eastern beauty from Westmill Omar and Badshah. McKean wanted this spelled out in the standard. He also believed the high tail carriage to be significant, having read an account of hunters supposedly following Afghan Hounds through the brush by means of their high tails. This is certainly one of the more questionable myths in the breed image, as sparsely fringed tails would scarcely make good "flags" considering the get-away speed of an Afghan, and the breed is certainly not suited to brush hunting, but Badshah's extremely high tail and McKean's beliefs encouraged acceptance of the model of the tall tail in the breed.

Through notation of the most pleasing aspects of the more successful dogs, a gradually detailed portrait of external breed character slowly developed, but did not gain unanimous acceptance. McKean's own sensitivity regarding pigment was obvious in the Gazette articles in which he denied any importance to nose or eye rim color. He claimed that the fierce, dark eye, which happened to be prevalent at Prides Hill, was of 'far greater value. Breeders plagued with light-eyed hounds, with dark masking and strong skin pigmentation, were understandably in discord with McKean. Unattractive blazes and the occasional occurrence of parti-colored Afghans put other breeders on the defensive. The fancy was unanimously against the unsound, the coarse or the puny dog, but could not agree on the boundaries of coarseness or size.

In 1941 the AHCA reviewed a copy of a trial standard submitted by Mrs. Porter to the *Bulletin*. At the February meeting of that year the members declared a ban on all *trimming of Afghan Hounds,* and the Gazette carried the following admonition: "The Afghans' whiskers are a characteristic of the breed, and he sheds his coat naturally where it should be shed, without benefit of the plucking knife. Let us leave him as he is!!" In those days an undersufficiency of hair was far more troublesome than any surplus, as indicated by Mrs. Boger's note to the effect that, "There should be a shed-off place at the pastern or knee joint on the front legs although dogs carrying the heavy coat down to the feet should not be unduly penalized." Revision of the standard was accompanied by a perpetual grumble growing louder when it was known that the English breed fancy had long ago abandoned the standard that roughly corresponded to the American document.

One inexplicable sentence of the standard calling for the body to have ample length caused concern. As a result of the indefinite phrasing, wide variation of ratio of back length to leg length was tolerated in the breed while some breeders strongly advocated a more compact hound. Marion Florsheim, writing an influential breed column in *Kennel Review,* pointed to the current English Standard which stated that the Afghan Hounds were "compact and well-coupled, agile, built for jumping and leaping endurance. Not the long-loined racing dog whose first quality is horizontal speed." From England then, came a statement, to the effect that the Afghan's height should about equal his length. As such a hound was balanced regardless of size, discouraging extremes of either body type, the concept of the square Afghan came into being. Acceptance was not wholehearted, as one writer maintained, "Ample length is open to personal interpretation, but it doesn't seem to mean 'square' no matter how one looks at it." In the midst of the furor, Mr. McKean suggested that the Standard revisions be shelved "for the duration" as America was being touched by the strife in Europe and had larger problems to worry about.

We are rushing past too many influential hounds and must back up a bit. In August of 1937 at Prides Hill Kennels a litter by Badshah ex Ch. Shireen of Prides Hill produced a noteworthy male pup christened Rudiki of Prides Hill. When Shaw McKean introduced the majestic Rudiki in the Fall of 1938, the dog was immediately acclaimed the finest Prides Hill specimen to date. After a quick round of Eastern shows, McKean rested his young champion and awaited coat maturity. A year later he took Rudiki to the West Coast where the sparkling dog etched his name at the top of many a hound group and in the memories of those who viewed him at the California shows. Some still recall his beautifully chiseled head in the tradition of Badshah, but black-masked on a clear gold background. So exquisite was his muzzle that his portrait signaled the Afghan Hound column in the *Gazette* at the debut of the column in 1940 and remained until 1965. With his fine, silken, red-gold coat,

81

Ch. Rudiki of Prides Hill, owned by Marion Florsheim.

Ch. Tanyah Sahib of Cy-Ann, owned by Cyrus Rickel, was Best of Breed winner at the first Parent Club Specialty in 1940.

an amazingly noble carriage and attractive gait, a grand career was prophesied for Rudiki.

The Afghan Hound Club of America held its first Specialty show in 1940, judged by Dr. Eugene Beck, who chose Ch. Tanyah Sahib of CyAnn from the kennel of Cyrus Rickel, noted multi-breed judge, as top winner. This dog, from the breeding of Ch. Amanullah of Kandahar to Kali of Prides Hill, went on to Group three as the Specialty was held in conjunction with the North Westchester all-breed show. In 1941, the Specialty, held at the same site, was judged by Dr. Combs who placed Dr. Gertrude Kinsey's young Champion bitch, Hazar (Ch. Agha Kush ex Westmill Taree) at the top of the breed.

Many fanciers with acknowledged success in other breeds were magnetically attracted to the Afghan rings. Ch. Kerrin Fachamo (Ch. Badshah of Ainsdart ex Zahera of Prides Hill) was a well-known Best in Show winner from the Weithoff's midwest kennel better known for fine "Kerrin Collies." Another Collie breeder, Lillian Miller, from the state of Washington stopped at Kerrin for a look at the Collies and adopted a promising Afghan named Kerrin Fachamur. Once back in Washington, her young male found practically no class competition but won honors for the breed by frequently topping Northwest groups and garnered the Best in Show award at Seattle in 1941. Ch. Kerrin Fachamur bred to Zar Sunni of Tazi forged a link between the Laurance Peters imports and basic American stock.

Charles Wernsman, long respected for Arken Collies, fostered a tribe of "Arken Afghans" based on Ku Mari Khyaam of Arken (Badshah ex Zahera of Prides Hill) and the imported English sire Ch. Garrymhor Zabardast of Arken. Zabardast was an upstanding hound with a magnificent head and Oriental expression and did some impressive winning. His great claim to fame was as the Arken stud. He and Sara (Ku Mari Khyaam of Arken) combined to raise a dynasty of famous black-masked red Arken hounds. Their first litter produced six notable champions: Bul Bul, Sultan, Pocono Persica, Mogul, Maharanee and Rajah. Miss Whelan, owner of Ch. Maharanee of Arken C.D.X. and Best in Show Ch. Mogul of Arken, C.D., firmly believed that Afghans were as bright as they were beautiful and well proved her contention.

Ch. Rajah of Arken, a hound of magnificently sound gait and

Ch. Garrymhor Zabardast of Arken (Garrymhor Ghalan Nubi ex Ranai of Istalif), imported from England.

Ku Mari Khyaam of Arken, bitch, owned by Charles Wernsman.

strong temperament remained at Arken, becoming the only Afghan Hound to ever win the Parent Club Specialty three times, in 1942, 1943 and 1944. The breeding was repeated with additional success. Quality Arken hounds stud the back lines of many fine American pedigrees.

In 1939, Rana of Chaman came from the war-threatened Scottish kennel of Molly Sharpe to the safety of America. The Royal Irish suffix was added by his importers, Mr. and Mrs. A. J. Baron. As an immediate group winner from the classes, Rana was acquired by Marion Foster Florsheim. Marion swiftly completed his title and a round of group wins, culminating in Rana's first BIS at National Capital Kennel Club in 1942.

Shortly before Mrs. Florsheim entered the breed with Rana, Mrs. Hayes Blake Hoyt of Blakeen Poodle fame, had been attracted to Shaw McKean's Rudiki whom she obtained together with a few select bitches to found Blakeen Afghans. Rudiki's success rivaled the Blakeen Poodles, and it was not unusual to find Rudiki and a Blakeen Poodle vying for top honors. Afghans at Blakeen were successful, but not lasting. Mrs. Hoyt retained a great fondness for the breed but by the end of 1941 the Afghan area of Blakeen was disbanded. Mrs. Hoyt had acquired an exceptionally lovely stud-fee puppy bitch (sired by Rudiki ex Lasca Klana) named Rudika of Blakeen. Rudiki, together with his gorgeous daughter Rudika, passed to the eager arms of Marion Florsheim joining Rana as the foundation of Five Mile Afghans in Connecticut.

World War II was diminishing the dog fancy in America by 1942. Gasoline and meat supplies were limited by ration cards. Dogs subsisted on commercial kibble and canned foods, sometimes of dubious quality. Suggestions for supplementing wartime diets included fish heads, breakfast cereals and incubator eggs.

As conscription took many of the men from their homes, kennel-keeping became the woman's responsibility. By clever and persistent efforts by dog lovers shows were not completely curtailed but were given over to the raising of monies for wartime charities. Defense stamps were given in lieu of trophies. Traveling on rationed gas was the biggest headache, and the 1945 AHCA Specialty was cancelled through fairness to those who could not make the trip.

In 1942, Dogs For Defense established the K9 Corps, enlisting dogs volunteered by selfless owners wishing to contribute to the effort in all possible ways. One of the few bench show champions

85

Ch. Rajah of Arken.

```
                                                      Khan Baber
                                      Ardmore Anthony
                                                      Dakkas Delight
                      Garrymhor Ghulam-Nubi
                                                      Ch. Ashna of Ghazni
                                      Ch. Garrymhor Souriya
                                                      Ch. Alfreda
        Ch. Garrymhor Zabardast of Arken
                                                      (Afghanistan)
                                      Ch. Sirdar of Ghazni
                                                      (Afghanistan)
                      Rani of Istalif
                                                      (Afghanistan)
                                      Shireen of Ghazni
                                                      (Afghanistan)
Ch. Rajah of Arken
                                                      (Afghanistan)
                                      Ch. Sirdar of Ghazni
                                                      (Afghanistan)
                      Ch. Badshah of Ainsdart
                                                      Taj Mahip of Kaf
                                      Ku Mari of Kaf
                                                      Sonee
        Ku Mari Khyaam of Arken
                                                      Danenda of Ghazni
                                      Westmill Omar
                                                      Surkh of Ghazni
                      Zahera of Prides Hill
                                                      Ch. Sirdar of Ghazni
                                      Asra of Ghazni
                                                      Shireen of Ghazni
```

Ch. Rudika of Blakeen, Best-in-Show bitch and dam of six champions.

Int. Ch. Rana of Chaman of Royal Irish (Ch. Westmill Bayezid Ansari ex Safiya) , dog imported from England by Mr. and Mrs. A. J. Baron, owned by Marion Foster Florsheim.

in the K9 Corps was Ch. Kerrin Fayunga, Afghan Hound. Mrs. Weithoff's Yunga was one of few Afghans in the Corps, serving with distinction, but never returning home as he succumbed to a hero's case of jaundice shortly before his time of discharge.

The Corps soon became more selective, accepting only specific breeds of value in particular duties. The Afghan Hound was not one of the desired ones. Some suspected that the Afghan had proved temperamentally unfit for Army life, but a later bulletin declared that breeds were dropped for a variety of reasons, one being their lack of availability as the rare breeds could not be procured in large numbers if the request should arise. The few Afghans in the K9 Corps did not become national heroes but managed to get their eye-catching selves into many of the Corps' publicity shots.

Dr. Marxmiller's Afghan, Red Ryder, a mascot of a Naval Bomber Squadron, was killed aloft in action on a South Pacific mission.

The Afghan Hound played its largest war effort role through raising impressive sums of money for charity. The AHCA Match Show of 1942 was held on the grand Florsheim estate in the form of a carnival which had a huge turnout of spectators who contributed over $350 to the United Nations War Relief. Incidentally, the Match was won by Mrs. Froelich's young Zannette of Elcoza, who later took her place on the line of Afghan greats.

As an aviatrix who ferried planes from field to field for Civilian Defense, Marion Florsheim managed to use her Afghans in her job. Ch. Rana, in a pair of long polka-dot pants, acted as Master of Ceremonies at the plush Calling All Dogs charity show. A Florsheim Afghan puppy named Freckles was raffled off to an elated new owner as a Bundle for Britain. She also penned an influential column in *Kennel Review,* passing on news from all over the United States, England and Canada. In addition to ferrying the planes, she was able to campaign champions Rudiki and Rana throughout the Eastern seaboard, Canada, and inland to Indiana and the deep South. Between them the two dogs racked up impressive quantities of top all-breed wins. These travels produced widespread puppy purchases and stud uses among fanciers able to glimpse these ambassadors of the breed. Rudiki was certainly the most popular Afghan stud in the United States during the war era.

Marion Florsheim's interests and duties multiplied. She was able to retain her beloved Rudiki and a few hounds at Five Mile, but most of her puppies and other hounds went to other fanciers. In 1945 Helen Bamberger of Salt Lake City, acquired Ch. Rana, spreading his stud effect over the Western United States.

Rudiki's daughter, Ch. Rudika of Blakeen, produced a small litter sired by Ch. Rana, containing Mrs. Bamberger's Ch. Zumerrud of Five Mile, Mrs. Gudgeon's Ch. Asri-Havid of Five Mile, and Ch. Yenghiz-Khan of Five Mile, campaigned some time by Mrs. Florsheim before he also was sold. The gorgeous Rudika moved to the home of Charles Costabile in Texas on a co-ownership and spent flying time commuting between Texas and Connecticut. Rudika was the top winning show bitch of the war years and those immediately following.

During 1943 and 1944 Afghan registrations understandably dropped to the pre-war level of 1940. But by the end of 1945, war pressure relaxed and registrations leaped from 134 in 1944 to 526 in 1946, a peak that was not passed again until 1957. Breeders frantically raced to put long-range breeding programs back on a schedule. Budding fanciers, eager for fun after the solemn war years, embraced the dog game as a delightful weekend recreation.

Ch. Ali Khyber, the first of the really extravagantly-coated, American bred Afghans, arose during the war years, making a record that was not clearly realized until after the national emergency. By the end of 1944, fanciers who avidly followed the *Gazette,* suspected that this young Rudiki son was running away with the honors in the New England states. Owned by Leah and "Macky" McConaha, the successful Khyber (pronounced, Keeber) was the family pet as was his mother, Pommel Rock Kashan.

The Pommel Rock hounds, imported property of Mrs. Lynde Selden, had quietly arrived in the United States during the late 1930s. Pommel Rock Kashan, whelped in America, had inherited some of the particularly heavy-coated genes developed through selection in England, coming down from Ch. Garrymhor Yenghiz-Khan (Ardmore Anthony ex Ch. Garrymhor Souriya). The mating of Pommel Rock Kashan to Rudiki represented a strong outcross from the Prides Hill type, unleashing a fantastic and heretofore unseen type of thick and long, stand-off-the-body coating that was to characterize Ali Khyber and many of his future get. Fortunately, Ali Khyber inherited refined chiseling of head from his sire.

Ali Khyber, born in 1941, had amassed 10 all-breed American

Ch. Ali Khyber.

```
                                                                (Afghanistan)
                                              Ch. Sirdar of Ghazni
                                                                (Afghanistan)
                        Ch. Badshah of Ainsdart
                                                                Taj Mahip of Kaf
                                              Ku Mari of Kaf
                                                                Sonee
          Ch. Rudiki of Prides Hill
                                                                Westmill Omar
                                              Ch. Kundah of Prides Hill
                                                                Asra of Ghazni
                        Ch. Shireen of Prides Hill
                                                                Ch. Badshah of Ainsdart
                                              Lakshmi of Prides Hill
                                                                Zahera of Prides Hill
Ch. Ali Khyber
                                                                Khan Babar
                                              Ardmore Anthony
                                                                Dakkas Delight
                        Nerone of Pommel Rock
                                                                Baber Khan
                                              Shiela Beg
                                                                Dakkas Delight
          Pommel Rock Kashan
                                                                Ardmore Anthony
                                              Garrymhor Yenghiz-Khan
                                                                Ch. Garrymhor Souriya
                        Hamara of Pommel Rock
                                                                Kulli-Khan
                                              Zinanna of Ghanistan
                                                                Natasha of Kuranda
```

Best In Shows by the end of 1947, cracking the record set by Ch. Amanullah of Kandahar a decade before. As a great sire Khyber founded Leah McConaha's Khanhasset Afghans and a formidable dynasty leading directly through the modern names of Majara and other offshoots noted for the great coats. The finest Prides Hill coats tended to be of a silky texture and were a slow growing proposition at their best on mature hounds, but coming down from Khyber, thick, full coats often grew at fantastic rates, creating puppy champions, but also on occasion fell off far more rapidly. In breeding combinations representing both types of coat, fantastically heavy and long coats sometimes resulted and, in less fortunate mixes, factors for slow growth and quick dropping combined to produce very poor coated specimens indeed. But the possibilities for Afghan show coats had been greatly advanced, and Khyber became one of the most successful American sires ever recorded, with 35 champions to his credit. Ali Khyber's lovely litter sister, Ch. Maharanee Kohibaba CD, was purchased, campaigned, and obedience trained by Marion Florsheim.

In 1944 the Rudiki-Pommel Rock Kashan breeding was repeated, producing Ch. Khanhasset's Kanda. Without seeing the dog, Charles Costabile purchased Ch. Kanda as a suitable mate for his famous bitch Ch. Rudika of Blakeen. The merger of Kanda and Dika formed the Kandika names seen on many modern pedigrees. Kanda astonished Texas and the nearby Southern states by winning six Best in Shows and numerous Hound groups when he arrived at the Costabile home. In consequence Kanda became the first Afghan Hound to win the valued Quaker Oats award as the top winning dog of all breeds in the Southern states during 1946.

Back at Khanhasset young Ali Khyber was put to Ch. Shibergam of Dunrobin (Ch. Westmill Humayun of Catawba ex Hamara of Pommel Rock), a further intensification of the European heavy-coated lines. In truth, much of this coat increase was in thickness and rate of growth on body and legs. Pasterns often remained completely bare, in the ballet dancer pattern. Feet were sparsely covered in many instances, giving a long-bodied, top-heavy look at first glance.

From the Khyber ex Shibergam litter, Ch. Karach and Ch. Karan of Khanhasset were retained by Mrs. McConaha. The youngsters developed quickly and when barely into his prime Khyber was tem-

Ch. Khanhasset's Kanda, dog, owned by Charles Costabile.

porarily retired to give his offspring greater opportunities. Ch. Karach matured magnificently, gaining exhibition success that bordered on the phenomenal, appearing ready to batter down all records set to date. From Best of Breed at the 1946 Specialty, he also took the group at Interstate where the Specialty was held. Five months later the AHCA arranged to hold its first independent Specialty judged by Charles Wernsman. Again Karach took the honors. In the next six months Karach had been chosen Best in Show three times and had taken seven Hound groups. But Ch. Karach of Khanhasset's career was in the nature of an explosion, for less than a year after he had gained his title, when at barely two years of age, Karach was defeated by leptospirosis, immediately fatal. The fancy was stunned. Many belatedly wished they had used the young male for stud, but Karach sired exactly one litter out of Far Away Loo, which was never offered for sale, being retained by the breeder, Mrs. Marjorie Jagger (later Mrs. Lathrop). This one-of-its-kind litter was the basis of "Majara." Peculiarly enough, it was more than Karach's personal quality that brought Mrs. Lathrop to him; it was the fact that she owned Karach's dam's sister, Ch. Dunrobin Daiquiri, but had been unable to get any issue from her when she was bred to Ch. Ali Khyber and other studs. Thwarted in obtaining the desired Daiquiri-Ali Khyber pups, Mrs. Lathrop bred Far Away Loo to Khyber's son from a similar breeding. The first Majara litter became the sole existing link from "Karach" to the future.

Leah McConaha was persuaded to bring out her great Ali Khyber again, as well as Karach's look-alike sister, Ch. Karan of Khanhasset. The now aging Khyber took control of the Eastern rings and won three of his total BIS when brought out of retirement. But he grew tired and soon left the banner to his daughter Karan who was to be reckoned with regardless of sex. She followed her brother's old footsteps by winning the Independent Specialty in 1948 under judge Ernie Ferguson who commented on her magnificent head and type. During the year she won nine Hound groups and Best in Show at Albany.

In 1948, the Afghan Hound Club of America decided to hold two Specialties, a Fall Show in conjunction with the Interstate All-Breed Club in September, and the Independent Specialty to follow in the Spring. The Fall show was somewhat experimental and was not repeated after the first try. At the extra Fall Specialty, with Leah

93

Ch. Karan (bitch) and Ch. Karach (dog) of Khanhasset, littermates owned by Leah McConaha.

McConaha as judge, young Ch. Majara Mahabat, from the lone Karach-sired litter, took the ultimate honors, which he repeated at the following Independent Specialty under a split judging assignment. Due to a tie vote in the judges' selection, Mr. McConaha judged the class dogs and Best in Show while Mrs. Boger did class bitches and Best of Winners.

We have come upon 1948 too soon and must back up a bit. At the end of WWII fighting broke out anew in the Afghan camps over revision of the Standard. Breed complaints had an age-old sound. In one area critics complained of all the "weedy little Afghans in the rings that couldn't catch a rabbit much less a deer." Elsewhere the complaint was that winning Afghans were much too large and distressingly coarse in head. Poor temperament was singled out as some specimens were dangerously headstrong while others were impossibly shy. Songs of judges' color prejudice against brindles and dark colors were sung, with a second chorus against the great variety of coat types and textures permitted on winners. The words "Afghan type" were becoming meaningless, it was moaned. A new and more highly detailed standard was seen by many to be the solution for all these sundry ills in the breed. Others politely suggested that a modicum of common sense, a little less kennel blindness and more attention to the current standard by judges and breeders might do as much good as a re-written standard. Tempers were rising again.

One thoroughly disgruntled fancier began to promote an International Afghan Hound Council to set up one standard for the United States, Europe and parts of Asia. This thought rang well with those impatient with cautious American efforts at serious revisions, and representatives from other countries gave the plan some serious consideration. In February of 1946 the *Gazette* announced that the group was meeting in New York City to write a standard "to emphasize the 'mountain type' of Afghan, with long slender skull, body balance and running gear to be stressed. This type of Afghan carries coat well down over the legs and is more elegant in profile . . ."

This, of course, was wild oversimplification of the existing problems embodying the inherent conflict between the early Bell-Murray type with elegant profiles and long slender skulls as opposed to the balanced, sturdier, long-coated Ghazni types. The embryo Inter-

95

ANNUAL A.K.C.
REGISTRATIONS
AFGHAN HOUNDS
1926-1948

1926....4	1937....80
1927....1	1938....125
1928....5	1939....148
1929....0	1940....135
1930....1	1941....217
1931....0	1942....218
1932....1	1943....138
1933....6	1944....134
1934....27	1945....310
1935....21	1946....526
1936....82	1947....444
1948....417	

national Group was immediately deadlocked in stubborn disagreement over what actually constituted the desired "mountain type." The International Afghan Hound Council stuck to its task for a few months, receiving a fair press and some highly unsympathetic rebukes from the AHCA correspondents in the *Gazette*. As the Council members continued to describe the mountain type in terms of their own most admired local types, the International concept came to a quick natural demise.

In 1946 the revised English Standard was adopted by the British Kennel Club and the Afghan Hound Association. This standard was not drastically different from its predecessor and the changeover was easily accomplished. Most of Europe adopted the British Standard shortly thereafter.

Simultaneously, but independently, in America the latest Standard Committee, with Mrs. Porter's ancient trial standard in hand and many suggestions to consider, drafted changes and additions. Requests, even pleadings, were sent to the membership for more opinions on what points needed clarification or addition. The committee was made up of thoughtful breeders of long years in Afghans and many more years in other breeds. Some of the guiding lights, in addition to Mrs. Porter, were Charles Wernsman of Arken, Muriel Boger of Doreborn, and Eve Miner of Laineux, working industriously to clarify and complete a new statement. The new standard was completed in 1947, but hashed over gently until the following Spring meeting where the final vote was taken and the revised Standard overwhelmingly accepted. On September 14, 1948, the Board of Directors of the American Kennel Club approved the current Standard.

5

Modern American
Afghan Influences

"So in just a few short years, the transition is complete from a wild dog of prey racing across distant plains under the banner of savage hillmen. He has now become a prancing exhibitionist at the nation's greatest shows, flaunting his beauty before the judges and winning his share of glory." Braden Finch (*Kennel Review* ad, June, 1949).

1948 brought a revised standard and a noticeable transition into the era of modern Afghan Hounds. The long-revered names of Prides Hill, Oakvardon, Five Mile, Arken and Khanhasset were over the top and gradually sliding back on the pedigrees. Rudiki at 10 years old died in 1947 of a broken heart, it was said, at being unable to accompany his beloved Marion Florsheim to Europe. Ali Khyber was retired and his younger brother Kanda, in Texas, broke off his leash and darted across a street into the path of a car, sustaining a crushed shoulder that sent him out to stud pastures. Ch. Rana, long retired, made his final home in California with Margaret Hawkins, siring a few twilight litters at the age of 11. In the New

Mexico sunshine, Amanullah lived out a full 17 years. Most of the pioneer importers and breeders had given up their hounds, passed on, or traded their exhibitor's passes for judging licenses.

Barberryhill Dolly saw her 15th birthday in the Grandeur Kennel of Sunny Shay. Two very fine bitches aged imperceptibly during the decade, continuing to challenge the youngsters on special occasions. In 1949, the nearly 10 year old Ch. Rudika of Blakeen was entered at Fort Worth, Texas, as a special treat for some of her human friends visiting from the East. A bitch of permanent and undimmed beauty, Charles Costabile's Dika won Best in Show before many misty-eyed spectators. Ch. Maharanee Kohibaba, sister of Ali Khyber, spent her Fall years with Amelia White in Santa Fe, teaching the youngsters a lesson by topping a New Mexico show the same year. But these proud ladies were well-preserved remnants of a fast fading era.

In 1948 registrations had settled back from the record high of 1946 into a period of quiescence, not to surge again until 1956. But the breed held its position, hovering around the 45th spot in total registration, rising and falling with dogs in general. As previously stressed, the Afghan Hound was decidedly an "exhibitor's breed" with an inordinately large number of entries in competition primarily in the coastal areas of California and New England. Point requirements were at minimums elsewhere. The New York area point schedule for 1948 required an entry of five dogs for three points, 10 dogs for four, and 15 hounds (dogs or bitches) for the maximum five points. California requirements in 1949 were eight males for three points, 10 for four points, and 13 dogs for five. Competition was keen across the continent, but by the early 1950s, the balance of heavy entries leaned from the East to the fast-growing West.

In 1947 the West Coast Afghan Hound Club had been formed with Mel Strann as President and Betsy Prior as Secretary. Membership leaped from 14 to 40 within the year. New impetus came to the West with the influx of the Priors and other fanciers from the East. The Club fostered organized enthusiasm for the hounds, advancing their popularity with breathtakingly brilliant bazaar wrappings and silken pillows surrounding tribes of exotic multi-hued hounds elegantly draped along show benches, catching the eye of many fanciers-to-be. June of 1948 found the young West Coast club sponsoring the

99

Annual A.K.C. Registrations of Afghan Hounds
(1965–1973)

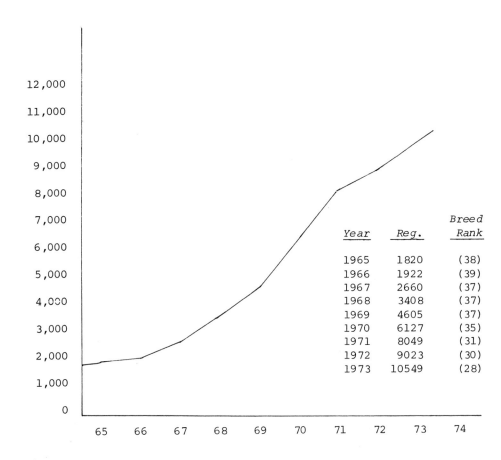

Year	Reg.	Breed Rank
1965	1820	(38)
1966	1922	(39)
1967	2660	(37)
1968	3408	(37)
1969	4605	(37)
1970	6127	(35)
1971	8049	(31)
1972	9023	(30)
1973	10549	(28)

Harbor Cities Kennel Club entry to the tune of 62 Afghan exhibits, easily winning first place for their striking bench decor.

By 1949, the American Kennel Club requested that the name be changed to the Afghan Hound Club of California.

The Afghans which won the most in the Golden State in 1948 were two group-winning bitches. Previous to the arrival of the Priors with their gorgeous coated black and tan Ch. Black Ryn of Donde, a lovely black-masked red bitch named Ch. Buzineh Tabidan of Jurahn had been holding the males in their places. Soon, ignoring the "boys," the two contrastingly colored bitches fought it out until touched by the challenge of young Felt's Thief of Bagdad, owned by a comparative newcomer to the breed, one Katherine Finch, well known in Yorkshire Terrier circles and as a ceramicist of note.

Not quite all the motion was from East to West, however. At the Los Angeles Kennel Club's 1948 show, a young lady held her pet hound by a length of clothesline rope as she embarrassedly glanced at the shimmering drape-coated Afghans on fancy leads led by highly-assured owners. Unable to escape from the benched showgrounds, she reluctantly entered the show ring with Punk and was both grateful and surprised to receive a blue ribbon. Soon the anxious steward pushed the pair back into the ring for Winners. That hound, not in the least embarrassed or flustered, "fit and strong without too many ruffles," was chosen Best of Winners for a five pointer under the noted judge, Dr. Wm. Ivens, Jr. The dog, later formally known as Ch. Five Miles Punjab Ben Ghazi, and his owner, Ruth Tongren, soon moved to the East Coast to found the famous Ben Ghazi Afghans. Punk became noted as a sire of champions including the famous Best in Show stud, twice winner of the Parent Club Specialty, Ch. Karli Ben Ghazi.

From 1948 onward, fanciers became breeders at the drop of a blue ribbon. Numerous names flash and go in the rings. Much as we would like to make mention of all these fine hounds, pay homage to their industrious owners and proud breeders, it would take several large volumes. Concentration on the development of the top winners and most prolific producers of champions is of the greatest value to the largest number of readers. Most well-bred Afghans of modern times are related to these great foundation sires. Refer to Chapter 7 for a list of top-producing sires, with names of their champion "get."

Int. Ch. Felt's Thief of Bagdad (Ch. Sinbad the Sailor ex Kara She-Ba), dog, owned by Kay Finch.

Ch. Black Ryn of Donde (Zenophon of Elcoza ex Ch. Laineux Dolly Deluxe) bitch, owned by Betsy Prior.

Through substitution of sibling names, the pedigrees within the chapter have an even broader application.

"Elcoza," a kennel of great interest, owned by Mrs. Lauer Froelich, was born of unexpected wartime developments. Attracted to the breed, Mrs. Froelich had arranged to purchase a bitch from the English kennel of Dr. Betsy Porter on a forthcoming trip to Europe, but, the year was 1939 and with bomb scares above Britain, Mrs. Froelich thought twice and turned West to California and New Mexico instead. When visiting pioneer breeder, Margaret Nison, Mrs. Froelich was quickly attracted to young Yusseff, a nearly white son of Ch. Tufan of Ainsdart ex Ch. Shabra, and took the handsome male back to Pennsylvania with her. On their arrival in the East, she discovered that Dr. Porter, unaware of the interim travels and frightened for the safety of her beloved hounds, had already shipped, not only a bitch, Rani, but also her litter brother, Sardar Khan el Kabul, to America via the "Somaria." Fortunately, the hounds arrived safely, but the ocean liner was sunk on the return trip.

Mrs. Froelich was more than a little surprised to find that the exquisite Rani el Kabul and her large raw-boned brother were brindles, very heavily coated with high black masks. The coloration was unfamiliar to her and a great contrast to the solid pale cream Yusseff. The imported pair were of strong Sirdar of Ghazni breeding, with the brindle coming from their exceedingly impressive fullcoated grandsire, Ch. Westmill Tamasar. Automatically finding herself "in Afghans," Mrs. Froelich adopted the affix of the family ranch, "Elcoza."

Yusseff and Sardar became champions in 1941. The charming brindle bitch, Rani, was mated to Yusseff, producing five champions including Ch. Zannette of Elcoza, who came into prominence as winner of the first Parent Club match on the fabulous Florsheim estate. Zannette joined the select roster of Best in Show bitches twice in 1946 and was topping the hound groups well into 1948. Said Mrs. Froelich, "Zannette was not the very best Afghan ever bred, but she was seldom denied placings for she came into the ring with a 'come hither look' and no judge could leave her unnoticed." This outgoing charm and spirit was a legacy from the born showman, Tufan of Ainsdart.

Mrs. Froelich, with Zannette and Yusseff, moved "Elcoza" to Indi-

Ch. Karli Ben Ghazi (Ch. Five Mile Punjab Ben Ghazi ex Trina Kush of Hazarat), red dog, owned by Mrs. Tongren.

Ch. Yusseff, C.D. (right above), dog, and Ch. Zannette of Elcoza (to left), bitch, owned by Mrs. Lauer Froelich.

ana, establishing the first Afghan kennel in that sector of America. Ch. Sardar Khan el Kabul remained in Pennsylvania with Elcoza's former kennel manager, Mr. Gruel, joining the ranks of great sires in the breed through his famous breeding with Flo Flo of Ghazni, resulting in nine champions, several being very handsome brindles.

In the quiet Indiana years, Ch. Yusseff, added C.D. to his name and, with his 10 champion offspring, became a valuable sire for other breeders as well as for Elcoza. Between campaigns, the sprightly Zannette was bred to Ch. Rudiki of Prides Hill, and also to his son, Ch. Ali Khyber, becoming the dam of four champions and other Elcoza offspring whose names pepper modern pedigrees.

Majara hounds invaded the breed through the lone litter sired by Ch. Karach of Khanhasset. The pedigree of Ch. Majara Mihrab ties into that of Ali Khyber, illustrating the relatively uncomplicated blending of Shaw McKean's imports with the later imported influences of the Pommel Rock hounds, plus a pinch of salt from Elcoza. Basic intensification of long muzzles, and great coat improvement met with marked success.

The fortunate Karach ex Far Away Loo litter produced Champions Majara: Mota Raja, Mahmoud, NurMahal, Mustapha, Mihri, and Mahabat. The last three perpetuated the growing tradition of producing BIS offspring. Pups from these hounds furnished impetus for other Eastern kennels. Mahabat's daughter, Ch. Lala Rookh of Estioc, owned by Patricia Leary, became the third bitch in history to top the Parent Club Specialty in 1956. In 1948 and again in 1949 Ch. Majara Mahabat, known affectionately as "Junior Bug," won the ultimate Specialty honors. It is said that when Mrs. Lathrop overheard that Mahabat's entry in the 1950 Specialty was frightening off the other Specials, she unselfishly withdrew his entry to encourage the participation of other champions. Best of Breed was taken by the imported Ch. Turkuman Nissim's Laurel, but the 14 months bitch Ch. Majara Mirza went BOS, and a black-and-tan Mahabat daughter, barely out of the puppy class, claimed the Winners Bitch trophy.

Majara followed a careful pattern of breeding by putting the black-and-tan Karach daughter, Ch. Majara Mihri, to Zombie of Dunrobin (litter brother of Ch. Shibergam of Dunrobin). The experiment paid off richly, giving rise to the remarkable Ch. Majara

```
                                                          Ch. Rudiki of Prides Hill
                                         Ch. Ali Khyber
                                                          Pommel Rock Kashan
                         Ch. Karach of Khanhasset
                                                          Ch. Westmill Humayun of Catawba
                              Ch. Shibergam of Dunrobin
                                                          Hamara of Pommel Rock
         Ch. Majara Mahabat
                                                          Ch. Badshah of Ainsdart
                              Shaitan Bedar
                                                          Zahera of Prides Hill
                         Far Away Loo
                                                          Ch. Badshah of Ainsdart
                              Cleopatra
                                                          Westmill Taree
Ch. Majara Mihrab
                                                          Ch. Sirdar of Ghazni
                              Ch. Badshah of Ainsdart
                                                          Ku Mari of Kaf
                         Ch. Rudiki of Prides Hill
                                                          Ch. Kundah of Prides Hill
                              Ch. Shireen of Prides Hill
                                                          Lakshmi of Prides Hill
         Zaritza of Elcoza
                                                          Ch. Tufan of Ainsdart
                              Ch. Yusseff, C.D.
                                                          Shabra
                         Ch. Zannette of Elcoza
                                                          Rama el Kabul
                              Rani el Kabul
                                                          Mem Sahib el Kabul
```

Ch. Majara Mihrab, bred and owned by Marjorie A. Lathrop.

Ch. Majara Mahabat (Ch. Karach of Khanhasset ex Far Away Loo), dog, owned by Marjorie A. Lathrop.

Ch. Majara Mirza (Zombie of Dunrobin ex Ch. Majara Mihri), bitch, owned by Marjorie A. Lathrop.

Mirza, only Afghan bitch to ever win the coveted Quaker Oats Award (Eastern division). During 1951, in the almost unbelievable short span of 10 months, Mirza took on the best all-breed competition the country had to offer, winning three BIS, one American-Bred BIS, and many hound groups. History proves her to be the last of the great show-winning bitches until the sex hoodoo was broken in 1964 by Ch. Pandora of Stormhill. Mirza, bred to her famous kennelmate, Ch. Majara Mihrab, produced four American champions and a bitch sent to Spain that not only became a Spanish champion but the first bitch of any breed to win a Spanish All-Breed BIS.

Majara Mihrab, a fine show dog, was an even better stud, producing 17 champions by just seven bitches. In 1953 his name was added to the roster of breed winners at the Specialty. He also earned three all-breed BIS's and 18 group firsts. His pups, Chs. Moornistan Shazenan, Shahriar, and Maymun, by the imported bitch, Djadji vom Falkenwalde, and owned by Dr. William Moore, established a famous strain leading to the spectacular modern Ch. Hassen Ben of Moornistan.

In 1953 Mahabat was mated with his famous aunt, Ch. Karan of Khanhasset, to sire the fantastically coated, black-masked red Ch. Majara Menelek ("Minky"). From such a background, Minky's prepotence was a foregone conclusion and he takes his place as a producer with 15 champions from six dams to lead Majara into the 1960s. The closely bred Majara hounds bear marked similarity in type, usually black-masked red, with some notable black-and-tans. Photos illustrate the profuse coating and fine carriage with other type marks of the kennel.

Development of the most successful Western kennel, "Crown Crest," is considerably more complicated. The story unfolds late in 1947 with Braden Finch's affectionate silver anniversary gift to his wife, Katherine, a "silver-blue" Afghan Hound named Felt's Thief of Bagdad. While not the first Afghan Hound at Crown Crest, the Thief, better known as "Thumper," was the beginning of the "great ones" and a continuing subtle influence on succeeding generations. "Thumper," a product of Western breeding, contained rare pedigree effects of the Peters' Afghanistan imports, Tazi of Beg Tute and Saki of Paghman, intermixed with McKean's Prides Hill hounds. The Thief's grandsire, Ch. Sahib of Prides Hill, was a handsome brindle litter brother of the great Rudiki owned by Dr. Frank Porter

108

Ch. Hassen-Ben of Moornistan (Ch. Zaamarakuri of Ghazni ex Ch. Maymum of Moornistan), dog, bred and owned by Dr. William Moore III.

Ch. Majara Menelek, dog, owned by Marjorie A. Lathrop.

Ch. Felt's Allah Baba (Int. Ch. Felt's Thief of Bagdad ex Felt's Fatima), Ch. Taejon of Crown Crest (Ch. Elcoza's Ponder ex Ch. Winomana of Rreks), Int. Ch. Jublee Julian of Crown Crest (Ch. Felt's Thief of Bagdad ex Ch. Five Mile's Banu of Rebel Hill), owned by Kay Finch.

Ch. Cha Cha Cha of Shamalan (Ch. Crown Crest Zardonx ex Kara Bash of Shamalan), black mask red dog, owned by Richard and Shirley Wainer.

Miller, famous race horse owner and all-breed dog judge. A trace of the practically extinct Kushan breeding of Ch. Barberryhill Phillip to Samson's English import, Jalalabad Kara, is also involved. This pedigree, while not overwhelming in either size or coat, excels in graceful dignified elegance, refinement and Eastern head type, in a wide array of the most fascinating tints and shadings to be found. Thumper's dam, Kara-She-Ba, was described as being pure white with a jet black nose and eyes. The grand Thumper is fondly recalled for his unforgettable, but unmatchable, shade of muted blue-gray.

The Thief of Bagdad was bred by Joe Felt who dearly loved exotic elegances of color and character. He also preserved rare traces of the precious Indian import, Fatima, in her breeding to Ch. Tufan of Ainsdart, through Felt's Fatima, who, when bred to Thumper produced a white-gold hound of unusual brilliance and majesty, Ch. Felt's Allah Baba. Both Thumper and Allah Baba enjoyed sparkling maturity under the guidance of Kay Finch, but were piloted by professional handlers Elsworth Gamble or Athos Nilson in the early days of their careers. Kay's breath nearly stopped on a wild afternoon when Thumper slipped his lead in group competition, dancing gaily around the ring while his handler frantically attempted to retrieve him. Despite the fact that he won the group, Kay vowed afterward to handle her own dogs. She developed an amazing rapport with both clay and fleshly Afghans which magically responded to each flick of her talented finger muscles.

Unfortunately for the preservation of these rare imported influences, the Felt dogs were rarely used for stud. Thumper sired seven champions with his daughters becoming especially influential on future pedigrees. Of Allah Baba's four champion offspring, Arnold Hartman's fine Ch. Rajah of Namtrah, a big red dog which produced delicately shaded brindles, is probably the best known son.

Late in 1948 the Thief of Bagdad took Crown Crest into the Best in Show rings at Pasadena, portending a future to come. Thief was the first Afghan in California since the reign of Oakvardon to stand alone before the top award marker.

Crown Crest hounds gained by the breeding of Thumper to Big Carmelita sister of Ch. Little Carmelita, owned by Dr. Frank Porter Miller and sired by Ch. Sahib of Prides Hill ex Fatima's Queen of Sheba. Of the produced litter, Ch. Egypt's Echo and Ch. Egypt's

Eudora, both of Crown Crest, play stellar roles in subsequent history. Eudora, a dark red brindle bitch, produced well for both Crown Crest and for her longtime owner John Buchanan. Echo, iridescent silver-blue like her father, lived out her days at Crown Crest. Kay and Braden Finch were impressed by Echo's very special quality and, in 1951, set off across country to find a similarly special stud for her.

On May 12, 1950, in Decatur, Illinois, Mrs. Leo Conroy attended the birth of a litter of silvers with black trims with fascinating possibilities. While on tour of the East, at the suggestion of Cissy Froelich, who had bred the sire of the litter, Kay and Braden paused to look at the yearlings. The couple from California had a fair idea of what they were looking for and were instantly struck by one regal silver-white, black-masked male pup with a remarkable flair and bearing. After striking a most remarkable bargain, young Taejon became Taejon of Crown Crest and was transported to the West Coast by his new owners.

Taejon, far better known as the great "Johnnie," hit California with shock impact. He won the breed under Dr. Frank Porter Miller and went on to BIS at Riverside Kennel Club when barely 17 months old. By his second birthday he topped groups with regularity, developing his famous long, bright-silver silken coat trademark, matched only by his sparkling air of superiority. While not a particularly large Afghan, he "looked big," seeming to tower over his competitors. "Johnnie" ruled the Western rings for the next four years, three spent without a defeat in the breed. When he retired in 1955 to make way for younger Crown Crest hounds, he had shattered all previous Afghan show records, standing high with 19 all-breed BIS and four Specialty wins, including the 1954 AHCA Specialty judged by Chris Shuttleworth. As the judges' choice for Best Hound at the prestigious Westminster show in 1954 and 1955, a gorgeous head study of him appeared in *Life* magazine. Always a great favorite with the gallery, Taejon and Kay Finch were voted as one of the ten best Dog-Handler Teams of the past 25 years by the New York World Telegram. There were ringside critics who preferred to see breed specimens with greater "reserve and aloofness" in the rings, but the flamboyant Taejon was never short on dignity. He had that indefinable something, made up in part by his glamorous, shimmering coat, his striking gait, coloration, and unshakable inner confi-

112

Ch. Taejon of Crown Crest, dog (sitting up), owned by Kay Finch, and Ch. Crown Crest Taejblu Minx, bitch, owned by Braden Finch.

```
                                                                Ch. Sirdar of Ghazni
                                            Ch. Tufan of Ainsdart
                                                                Ku Mari of Kaf
                        Ch. Yusseff, C.D.
                                                                Ch. Badshah of Ainsdart
                                            Shabra
                                                                Zahera of Prides Hill
            Ch. Elcoza's Ponder
                                                                Ch. Ali Khyber
                                            Ali Zhyber of Elcoza
                                                                Ch. Zannette of Elcoza
                        Kenya of Westgham
                                                                Ch. Yusseff, C.D.
                                            Laineux Coming Event
                                                                Natasha of Allsworth
Ch. Taejon of Crown Crest
                                                                Ch. Badshah of Ainsdart
                                            Ch. Rudiki of Prides Hill
                                                                Ch. Shireen of Prides Hill
                        Ch. Mo-Qua-Hee's Remus
                                                                Lakhsman of Enriallic
                                            Mo-Qua-Hee's Fantasy
                                                                Sitana of Prides Hill
            Ch. Winomana of Rreks
                                                                Ch. Tufan of Ainsdart
                                            Ch. Yusseff, C.D.
                                                                Shabra
                        Zuleika of Elcoza
                                                                Rama el Kabul
                                            Rani el Kabul
                                                                Mem Sahib el Kabul
```

dence, and bolstered greatly by his owner-handler. Taejon of Crown Crest was a show dog of the first order, responsible for a decided upsurge in the breed's popularity and a heavy demand for the silver Afghan with the flashing black trim. In pedigree, Johnnie was the result of various combinations of Ch. Yusseff with different bitches. He was used as stud for the "Thief" daughters, Egypt's Eudora and Egypt's Echo. The multi-hued Echo litter ran from black to the white of Ch. Taejanne of Crown Crest, foundation bitch for Hobart Stephenson's Patrician Afghans. Braden Finch claimed Ch. Crown Crest Taejblu Minx as his own personal pet, enjoying her coloration and character which was so like the blues behind her. The black-masked silver daughter, Ch. Crown Crest TaeJoan, marked like her sire, carried on the Crown Crest breeding program.

Johnnie produced over 30 champions from the many bitches put to him. His best known sons of the era, famous for similar dark masks, silken silver coats, and free striding gaits, were Ch. Desert Chieftain of Mikai, owned by Virginia Mika, and Ch. Stormhill Silver Dream, foundation stud for Bill and Virginia Withington. Johnnie furnished valuable studs for other breeders, but at Crown Crest his daughters carried on for him.

In 1954 Kay Finch imported the German, Belgian and Dutch Ch. Ophaal from the Von de Orange Menage Kennels of Eta Pauptit, famous for show winning and racing Afghans and Salukis. The V.D.O.M. kennel adhered to a strict breeding program, with the greatly admired Sirdar of Ghazni as model. The only foreigner at V.D.O.M. was the silver-colored Chota, imported directly from the East, but who resembled the Sirdar type and did not disturb the established balance. With a firm picture of a close-coupled, working mountain hound in mind, Eta Pauptit bred for great structural strength and prominence of brisket with strong, upright head carriage in a highly maneuverable frame. Her hounds exhibited length of stride and shoulder angulation rarely found to such a marked degree in America. While there was very little emphasis on coat at V.D.O.M., most of the males came by excellent long, thick fur as a natural heritage from Sirdar.

In spite of being a BIS winner, Ophaal's fame was not to come from show records but, as with so many of the notable imports, as a remarkable prepotent stud. As the private stud of Crown Crest, un-available to the public, Ophaal produced 27 champions from just

114

Ch. Stormhill Silver Dream, dog, owned by Virginia Withington.

Ch. Desert Chieftain of Mikai C.D. and owner, Virginia Mika.

Am., Ger., Belg., and Dutch Ch. Ophaal of Crown Crest (Int. Ch. Nereus V.D.O.M. ex Pythia V.D.O.M.), dog, owned by Kay Finch.

five litters, a remarkable record. Bred to Ch. Crown Crest TaeJoan twice, 14 champions resulted from the now famous "gem" and "K" litters. By the late 1950s the produce of these two litters filled a section of Who's Who in Afghans, as litter brothers, Zardonx, Rubi and Topaz, all appear simultaneously in the lists of the top ten Afghans for 1957 and 1958. A member of the "gem" litter, named for Zodiac jewels, Zardonx made his name as winner and sire at Crown Crest. Rubi, when owned by Ruth Tongren, combined well with Ben Ghazi daughters. Topaz, heartbroken at the death of his beloved owner Al Hewitt in a plane crash, found solace and a permanent home as the stud of Gordon Miller's "High Life" hounds in Northern California.

By 1958 Ch. Crown Crest Kabul of the "K" litter owned by Mary Stephenson, who had been seriously injured in an automobile accident during the year, was added to the list of the Top Ten. Sentiment clouded the eyes of many who watched Kabby stride to BIS at Beverly-Riviera, courageously handled by Mary who had finally overcome multiple leg injuries that had confined her to a wheelchair for many months.

As Charles Costabile watched Zardonx win the 1957 AHCA Specialty in New York, he was immediately convinced that mating his lovely Taejon-daughter, Ch. Hope, to Ophaal would produce exceptional quality. After lengthy discussion with Kay Finch, who was highly appreciative of Hope's many virtues, but preferred not to have her red imported dog at public stud, a co-breeding arrangement was worked out. As part of the contract, Ch. Hope went to Crown Crest. The Ophaal-sired litter was born in June of that year with a lopsided whelping of nine females and one male. Five of the bitches became titled, but the lone male, elected by Kay as *the* bearer of greatness almost from birth, outdistanced them all, under the joint co-ownership of Finch and Costabile. This black masked golden male, Ch. Crown Crest Mr. Universe, appropriately named due to his arrival into the world with the Miss Universe pageant in progress on television, was familiarly known to all as "Mr. U." The maternal half of his pedigree is shown below; for sire, refer to the pedigree for Ch. Crown Crest Khalifah.

By 1959 the meteoric rise of Mr. U marked him as the Afghan Hound to be reckoned with, and he went on to amass a record-

Am., Can., and Mex. Ch. Crown Crest Zardonx (Ch. Ophaal of Crown Crest ex Ch. Crown Crest TaeJoan), dog, owned by Kay Finch.

Ch. Crown Crest Mr. Universe (Ch. Ophaal of Crown Crest ex Ch. Hope), black masked golden dog, bred and owned by C. Costabile and Kay Finch.

Ch. Taejon of Crown Crest

Ch. Kandika's Kanda

Ch. Khanhasset's Kanda

Ch. Kandorissa of Aldachar

Ch. Rudika of Blakeen

Shelgrove Orissa

Ch. Shelgrove Jhalia of Five Mile

Shelgrove Sanadja

breaking score of 28 all-breed Bests in Show, 96 Hound Group firsts, four independent Specialties, and top awards in Canada. He was handled throughout by Mrs. Finch, and the team of Kay and Mr. U clicked as had the teaming with Taejon in years past, bringing the Gaines Award for Best Owner/Handler in 1960.

The Florida circuit was enlived in 1961 by competition between the two fabulous breeder-owner-handler personalities, Kay with Mr. U and Sunny Shay with Ch. Shirkhan of Grandeur. By the final day of the circuit, each pair had taken six Bests of Breed and three Hound Group firsts. Kay recalls Percy Roberts doing the breed judging in a large ring containing two bright patches of sunlight. As Mrs. Finch "happened" to stop Mr. U where the sun would best spotlight his proud bearing and glimmering gold coat she looked around for Sunny, and there she was—with the magnificent Shirkhan posed directly in the other sunlit spot. They shared a good laugh over it. On that day the younger Mr. U won out, culminating the day for Afghanites by winning the BIS.

With 31 American champions to his stud credit, Mr. U became the top ranking stud at Crown Crest until his death in 1968. Always an inspired showman, with glistening silken tawny coat, and firm outstriding front quarters, Mr. U was definitely reminiscent of his grandsire, Taejon, thereby giving many observers a tighter concept of "Crown Crest type" than was actually the case. Over two decades, from the late '40s through the '60s, via Thief, Taejon, Ophaal and his sons, Crown Crest was responsible for over 100 Afghan Hound champions, most of which took their pedestals as foundations or improvers of stock for owners throughout this country and in England.

In America, and to a lesser degree in Britain, the pedigree impact of Crown Crest cannot be overstated, although it became generally enmeshed with local or other acquired lines in a few short generations. Among the myriad Crown Crest spin-offs, one of the purest was Leo Goodman's Belden Kennel, based pretty exclusively on the matings of his Ch. C.C. Vegas Ghamblr of Belden (Ch. Crown Crest Khanazad ex Ch. Crown Crest Safari Sand-Star) to his Ch. Crown Crest Sancy (Ch. Crown Crest Dhi-Mond ex Ch. Hope) plus the later incorporation of Ghamblr's own dam, Sand-Star. Primarily, from the five different matings to the lovely Sancy, Ghamblr has sired 23 champions.

"Dahnwood" (Forrest Hansen and Don McElvain) noticeably intensified existing Crown Crest influences in the Northwest with their winning studs, Ch. Crown Crest Mr. California (Ch. Crown Crest Mr. Universe ex Ch. Crown Crest Eve Queen) and Ch. Crown Crest Zardani (Ch. Crown Crest Zardonx ex Mikai Tai Temple Doll). Zardani is probably best known as the sire of the highly impressive Ch. Dahnwood Gabriel that, in 1968, topped the National Specialty and won the Quaker Oats Award as Top Hound in the United States under the ownership of Judy and Herman Fellton in Georgia.

Various combinations of Crown Crest with other lines will become evident as this chapter continues, it being a rare modern pedigree that does not contain some of these threads.

Ch. Shirkhan of Grandeur, born in August 1954, became one of this country's most famous and beloved hounds. Holder of the record number of BIS's for an Afghan between the times of Taejon and Mr. Universe, Shirkhan gave the breed one of its most unforgettable thrills when he was signaled by judge Bea Godsol to the supreme award at the world-famous Westminster show at Madison Square Garden in 1957. This magnificent pewter-gray dog became the third Afghan in history to take the Quaker Oats award, winning the Eastern division in both 1958 and 1959. As late as 1963, marked with a graying muzzle but with a youthful step, the nine year old Shirkhan forsook retirement to again top the breed at Westminster. Owned by the colorful Sunny Shay, Shirkhan is a product of Grandeur breedings, a name long established in Afghan Hounds.

In 1947 Sunny Shay and Sol Malkin jointly imported the handsome black Ch. Turkuman Nissim's Laurel from Juliette de Bairacli-Levy in England, a transaction that put Grandeur in the limelight. The exotic black hound, with a marvelously effortless gait, won Best in Show at Cincinnati in 1950, handled by Jerry Rigden. As a

119

Ch. Shirkhan of Grandeur, dog, owned by Sunny Shay and Barbara Caminez.

```
                                                           Burma Kush el Myia
                                         Nehru of Ku
                                                           Nidja of Chaman
                         Ch. Taj Akbaruu of Grandeur
                                                           Chad of Prides Hill
                                         Doreborn's Karya
                                                           Amita of Prides Hill
          Ch. Blue Boy of Grandeur
                                                           Ch. Rudiki of Prides Hill
                                         Ch. Ali Khyber
                                                           Pommel Rock Kashan
                         Ch. Khanhasset Ginger of Grandeur
                                                           Shaitan Bedar
                                         Far Away Loo
                                                           Cleopatra
Ch. Shirkhan of Grandeur
                                                           Amanullah
                                         Ch. Umberto
                                                           Shiela Beg
                         Ch. Oakvardon Charon
                                                           Ch. Garrymhor Kishtwar
                                         Sita of Oakvardon
                                                           Morgiana of Kandahar
          Mahdi of Grandeur
                                                           Westmill Razuran
                                         Oakvardon Banneju
                                                           Ch. Westmill Natanz
                         Adera
                                                           Ch. Fatima's Son Tufan Khan
                                         Oakvardon Dera
                                                           Ch. Barberryhill Dolly
```

valuable imported stud force, he produced from various bitches many champions with notable fine hound type and interesting colors, but does not appear on the written pedigree of the great Shirkhan. Never one to follow fad or fashion in the breed, Grandeur successfully preserved, enhanced and united some of the exotic hound assets of the very earliest American imports. Grandeur prides itself on a remarkable array of hound colors from Turkuman Black through Shirkhan Gray to the palest creams and bi-colors.

Shirkhan's pedigree illustrates a fascinating conservation of nearly extinct imports, seen on few other contemporary pedigrees. Behind his dam, Mahdi, is the great Ch. Umberto, preserved through Dr. Iven's handsome black-masked light-red Ch. Oakvardon Charon who also sired Dr. Iven's own Ch. Tamerlane II. The immigrant names of Ch. Garrymhor Kishtwar as well as Westmill Razuran and Ch. Westmill Natanz are seen as is offspring from the Tufan and Fatima merger; all in addition to the Prides Hill basics and Khan-hasset influences, in a remarkable blending-pot of Afghan history. A very popular stud dog, famed for his gait, character and chiseled muzzle, Shirkhan has been used in various outcrosses, spreading his genes effectively across the nation. The unequalled number of 43 champions were sired by Shirkhan from the various bitches put to him.

In January of 1958, Sunny flew to California with Shirkhan for the Northern California Afghan Hound Specialty, held in conjunc-tion with the Golden Gate Kennel Club benched all-breed show. Shirkhan gained another BOB, a Group first, and the opportunity to sire two California litters of marked future pedigree importance.

Hobart (Bud) Stephenson, Jr. took advantage of the visit to breed his exquisite Ch. Crown Crest Taejhanne (Tae-Joan's litter sister) to Shirkham, to obtain the well-known "blue" stud, Ch. Patrician Sherwood.

During Sunny's stay, Lois Boardman was able to mate Genii al Paraa (granddaughter of both Ch. Rana of Chaman of Royal Irish and Ch. Felt's Allah Baba) directly to Shirkhan. This breeding became the cornerstone of "Akaba" and its fantastic rise to emi-nence through the immediate production of the magnificent and sound-moving smoky brindle, Ch. Akaba's Top Brass, plus his lovely

121

Ch. Blue Boy of Grandeur (Ch. Taj Akburuu of Grandeur ex Ch. Khanhasset Ginger of Grandeur), sire of Ch. Shirkhan of Grandeur, owned by Sunny Shay.

Ch. Tamerlane II (Ch. Oakvardon Charon ex Ch. Riverside Tuck of Pocono), dog, owned by Mrs. George Skinner.

black-and-tan brindle-pointed sister, Ch. Akaba's Know It All. The famed Brassy became the proud sire of 25 champions. In 1962, Lois took him back to the AHCA Specialty, where he topped the huge breed entry on Sunday, and further distinguished himself by winning the BOB and Hound Group at Westminster the following day.

In 1961, Lois Boardman decided to intensify her strain by sending Akaba's Gigi in White back to be bred to Shirkhan. Gigi was a striking daughter of the very handsome all-cream Abez (littermate to Ch. Hope and Ch. Stormhill Silver Dream). An exceptionally fine, but never exhibited (due to superficial injury) young male named Akaba's Royal Blue emerged from the breeding. As a strong believer in "inbreeding," and one of the breed's most successful exponent of it, Lois continued to further Akaba through the close interweaving of the members of the two Shirkhan-sired litters. In such breedings Akaba was soon specializing in the more exotic areas of the color spectrum, particularly the "blues" brindles, and creams. Akaba's Royal Blue (the only non-champion stud in the Top 50 Studs: he has 14 champions to date) was bred to Ch. Akaba's Know It All ("Smarty"). Out of this litter came Champions Akaba's Blue Devil and Akaba's Sterling Silver, both destined for stardom in the breed, but being of such dissimilar external appearance they sprouted quite disparate groups of partisan fanciers. As owner of "Devil", and co-owner with Donna Bandy of "Sterling Silver", Lois Boardman took both dogs to New York in 1967, and astonished her competition by showing Silver to BOB at the AHCA Specialty, and switching over to win BOB and Group 1 at Westminster with Devil. This left a trail of arguments behind as to which was the better dog. Silver was a tall, leggy, angular sort with a fantastic springy gait and carrying a close-lying cream-and-gray brindle coat. Devil was more "exotic," being fierce and wild in eye and expression, highly angulated, a mysterious dark gray blue color, and rather short in stature. Devil was nearly asphyxiated in an unfortuate accident with a hot dryer over his crate, but somehow survived to later make a Specialty comeback. The ageless Sterling Silver was able to win good-sized shows at the age of 8 years. Both are well-remembered for their individual arresting appearances, as well as for their "get". Not too much later, the handsome brindle Ch. Akaba's Royal Flush

```
                                                 Ch. Barukhzy's Khan
                                 Ch. Achmed Sjach VDOM
                                                 Ch. Aruna of Enriallic
                  Ch. Nercus VDOM
                                                 Original Nae
                                 Rashna du Chateau de Roches
                                                 Nakhia of Pushti Kuh
      Ch. Ophaal of Crown Crest
                                                 (Afghanistan)
                                 Ch. Chota
                                                 (Afghanistan)
                  Pythia
                                                 Ch. Achmed Sjach VDOM
                                 Koula VDOM
                                                 Rashna du Chateau de Roches
Ch. Crown Crest Khalifah
                                                 Ch. Yusseff, C.D.
                                 Ch. Elcoza's Ponder
                                                 Kenya of Westgham
                  Ch. Taejon of Crown Crest
                                                 Ch. Mo-Qua-Hee's Remus
                                 Ch. Winomana of Rreks
                                                 Zuleika of Elcoza
      Ch. Crown Crest Tae-Joan
                                                 Ch. Sinbad the Sailor
                                 Ch. Felt's Thief of Bagdad
                                                 Kara She-Ba
                  Ch. Egypt's Echo of Crown Crest
                                                 Ch. Sahib of Prides Hill
                                 Big Carmelita
                                                 Fatima's Queen of Sheba
```

Ch. Crown Crest Khalifah, foundation bitch of Sahadi Ks., owned by J. Brearley.

Ch. Sahadi Shikari (Ch. Shirkhan of Grandeur ex Ch. Crown Crest Kalifah), black dog, bred by Joan Brearley, owned by Dr. and Mrs. E. F. Winter.

Ch. Akaba's Top Brass (Ch. Shirkhan of Grandeur ex Genii al Paraa, bred and owned by Lois Boardman.

Ch. Akaba's Kharma of Torrekesh (Ch. Akaba's Top Brass ex Akaba's Gigi in White), black-masked gray brindle dog, owned by Bill Spivey.

Ch. Shalimar's Sweet Surprise (Ch. Akaba's Top Brass ex Ch. Athena of Windswept), bitch, owned by Lewis A. Rosenbaum and Sheila M. Leaman.

(Akaba's Royal Blue ex Ch. Akaba's Brass Bangle) took his place as an important Akaba stud.

Fire was a tragedy for the Boardmans. Not long after they had laboriously trucked all dogs and possessions from California to Illinois, their home and kennels were gutted by fire. Some very fine Afghan Hounds and a lifetime of memorabilia were lost. A few studs and brood bitches were fortunately saved, and once the tragic interval had softened with time, Lois was again producing quality Afghan Hounds in a saga that is far from complete at this writing.

During the lull in Akaba a fairly pure derivative, "Coastwind" (Michael Dunham and Richard Souza), rose to prominence. Their record-breaking Best in Show and Specialty winner, Ch. Coastwind Gazebo, had been sired by an unexhibited littermate to Devil and Silver. The beautiful Ch. Coastwind Serendipity, litter sister to Gazebo, also at Coastwind, was bred to Akaba's Geronimo Blue, one of the males lost in the tragic fire. When Donna Bandy was forced to give up her Afghan Hounds, Ch. Akaba's Sterling Silver moved to Coastwind intensifying the "Akaba" influences, a practice that has been continued in all due deliberation.

The foregoing kennels tended to blend Shirkhan-blood with what in California is called "pre-Dutch influences". But mixtures heavy with Ophaal in combination with Shirkhan were also found to be successful. At Sahadi, in 1959, Joan Brearley united Shirkhan and her beautiful red Ophaal-daughter, Ch. Crown Crest Khalifah, to produce several noted champions and the upstanding, elegant black Ch. Sahadi Shikari, owned by Dr. E. F. Winter of Wisconsin. Dr. Winter unhesitatingly shipped his fine hound from East to West to the areas of the largest competition. "Sheik" became a noted multiple Specialty winner and formidable Best in Show contender. From the same litter, Ch. Sahadi Sessu, as will be seen later, left strong influences as a stud.

In the early 1960s a remarkable bitch came to the fore, after more than a decade of male domination in the top show awards, in the body of the stately brindle Shirkhan-daughter, Ch. Pandora of Stormhill. "Pan", bred and handled by loving owner, Virginia Withington, was from a litter sired by Shirkhan ex Ch. Stormhill San Dhal (homebred daughter of Ch. Stormhill Silver Dream).

127

Ch. Pandora of Stormhill (Ch. Shirkhan of Grandeur ex Ch. Stormhill San Dhal), gray, gold and mahogany brindle bitch, bred and owned by Virginia Withington.

Ch. Bacha Khiva of Kubera (Ch. Hassan-Ben of Moornistan ex Ch. Majara Munshi), dog, owned by Erman M. Moore.

Ch. Javelin of Camri (Jonte of Stri-Mar ex
Karma's Jamil Khanum), gray brindle dog,
owned by Betty and John Richards.

Ch. Pamir Storm Ho (Cho. Stormhill Silver Dream ex Ch. Patrician's Victoria),
dog, bred by Joe and Ruth Emmert, owned by Miss Mary E. James.

While Pan was eagerly battering down the Best in Show jinx for her sex through vigorous campaigning, "Gini" Withington was keeping a watchful eye for a suitable mate for this exceptional bitch. Gini had a clear picture in mind of a quality male that generally resembled Pan, specifically possessing the same type of free-flowing gait, with a pedigree that included a good measure of the Shirkhan-combined-with-Dutch blood. Once seen, the handsome brindle Ch. Holly Hill Black Magic (sired by Ch. Sahadi Sessu) was selected to sire Pan's first litter. At the age of five, Pan stepped from her exalted rank as all-time top-winning Afghan Hound bitch (to that date) into the whelping box. The chosen combination proved so successful that it was later repeated. The net results included a number of well-known Stormhill champions plus International Champion Panameric of Stormhill, a top winner and producer in Scandinavia.

To enlarge Stormhill's breeding base but still retaining Pan as the focal point, for her third and last litter "Gini" settled upon the proven producer of quality, Ch. Mecca Tajma Khan of Tajmir. "Snoopy", as this male was affectionately called, carried 'Tajmir' from his dam, Ch. Tajmir's Desert Dream, a bitch bred by Pat Sinden Wallis out of solid post-Ophaal Crown Crest background. "Snoopy's" sire, Ch. Infashia of Grandeur, was responsible for Mary and Jim Nesbitt's "Mecca" Kennels; a name that was fast gaining distinction in the breed until Mary Nesbitt's tragic death via an automobile accident in 1971. (Snoopy's brother, Ch. Tajmir Gunsmoke of Mecca, remains a noted stud dog for Mr. and Mrs. Dick Stoll in Texas.)

From the Snoopy-Pandora breeding, Ch. Pandora Sheik of Stormhill took his place as show winner and stud, together with "Panjet" and "Panther" from the previous Black Magic breedings. Out of deference to his sire "Snoopy" and Charles Schultz' fabulous gang of "Peanuts" characters, Pandora's Sheik is far better known as "Linus." Pandora daughters from the three breedings continued to produce well within the maternal breeding framework that had been established. With her twelve champion offspring (11 American), Pandora became the most outsanding BIS Afghan Hound bitch to achieve such remarkable success at both the upper show levels and in the whelping box. Pan is presently one of the top producing Afghan Hound bitches of all time. After her third litter, a series of small strokes turned the highly vigorous Pan into a semi-invalid, but with great strength of spirit she lived out her years relaxing under favorite tree at Stormhill. In addition to the Stormhill champions and show laurels, "Gini" can boast of another achievement in the form of her exceptionally graceful daughter "Sandy," who now handles, and wins with, the current Stormhill pack.

Those that claim brindles and "dark dogs" are discriminated against in the show rings—and that song has been sung off tune since Badshah arrived in America—must explain why so many dark dogs are currently among the top winners in the nation. The percentages of light to dark winners shifted steadily through the 1960s. In Northern California, campaigned sparingly, never leaving the state but never ducking the toughest competition, the proud grey-brindle Ch. Javelin of Camri made his presence known at the BIS and Specialty level. Javelin would seem to be another of those rare lucky accidents of fate, being from two non-champion parents. His sire was a quality unexhibited son of Taejon (Jonte of Stri-Mar), and his dam, Karma's Jamil Khanum, was daughter of Ch. Rajah of Arken. Rarely used at stud, mostly due to his definite preference for only a few specific bitches, Javelin, nevertheless, proved remarkably prepotent in transmitting his magnificent headpiece, powerful driving rear quarters, and arrogant "type" of the old Badshah flavor. Bought as a family pet, Javelin—with his haughty bearing—was instrumental in making a first-rate handler out of his owner, Betty Richards. Traces of Javelin, especially through his breedings to the black-and-tan Top Brass daughter, Akaba's Brass'N Soot of Camri, C.D., spice many a fine Afghan Hound pedigree.

A spectacularly successful kennel built on a strength from one truly prepotent bitch is that of "Holly Hill" in Ohio. The story begins in Pennsylvania where Dr. William Moore III put his imported Djadji vom Falkenwalde to Ch. Majara Mihrab to form "Moornistan." From the resulting litter, Dr. Moore chose to mate his beautiful Ch. Maymun of Moornistan to Ch. Zaamarakuri of Ghanzi—a male that respresented a pure early American line through Ch. Zaadulla of Arthea and Winonie of Ghazni (Taejon's litter sister). An outstanding type with lovely heads, and practically unparalleled coat profusion, emerged from the blend, providing

131

"Moornistan" with the famed Ch. Hassan-Ben of Moornistan. His litter sister, Samaris of Moornistan, went to Holly Hill where her prepotence and exceptional qualities were wisely nurtured by Ned and Sue Kauffman.

Born in 1957, and quickly achieving her title, "Sam" made her brood presence known in her first litter sired by Ch. Dureigh's Golden Harvest. Two of the litter, Holly Hill King Lear and Holly Hill Vanity Fair, were called up from the 9 to 12 month Puppy Classes at the 1960 AHCA Specialty by judge Robert Boger to win both Winners Dog and Winners Bitch awards. This was just a sample of what Sam had to offer the breed. Whether outcrossed or linebred, under the Kauffmans' guidance, Sam proved to be a path to the shining lights. When put to Ch. Moonshyn of Moornistan, she produced the BIS Specialty winner, Ch. Holly Hill Draco. With Ch. Khabiri of Grandeur out popped the fantastically famous red Ch. Holly Hill Desert Wind, later owned by Mrs. Cheever Porter and piloted to such great show laurels by Jane Kamp Forsythe. As the dam of 17 champions, Sam is the top producing Afghan Hound bitch of all time. Sam provided additional fame for Holly Hill by producing the foundation stock for many other breeders, one of the most notable being "Ammon Hall." BIS Ch. Ammon Hall Nomad is the product of Ch. Holly Hill Desert Wind ex Ch. Holly Hill Lorna Doone. Samaris' daughter, Holly Hill Indus (sired by "Moonshine"), has continued this trail of maternal dominance by almost equalling her dam's production record. Indus has produced 16 champions through 1972, with pointed offspring still in the running. Through the decade of the 1960s, "Holly Hill" became a name in lights, adding considerable pedigree influence to the melting pot until Mr. and Mrs. Kauffman fully retired from active breeding of Afghan Hounds to become highly respected judges.

An area continually noted for its spawn of fine Afghan Hounds, Ohio is also home to Dewey and Reigh Abrams (Du-reigh), whose tenacious hold on the virtues of such dogs as "Rudiki", long after fad and fashion had passed the once-famed stud, have preserved much of current value to the breed. The very "typy" black-and-tan Specialty-winning bitch, Ch. Eljac's Dragon Lady of Dureigh, invariably received marked commendation from breeder-judges. Through "Dragon Lady" and the elegant Dureigh Champions Dark Victory, Randy of Hillbanks, Golden Harvest, and Swan Song, a

Ch. Samaris of Moornistan, owned by Sue and Ned Kauffman.

```
                                                              Ch. Agha-Kush
                                         Ch. Rama Bhajan of Arthea
                                                              Ch. Zudiki of Arthea
                        Ch. Zaadulla of Arthea
                                                              Ch. Rudiki of Prides Hil
                                         Ch. Arthea Bathsheba of Five Mile
                                                              Ch. Zudiki of Arthea
      Ch. Zaamarakuri of Ghazni
                                                              Ch. Yusseff, C.D.
                                         Ch. Elcoza's Ponder
                                                              Kenya of Westgham
                        Winonie of Ghazni
                                                              Ch. Mo-Qua-Hee's Remus
                                         Ch. Winomana of Rreks
                                                              Zuleika of Elcoza
Ch. Samaris of Moornistan
Ch. Hassan-Ben of Moornistan
                                                              Ch. Karach of Khanhasset
                                         Ch. Majara Mahabat
                                                              Far Away Loo
                        Ch. Majara Mihrab
                                                              Ch. Rudiki of Prides Hill
                                         Zaritza of Elcoza
                                                              Ch. Zannette of Elcoza
      Ch. Maymun of Moornistan
                                                              Samindarwar's Cronos
                                         Azar v. Onkel Tom's Hutte
                                                              Rhani v. Weissen Hirsh
                        Djadji v. Falkenwalde
                                                              Emir v. Jugenheim
                                         Baroness v. Schonen Rhein
                                                              Aruna v. Falkenstein
```

Ch. Dureigh's Golden Harvest, bred and owned by Dewey and Reigh Abrams.

```
                                                    Chota Nissim of Ringbank
                                         Ch. Turkuman Nissim's Laurel
                                                    Turkuman Camel Thorn
                            Ch. Turkuman Tar of Grandeur
                                                    Duke Alfrieda of Cyann
                                         Tahtara of Grandeur
                                                    Far Away Loo
              Ch. Dureigh's Dark Victory
                                                    Ch. Sardar Khan el Kabul
                                         Ch. Kandar of Riverside
                                                    Flo Flo of Ghazni
                            Ch. Dureigh's Dey Abrama
                                                    Ch. Rudiki of Prides Hill
                                         Ch. Bey Bombay of Five Mile
                                                    Shireen of Ainsdart
CH. DUREIGH'S GOLDEN HARVEST
                                                    Westmill Bayezid Ansari
                                         Ch. Rana of Chaman of Royal Irish
                                                    Safiya
                            Ch. Venghiz-Khan of Five Mile
                                                    Ch. Rudiki of Prides Hill
                                         Ch. Rudika of Blakeen
                                                    Lasca Klana
              Ch. Dureigh's Dawn
                                                    Ch. Badshah of Ainsdart
                                         Ch. Rudiki of Prides Hill
                                                    Ch. Shireen of Prides Hill
                            Ch. Bey Bombay of Five Mile
                                                    Ch. Badshah of Ainsdart
                                         Shireen of Ainsdart
                                                    Ch. Shireen of Prides Hill
```

134

Littermates, Ch. Patrician's Victoria, cream and blue brindle, and Ch. Patrician's Myles, light red dog, owned by Ruth and Joe Emmert.

Ch. Zaamarkuri of Ghazni (Ch. Zaadulla of Arthea ex Winonie of Ghazni), dog, owned by Mrs. Mary K. Blecker.

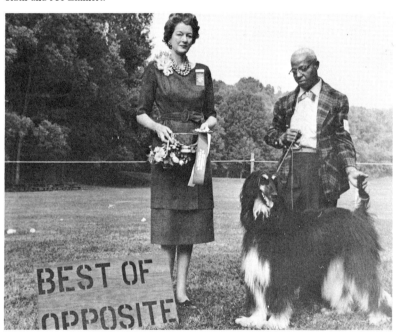

Ch. Eljac's Dragon Lady of Dureigh (Ch. Dureigh's Dark Victory ex Ch. Dureigh's Fai of Hillbanks), owned and bred by Mr. and Mrs. Dewey Abram.

sizeable pinch of "Dureigh" adds quality and "type" to many a show pedigree.

Quantity was never particularly evident in Afghan Hounds in the Southern States, but quality could usually be found in a few individual dogs that were quite capable of holding their own in any competition. The revered names of "Longlesson" and "Mandith" are based in Georgia. In Tennessee, Ch. Pamir Storm Ho has quietly amassed an enviable number of all-breed BIS wins. Owned by Miss Mary E. James, this flowing-coated hound was California bred by Ruth and Joe Emmert, sired by Ch. Stormhill Silver Dream ex Ch. Patrician's Victoria. "Pamir" as a kennel name was later transferred to Mr. and Mrs. Don Jensen, who continued the strain through a program of close line-breeding, leading to the striking winner, Ch. Pamir Ho Chester.

Once the home of "Kandahar", New Mexico had its modern counterpart in the Joh-Cyn kennels of John and Cynthia Guzevitch. From Sweden they imported a spectacular breeding pair of International Champions that were to have profound pedigree effect in America. The male, Tanjores Domino, was a handsome and very unusual-appearing dog, sporting a rare blue-and-cream coloring, marked in what is now called—in his honor—the "Domino pattern" (better known as "grizzle" in Salukis). Imported with "Domino" and bred to him was the glorious black-and-tan bitch, Tajmahal Kenya. These hounds were not greatly dissimilar in background, from the Dutch V.D.O.M. Afghan Hounds. They excelled in angulation, length of neck and elegant character, as did their offspring. Due to business pressures, within a few short years Afghan Hound breeding came to a close at Joh-Cyn, and Mrs. Guzevitch confined her Afghan Hound activity to painting, sculpturing and judging. Nevertheless, the Joh-Cyn dogs have found their way into a number of notable modern pedigrees, and the current craze for "Dominoes" may well increase this effect in the near future.

Brandt and Dorthy Houtsma, in California, put their beloved black-and-tan Ch. Sandhihi Dominja Joh-Cyn to her kennel mate, Ch. San-Dhi's Hatim Isi of San-Dhihi, C.D. (a son of Ch. Crown Crest Kabul). This planned mating produced the most "glamorous" Afghan Hound to grace the middle and late 1960s in the form of the popular "Baba" (Ch. Sandhihi Joh-Cyn Taija Baba). While being handled to multiple Bests in Show and Specialty wins by

Brandt, Baba acted as press agent for the breed, especially in the Group and BIS lineups. He was too "pretty" to be believed, lovely head and eye, regal carriage, invariably immaculately groomed with shimmering pale gold coat accented by a dark mask, and an eye-catching flowing gait. Baba was a gentleman, totally attuned to Brandt's every move. Wherever he was shown, the requests for "one just like him" piled up. But Baba was never at public stud, for his owners were having too much fun campaigning him to trouble themselves with visiting bitches or litters. Destiny decreed that there were never to be any males "just like Baba", for his only legacy to the breed came in the form of a unique daughter, lone survivor of his only litter.

But what a daughter she turned out to be! In 1967, Baba was mated to Dr. Gerda Kennedy's Ch. Shangrila Pharahna Cleopara (sired by Ch. Swedveikas Joh-Cyn—making this a linebreeding on the Joh-Cyn imports). The single survivor of the litter was Ch. Shangrila's Pharahna Phaedra ("Phaedra"), top-winning bitch since the days of Pandora, owner-handled to the dazzling heights of 11 BIS's, and the final count of her successes are not yet in.

Under the hand of Dr. Kennedy, "Shangrila" has become an active kennel of considerable size, combining the basic stock of Joh-Cyn, Akaba and Scheherezade into a recognizable strain now filtering across the country.

Lt. Col. Wallace H. Pede brought the English winners, Ch. Bletchingley Ragman of Scheherezade, and son Ch. Alibaba of Scheherezade, C.D., together with some fine English bitches, to the American show scene in 1962, providing new pedigree blood. "Ragman" was a rather sedate black-masked red, while "Ali" was a very flashily marked black-and-tan. Scheherezade breeding has remained unusually pure and closely linebred on the basic imported stock, characterized by strong-jawed "English" heads, long necks, and exceptionally well-angulated quarters, fore and rear. Via the public use of his studs and sales of puppies, this bloodline has seeped through the United States. "Wally", now a retired Air Force Lieutenant Colonel, has become one of the few Afghan Hound breeder-judges to adjucate in England, Australia, Finland and the United States.

The Canadian kennel of Mary Matchett should be mentioned in the roster of notable American pedigree influences, for through the

137

Ch. Alibaba of Scheherezade (Ch. Bletchingley Ragman of Scheherezade ex Tasha of Zabul) British import, dog owned and bred by Lt. Col. W. Pedé.

Am., Aust., Nor., Swed., Fin., North and Int. Ch. Tanjores Domino (Xenos VDOM ex Tanjores Senorita), imported blue and cream dog with "domino" pattern, owned by John and Cynthia Guzevich.

years some of the "El Myia" hounds have found their way into American pedigrees. The hounds of "El Myia" were originally imported from the "Chaman" line of Molly Sharpe in England. The Lophi kennels of Greata and Myles Phillips has also produced dogs whose influence is being felt in American pedigrees.

The American Afghan Hound eventually found his way north to the state of Alaska, where several members of the breed have won BIS awards, acclimatizing themselves well. Mrs. Nosky's Ch. Khy's Sheik and later Marge Webber's Ch. High Life Bibbi have taken the awards. These two dogs were good friends, as were their owners, with one living in Anchorage and the other in Fairbanks. When Khy's Sheik broke loose from a handler's car and roamed an Alaskan forest, refusing to come to strange human beings, Marge Webber put Hi Bibbi into the car and raced for the area where the other Afghan was last seen. At the site, she let her Afghan loose, mindful of the chance she was taking, but the dog found his friend and, once in sight of someone he knew, the panicky lost dog allowed himself to be retrieved by Marge and soon was heading on to Anchorage where his owner awaited him.

In this chapter we have attempted a roster of breeders that were responsible for an overwhelming percentage of Afghan Hound champions in the expanding 1950s and '60s, either directly through the use of their stud dogs, or by breeding stock they supplied to others. Limits of space prevent our mentioning many other worthy dogs, including some that were, or are, among our personal favorites. We are distressingly aware of promoting that rather faulty impression that these Afghan Hounds were "kennel dogs". Do not be misled. Kennel names did not necessarily a kennel make. Through these decades, well into the late 1960s, the top winning and producing hounds were—more often than not—beloved house pets, proudly handled in the rings by their owners. Only the very large kennels, such as Grandeur and Crown Crest, averaged more than a couple of litters per year, and even at Crown Crest, the dog Mrs. Finch was actively campaigning took its place as the "indoor dog", spending many hours by her side and sleeping in her bedroom. The usual successful fancier adopted a kennel name out of pride of identification. He (or she) bred an occasional litter, keeping the

139

promising pups within a crowded household situation until "show homes" could be found for the extras. Bitches were placed under "breeders' terms", requiring the return of some puppies that would carry the home kennel name before being sold. Stud owners eagerly accepted "stud fee puppies" in lieu of at least some of the monetary fee, placing their brand on them before selling, and proudly following their "kennel name" in the AKC *Gazette*. The fact that this type of activity would lead to an inverse pyramid of puppies was not yet evident. As a delightful Sunday afternoon hobby, the breeders hoped only to have their hands on another "good one", as worthy as the one just retired to the hearthside. They had little hope of breaking even financially, readily accepting the challenge and camaraderie as the biggest part of the profits.

As should be quite evident to the reader by now, the tendency to use professional handlers was very low. A special pride came from personally winning above the Breed level with an Afghan Hound. Some of the very best handlers—all owner-handlers—in the dog game arose from the ranks of Afghan Hound enthusiasts. Pervasive awareness that the sensitive Afghan Hound should, and does, disport himself most proudly in collaboration with his loved ones was accepted. An inspiring breed memory was furnished by young Jennifer Sheldon who, when only 11 years old, successfully led her much-loved black Ch. Khabiri of Grandeur to BIS at Lackawanna Kennel Club in 1962. Edith Tichenor of "Dea Zanga" regularly finished champions, carrying them into the group ring while in her teens. The tendency for novices, as well as veterans, to handle their own Afghan Hounds promoted a close-knit "family" atmosphere around the rings.

The volcano loudly erupted in the middle 1960s, but few were aware of the extent of its disturbance. Seasoned exhibitors stood glued to the Afghan Hound rings, chatting with old friends, idly wondering where all the new dogs and strange people were coming from. They were vaguely aware that an upsurge in all-breed registrations had hit, reflected in fewer parking spots, greater show bedlam, and the demise of the sadly outgrown benched show (except for such stalwarts as Westminster, Golden Gate, and Santa Barbara).

Gradually the realization came that the once "rare" Afghan Hound had quietly become commonplace at shows in almost every

140

Ch. Pamir Ho Chester (Ch. Pamir Storm Ho ex Ch. Kabul's Carol of Patrician), black mask silver dog, bred and owned by Donald A. and Georjean N. Jensen.

Ch. Patrician's Sherwood (Ch. Shirkhan of Grandeur ex Ch. Crown Crest Taejhanne), blue dog, bred and owned by Hobart (Bud) G. Stephenson, Jr.

Ch. Holly Hill Black Magic (Ch. Sahadi Sessu ex Ch. Samaris of Moornistan), brindle dog, bred by Sue A. Kauffman, owned by Sharon R. Watson.

Ch. Mecca Tajma Khan of Tajmir (Ch. Infashia of Grandeur ex Ch.
Tajmir's Desert Dream), black with white on chest dog, bred by James
Nesbitt and Pat Wallis, owned by James Nesbitt.

state of the Union, including Hawaii and Alaska—and was reaching out even into Puerto Rico. Pleasantly enough, the breed was garnering more than its share of Group and BIS trophies. Puppy calls for "show stock"—in person and via mail order—were high. Entries ballooned at the Specialties, passing 100 and then the 200 mark, until the selection of two judges became a necessity for the breed clubs.

Our registration chart for 1965 through 1973 portrays some of the startling growth of the breed. In 1973 alone, there were more Afghan Hounds registered (10,549) than in the 16-year period from 1949 through 1964 (10,409).

The ratio of the number of Afghan Hounds being exhibited as compared to the number registered had long been lopsided, but turned ridiculous by the 1970s. The Afghan Hound ranked 31st in AKC registration figures in 1971, but in many areas hovered around No. 3 or 4 in the numbers exhibited at all-breed shows. Only the German Shepherds (2nd in registrations), Great Danes (17th) or Doberman Pinscher (13th) were apt to tie or exceed the Afghan Hound in show entries.

From short hours to full days, the blurring parade of Afghan Hounds gaited by, and sometimes, circuslike, fanciers were forced to watch two rings at the same time. Open classes turned into endurance tests for dogs and handlers alike. Jumps in major point requirements reflected the fantastic increase in entries, especially in California—the bellwether state. Inland states were affected, to a marked extent, not only by their own increase in the breed, but by the "circuits", in that dogs in need of "majors" tended to pile up in areas of fewer Afghan Hounds and easier point requirements.

A chart of the rise in the California point requirements for a 3-point major, over a span of five year intervals, best illustrates the point:

Year	Dogs	Bitches
1955	7	6
1960	14	14
1965	18	17
1970	35	29
1974	42	40

Obviously, these rapid jumps in major requirements deterred no one from breeding and/or exhibiting. In point of fact, the chances of "finishing" champions became greatly reduced as more and more pointed dogs vied in the classes. We have seen Open Classes containing over 20 dogs, with practically every entry claiming some points toward their championship. The mathematical implications that each Afghan faces in finishing is awesome. A quick trip to the "boondocks" with a well-known handler seems to have become the modern prescription for finishing—and the "boondocks" are becoming harder and harder to find.

Two disturbing changes in the complexion of the breed had become screamingly evident by 1970. A high percentage of the seasoned breeder-owner-exhibitors mentioned in this chapter had retired from active breeding, or at least curtailed their programs, in favor of becoming licensed AKC judges. That's as it should be. But as a result, the roster of current Afghan Hound exhibitors was now made up of comparative newcomers, lacking perspective hard-won over the years, pursued by a naive wish for quick champions—and a litter of quick champions—spurred by the knowledge that theirs was "show stock" from pedigrees rich in champions. The relaxed apprenticeships gained by showing one's own dog and glowing over minor point wins, so readily available in the years preceding the mid-1960s, became scarce. In desperation and frustration many first and second generation novices sought, or were advised to seek, the use of professional handlers in the ever-increasing show tempo. Suddenly the Afghan Hound most emphatically became the professional handler's "darling".

The happy concept of the Afghan Hound as a combined "Pet-and-Show-Dog" slowly faded. In too many instances, the Afghan Hound had now become a manufactured, handler-guided "hothouse rose", every hair protected, living in padded crates, and exercised by means of a Jog-A-Dog. Those that fondly recall the independent, even stubborn nature of the rugged Afghan Hound, and his penchant for emotional bonds only toward his special chosen people, saw in the widening acceptance of a lifeless statuary type of superficial perfection, a terrifying result of the show world frenzy.

Novice or over-eager exhibitors would do well to remember that show wins, now more than ever, represent not only good dogs but a considerable outlay of time and money. In many instances, the emergence of a plethora of regional Afghan Hound "stars" at the Hound Group and BIS level actually signifies well-managed show careers by persons skilled in Madison Avenue methods of merchandise projection. The untraveled, unadvertised, but respected dog, remains all but invisible in the welter of shrieking exhibits. At one time the news of *any* Afghan Hound taking a BIS, or winning a large Specialty, spontaneously flashed through the underground of the fancy. Full page cannon blasts now drown out the modest whispers. Like all hobbies, this one can—and often does—get out of hand. The dizziest merry-go-round a fancier can climb onto is the tail-chasing game of trying to better a record already set by one of his own dogs, for fear that someone else might usurp his momentary prominence. Admittedly, the well-advertised winning hounds get the most frequent calls for stud services, often to the best bitches, and their puppies are the most in demand. But in a surprisingly short time once-famed names fall off the ends of pedigrees, and temporary records are remembered only by those who set them.

In these days of overflowing Afghan Hound population, and lack of opportunities for natural challenge or real purpose in their lives, the least we can do is to deliberately supplant that void with respectful understanding and affectionate attentions, completely free of concern for the blue ribbons our dogs do or do not win for us.

Ch. Ninth Turn Argus (Ben Ghazi's The Silver Shadow ex Ninth Turn Black Market), black dog, bred by Susan H. Hamlin, owned by Frank A. and Diane La Greca, Afghan Hounds of Gran Salaam.

6

Conformation and
Official Breed Standard

UNLESS rough standards are available from the land of any breed's major development, and such is definitely not the case with Afghan Hounds, establishing a detailed breed standard can be a perplexing task. In Afghanistan, the hounds developed through a process of natural selection within isolated tribes, creating various geographic types. With a broad range, the gaze hound physical type was preserved for the elementary reason that any pup who strayed too far from this functional build forfeited his natural ability to overwhelm fleet game, thereby destroying his value as a hunter.

The newspaper article from Kabul, by Gulbaz, describing the three *tazi* coat types, is as near to an Afghanistan standard as has been found. Dated August 1962, it could scarcely be applied to past generations without caution, but its brief comments are provocative and compatible with Western concepts of correct breed type: "The animals should have a long, pointed muzzle, a prominent protuberance over the dome of the head, and the distance between the two

146

pelvic bones should be at least four fingers placed side by side. Crooked legs, a short muzzle, and narrowness of the 'Kargas' (rhyming with 'bus'), meaning the diaphragm or breastbones, are disqualifications. Large breastbones are an asset on the grounds that the animal has large lungs and therefore a great 'wind.' 'Tazis' are neither docked nor are their ears cut." (The last sentence differentiates the "Tazi" from the "Siahbundy" or Afghan Sheepdog, which do have ears cut and tails docked.)

Lacking basis for a cohesive breed standard from Afghanistan, early descriptions were logically based on notable Eastern specimens that impressed canine authorities of the day. In England, the outstanding Zardin was given the banner of leadership. The Afghan Hound type in America was derived from British stock and a written standard based on a British document.

In this book we are mainly concerned with the current American Standard but have included reference to some obsolete standards for the historical insight they provide. Dates show the divergence in concepts between English and American documents in the 1930s and the 1940s and despite undeniable British influences on the current American Standard, the document stands very well by itself, not as an imitative copy, but as a well-thought out description of a majestic, unique and useful breed of dog.

The basic purpose of the breed standard is twofold. The foremost duty is the *delineation of the breed's characteristics* in such a clear fashion that a reader who knows next to nothing about dogs could stroll into his first show and pick out a representative of the breed. Such breed characteristics include structural outline, range of size, coat type, coloration, head shape, ear and tail formation, and expression. The other duty of the breed standard is to set up criteria for the recognition of superior specimens within the breed. Breed-judging consists ideally of comparing several highly similar individuals against a Standard of perfection, but, in actuality, the dogs are compared against each other, and against the judge's image of other noteworthy specimens. Ruling factors here are not angles and inches so much as elements of "type" (the hallmark of the breed) plus the total balanced appearance and working efficiency of the dog's standing and moving parts. There is certain to be honest disagreement in the manner in which different knowledgeable human beings value these factors, and in Afghan Hounds the dog's struc-

147

ture is virtually hidden by a long coat. For this reason we have included, not only an expanded Standard section, complete with the authors' interpretations, but also a small dose of anatomy to help the thoughtful fancier better understand the underlying form involved.

In reading the following discussion of the Standard, it would be well to hold firmly in mind the sage advice written by the President as of 1964 of the Afghan Hound Club of America, Donald A. Smith: ". . . in studying the standard and in evaluating dogs, always try to get back to the complete entity. Study the standard in detail—not for the sake of details nor in order to talk about your dog's virtues and my dog's faults—but to fix in your mind a clear and complete picture of how a truly good Afghan is put together . . . how he should look, stand, move and act."

OFFICIAL AKC STANDARD
FOR AFGHAN HOUNDS

The current Afghan Hound Standard was drafted by the Afghan Hound Club of America and adopted by the American Kennel Club on September 14, 1948:

General Appearance—The Afghan Hound is an aristocrat, his whole appearance is one of dignity and aloofness with no trace of plainness or coarseness. He has a straight front, proudly carried head, eyes gazing into the distance as if in memory of ages past. The striking characteristics of the breed—exotic, or "eastern," expression, long silky topknot, peculiar coat pattern, very prominent hip bones, large feet, and the impression of a somewhat exaggerated bend in stifle due to profuse trouserings—stand out clearly, giving the Afghan Hound the appearance of what he is, a king of dogs, that has held true to tradition throughout the ages.

AUTHORS' COMMENTS—The primary purpose of breed identification has been covered here. Included are the notable attributes that place the Afghan Hound apart, from even the closely related Saluki. Topknot, exotic expression, hip bones, cowboy chaps, and his king of dogs demeanor contribute little to hunting efficiency, but they are priceless in preserving the uniqueness of the breed. About the only explanation that is missing is the term "straight front" which refers to the dog's appearance from the straight-on view.

Head—The head is of good length showing much refinement, the skull evenly balanced with the foreface. There is a slight prominence of the nasal bone structure causing a slightly Roman appearance, the center line running up over the foreface with little or no stop, falling away in front of the eyes so there is an absolutely clear outlook with no interference; the underjaw showing great strength, the jaws long and punishing; the mouth level, meaning that the teeth from the upper jaw and lower jaw match evenly, neither overshot nor undershot. This is a difficult mouth to breed. A scissors bite is even more punishing and can be more easily bred into a dog than a level mouth, and a dog having a scissors bite, where the lower teeth slip inside and rest against the teeth of the upper jaw, should not be penalized. The occipital bone is very prominent. The head is surmounted by a topknot of long silky hair.

Ears—The ears are long, set approximately on level with outer corners of the eyes, the leather of the ear reaching nearly to the end of the dog's nose, and covered with long silky hair.

Eyes—The eyes are almond shaped (almost triangular), never full or bulgy, and are dark in color.

Nose—Nose is of good size, black in color.

Faults—Coarseness; snipiness; overshot or undershot; eyes round or bulgy or light in color; exaggerated Roman nose; head not surmounted by a topknot.

149

AUTHORS' COMMENTS—The head of the Afghan Hound is unabashed in its show of bone, veins and character. It is of the utmost importance in matters of beauty and utility and should never be softened with pads of fat, loose skin, or evidence of grossness. In head type, the Afghan, in a league with the other sight hounds, is *dolicocephalic* (head considerably longer than broad, as differing from the *brachycephalic* or shortheaded breeds). This long bony muzzle fronted by powerful jaws and large teeth is the prime maiming tool of the gazehound for grasping or slashing at victims or opponents. While some Afghan Hounds rip for the jugular veins, others "hamstring" victims by severing heel tendons and a few have been known to spring like great cats onto the back of their victim crunching the backbones. The usual disposal method with hares, rabbits, and vermin is to grasp them by the spine and shake them until the vertebrae snaps.

The Afghan's nasal bone should be as long as possible ending in large black nostrils, capable of full and rich intake of air (so necessary for hunting endurance) set into a heavy black nose leather. (Note: "nose" means the leather, not the whole muzzle. Dark masks are attractive but nowhere specified in the standard.)

Looking down from above the impression is that the long nasal bone serves as a well defined ridgebeam from which the sides of the muzzles drop abruptly. For the touch of Roman nose, the nasal bone has a slight rise to it. The flat or concave muzzle ("dished") is incorrect as is any gross exaggeration of the Roman convexity. The mildly arched nasal bone is forced to meet the frontal bone at a slight downslope causing a noticeable incurve just in front of the eyes—that should never be confused with a true stop (an abrupt rise and fill-in of the frontal bone in a stair-step effect). The very important frontal bone should form a well-defined upstanding triangle, based at the eyes, rising in a domed apex, to a ridgy saggital crest that leads to the very pointed occiput. The sides of the skull should drop away from the frontal bone and "crest" fairly steeply. Any dip, depression, or lack of distinct formation of this frontal triangle is a fault, distorting the total head shape as well as the ears and eye type.

Lips ("flews") should be tight and not hang below the mouth line.

150

The request for a skull "evenly balanced with the foreface" refers, in part, to the fact that the midpoint of head length, from occiput to nostrils, falls between the eyes. Aside from any illusion provided by topknots, the head, upon examination, should illustrate such total balance, with muzzle and skull parts joining smoothly. Rounded and broad backskulls or disproportionately short, narrow or thin ("snipey") muzzles seriously disrupt the aristocratic head line.

The widest part of the skull necessarily falls at the broad point of the zygomatic arch where it passes the point of lower jaw attachment. This arched bone runs back from the base of the eye, protecting the eyeball within its hollow, to the ear opening, and is analogous to the human cheekbone. For the sake of refinement, the Afghan Hound head should have as smooth, low-curved and inconspicuous a zygomatic arch as is possible.

Topknots, receding at the temples until the broadest point of the zygomatic arch is revealed, create illusionary coarsening effects. Profuse topknots, hanging well over the eyes, blur easy perception of correct skull and eye form. Some judges mistakenly believe that what doesn't show can't matter much, but the lack of classically shaped heads and eyes is a matter for serious breed concern.

Faults of round, large or bulging eyes result from incorrect head shapes. The eyeball must lie in a deep oblique plane along the zygomatic arch to form an almond shaped aperture, necessitating definite "fall-away" of the nose from the nasal ridge in front of the eyes and a well-defined frontal triangle.

Eye expression depends on a variety of factors: size, shape, and placing of eye frame as well as the dog's mental attitude. Color of eye and fur surrounding it must be considered. The natural occurrence of dark eye-pencilling with slanted outer-eye lines (so commonly found on masked hounds) or orange dashes over the brow of black-and-tan hounds give "Oriental" aspects. Dark eyes tend to recede and appear deep, being preferred in Afghans as in most breeds. The light eye with its yellowish iris is aesthetically undesirable, often giving its wearer a startled look. Unfortunately, the really deep dark, hard eye of Shaw McKean's time has become a very scarce item today.

Proper Afghan expression, not easily described in words, varies with the specimen somewhat, but must be in keeping with the Oriental character of the breed. It might be a look of complete in-

151

This drawing illustrates a head with excessive stop, rounded skull, circular eyes, coarse bone, and insufficient muzzle length.

The structure of this head is very desirable. Note the excellent chiseling of a long nasal bone, the presence of a frontal triangle above the eyes, and a smooth zygomatic arch from eye to ear. These characteristics form the proper slant-back skull and small, deep-set almond eyes. Both this drawing and the one on the opposite page were made expressly for this book by Lois Gossner.

scrutability. Some handsome hounds have a piercing, warlike stare that freezes the advances of strangers—while others have a gentle-wise gaze in character with the timeless passive wisdom of the Orient. The addition of Mandarin chin whiskers certainly contributes to the Eastern aspect. Pleading, trusting, puzzled, surprised or vacant expressions are foreign to the King of Dogs.

Being far sighted, the Afghan Hound tends to pull back his head and "look down his nose" at close objects, contributing to the highly desired, arrogant air.

The outer ear occurs at the rear point of the zygomatic arch, with the leather curving above it, tying ear placement into the important zygomatic arch effects. The ears should be set as low and far back as possible to create the leanest head effects. In this day of over-whelming topknots, however, the length of ear and its fringes do more for the flat ear effect than the actual set. The Standard's request for ear leathers that reach nearly to the end of the nose would seem to be stretching the word "nearly," for any ear leather that falls much below the beginning of the lip line on an adult dog is of good average length. The silky hair fringes that line the ear leathers can grow to fantastic lengths and, with luck and meticulous protection, fall well down onto the mature dog's shoulders.

The importance of large, powerful teeth and a tight, punishing bite could hardly be overemphasized on a gazehound. Both the level bite and the scissors bite are efficient weapons for slashing, tearing, biting or gripping. The scissors has one advantage in that the incisors grind down more slowly with age, not being in constant working contact as in the level bite. The undershot bite (lower teeth projecting beyond uppers as in the Bulldog) may be useful for gripping but not for much else. The overshot bite (teeth of upper jaw closing well ahead of the lowers) is entirely too loose for effective holding power. A good bite calls for a well-fitted lower jaw as well as upper. Any sign of shallow, narrow, or poorly fitted under-jaws is seriously detrimental to a game dog.

Neck—The neck is of good length, strong and arched, running in a curve to the shoulders which are long and sloping and well laid back.

Faults—Neck too short or too thick; an ewe neck, a goose neck; a neck lacking in substance.

AUTHORS' COMMENTS—The demand for a long-strong-powerful arched neck is common to all gazehounds for not only does it add great nobility to the structure, it is essential for any animal that is expected to reach out, from a full gallop, to grasp or bite his prey. Necks that are short appear thick and unattractive and, while such necks do not lack power, they lack length of reach for picking up the skittering hare and are dangerously ineffective in keeping the dog's vulnerable body away from the teeth and claw of adversary.

The neck may appear short for two reasons, one of which is illusionary but no less undesirable. The seven cervical vertebrae may actually be short—or the vertebrae might be of the desired length but the shoulders placed well forward on the body bringing the vertebrae point between the shoulder blades well up onto the neck area. Obviously, in the latter case the fault is more with the shoulder placement than with the neck itself, and clear reason for the necessity of a well-sloped shoulder blade. A rule of thumb states that the neck, when measured from occiput to withers, should match the length of the head from the occiput to the tip of the nose. Profuse coat around the neck and upper shoulder can also give the illusion of foreshortening of the neck. The "ewe neck" is concave on the upper surface and the undesirable "goose neck" is long, but loose, lacking in substantial muscle. Shoulders will be further detailed under "legs."

Body—The backline appearing practically level from the shoulders to the loin. Strong and powerful loin and slightly arched, falling away towards the stern, with the hip bones very pronounced; well ribbed and tucked up in flanks. The height at the shoulders equals the distance from the chest to the buttocks; the brisket well let down, and of medium width.

Faults—Roach back, sway back, goose rump, slack loin, lack of prominence of hip bones; too much width of brisket causing interference with elbows.

AUTHORS' COMMENTS—In 1929 Jean Manson wrote an article for the *American Kennel Gazette* describing the characteristic Afghan body type that bears repetition today. We quote: "Another thing 'outsiders' do not realize and this is the Afghan's enormous strength and power. This is due to their graceful outline and rather chiseled appearance and elegance. A hound which is well developed

155

should possess hard muscle and a great deal of it should be in the hind quarters; the shoulders are not so well equipped, but should slope into the long, strong neck. Bones should be heavy and the feet as large as possible, all joints very flexible, and the greater the depth of brisket the better, with a neat tuck-up under the loin.

"The great thing in breeding is to keep this strength, muscle and bone without producing coarseness. Thick heavy shoulders, thick loins, and a wide chest, etc., give a general appearance of cumbersomeness. A hound of this variety might be heavy and strong, but his lack of agility would be far too great a handicap to him, apart from his unattractive appearance.

"On the other hand, weedy, light-boned hounds are not coveted, however pretty and graceful they may be. It has to be remembered that they are sporting dogs, not drawingroom pets. Their forefathers have done rough work, and it will be a thousand pities if we allow them to degenerate into ornaments."

To this sage description we might add that a good Afghan is lean at all times, but never scrawny. A rule of thumb says that just the tops of three dorsal vertebrae should stand above the backline as evidence of proper weight. There should never be deep valleys between ribs, but neither should they be filled smooth with fat layers.

The Standard description of "topline" requires very careful reading, calling for a "practically level line from shoulders to loin." This all-important loin contains a thick cable of telegraphic muscles, surrounding the lumbar vertebrae, transmitting the "drive" from the rear quarter to the front end of the dog. At the loin, the hound's "power pack" is at surface level, forming a broad muscular ridge that is slightly above the topline—in some semblance of an arch. "Roaching" (obvious arching of the vertebrae at the loin), humping, sagging or dipping is generally indicative of slack musculature. However, a slight apparent dip between the withers and back vertebrae (between 8th and 9th vertebrae), on an otherwise firmly muscled back, is quite different from a true "sway back", since it is caused by the down-slope of the shortening spires above the withers vertebrae, and has been noted on many a fine hound since Zardin's day. Efforts to avoid this natural low point behind the shoulders have, in some cases, resulted in hounds with shortened hind legs, placing hip bones lower than withers, forming a "downhill" topline. Neither uphill nor downsloped backlines should be encour-

156

aged in this level-backed hound whose withers and hip bones should be at approximately the same level.

The loins usher in the hip section. The hip bone, correctly called the pelvis, is a stationary bony formation through which the fused sacrum section of the vertebrae passes. The actual hip joint is in the lower half of the pelvis, joining the hind leg in a ball and socket connection. The "seat bones" make up the rear ends of the pelvis. Those points, commonly called "hip bones" that project above the backline, are the upper prominences of the pelvis as it curves away from the sacrum. In the traditional rawboned Afghan Hound frame, these appear as bony knobs, typically large and well-developed, visually accentuated by the demarcation line of the fur pattern. These bone-tips should never be hidden by pads of fat. The entire pelvis should be quite broad with the seat bones well separated. Any narrowness of rear quarters through the loins or the pelvis is to be strongly discouraged. Contrary to circulated propaganda, the Afghan is no more double jointed nor structurally swivel hipped than other breeds.

The largest difference, aside from coating, between the Afghan and related gazehounds such as the Borzoi or the Greyhound, is in the full profile. The Borzoi outline has a grand curving flow to it. The Afghan backline is considerably more angular, from its abrupt high head carriage, through the level back, past the bony pelvic protrusions, to a rather stark rumpline and a tail that curves out and thrusts itself upward. A portion of this difference emanates from the shoulder area, where on the Afghan Hound, the spinion processes (spires that project above the vertebrae as muscle anchors) are shorter, placing the spinal column nearer the surface and contributing to the extreme high head carriage and level back of the breed.

Like the Borzoi, the Greyhound has the drawnout horizontal "S" curve of vertebrae from neck to line of tail, with a spinal curvature that tucks the pelvis into a steeper grade than is found on average breeds. It is interesting to note that Track Greyhounds, often less pronounced in "roach" are apt to have somewhat more definite hip bones and higher tail carriages than their more fashionably built show brothers.

In the eyes of some writers and judges, the Afghan Hound with his harsh rumpline is considered "goose rumped" as a breed, but the goose rump is listed as a fault—with reference to any pelvis that drops unduly sharply, creating a restrictive angle at the point of hind leg attachment. Such a narrowed angle cuts down the possible backward extension of the hind leg in action. The impression of the goose rump in Afghans when not actually present comes from the decisive incline from prominent pelvic tips to the seat bones, in the absence of a fat-softened croup drop. This is demonstrated by the overweight Afghan whose pelvic angle has not changed but, with invisible hip bones and rounded rump, suddenly appears to have gained a decidedly more horizontal pelvis than when in a leaner state.

The Afghan Hound, being less drawn-out in line than the Greyhound and built for maximum maneuverability is expected to fit the standard request for a square dog, a challenging feat to achieve in conjunction with maximum angulation of quarters. In complicated matters of proportions, owners may find it most informative to take actual measurements. Factors of angulation, body type and coating create some amazing constant and sometimes changeable proportion illusions. Judges see only how the hound looks to them and there is no point in arguing that the dog is pure square, when they say "too long." Seek the underlying reasons for the disproportionate appearance instead.

As with all gazehounds, the Afghan must have great depth of ribs ("well let down" brisket) and, at maturity, on a level with the dog's elbows. His body breadth is medium with the important rib cage, housing heart and lungs, never to form such a broad oval (barrelled) as to cause interference with elbows gliding back and forth in motion. Certainly the rib cage should not be narrow or flat ("slabsided"), fully as serious a fault as too much width. Ribs themselves should be broad and long, well carried back onto the dog's body, softly arching outward for maximum breathing capacity.

The breastbone (sternum or keel) deserves mention. The sternum, connecting the right and left sides of the ribs, begins as a prominent projection at the base of the throat and runs in a downcurve between the front legs to form the floor of the brisket. Examination of the forechest area indicates the actual breadth of the forequarters. The old reliable rule of thumb asks for about four fingers' width between front legs. A shallow or narrow sternum indicates skimpy front ribs, a "pinched" brisket, and lack of lung room.

158

Afghan Hound skeleton, drawn from X-rays by Lois Gossner.

Tail—Tail is set not too high on the body, having a ring or curve on the end; should never be curled over, or rest on the back, or be carried sideways, and should never be bushy.

AUTHORS' COMMENTS—Most of this is crystal clear except for the problem of the tail set. "Set not too high on the body" is open to diverse interpretation but hardly substantiates the popular concept that the Afghan's tail should be "set low but carried high," calling for a rather improbable spine, the tail being merely the outside extension of the spinal column. Factors to be considered are pelvic lengths and angle of inclination plus the nature of the tail itself. A pelvis that is unusually tilted towards the horizontal automatically produces a "high set" tail, while the "goose rump" rear cants the tail into a "low set" position. Greyhounds, with their spinal curve and tucked-under pelvis, come by a true low set (and low carried) tail quite naturally. Afghans should have neither low nor high set tails, but good middle-of-the-road caudal appendages indicating a functional 30° pelvis. The curl of the tail is of remarkable visual importance. Any tail that begins its tight curl near the body appears considerably higher-set and shorter than the tail that does not take much of a swing until past the midpoint. The tail with the tiny doughnut on the end looks far longer than the broad loose curl. The straight tail just looks terrible. In spite of great apparent variation in Afghan tail lengths, most of them, when stretched full length along the hind leg, finish about one to one and one-half inches above the hock tip in mature hounds somewhat shorter than the tails of other gazehounds. Tails vary in tensile strength, and the good Afghan tail has considerable "spring" to it. (Note: There is not one word in the Standard implying that any Afghan Hound must hold its tail high, either naturally or as aided by the handler, when the dog is standing in a show pose.)

Legs—Forelegs are straight and strong with great length between elbow and pastern; elbows well held in; forefeet large in both length and width; toes well arched; feet covered with long thick hair; fine in texture; pasterns long and straight; pads of feet unusually large and well down on the ground. Shoulders have plenty of angulation so that the legs are set well underneath the dog. Too much straightness of shoulder causes the dog to break down in the pasterns, and this is a serious fault.

All four feet of the Afghan Hound are in line with the body, turning neither in nor out. The hind feet are broad and of good length; the toes arched, and covered with long thick hair; hindquarters powerful and well muscled with great length between hip and hock; hocks well let down; good angulation of both stifle and hock; slightly bowed from hock to crotch.

Faults—Front or back feet thrown outward or inward; pads of feet not thick enough; or feet too small; or any other evidence of weakness in feet; weak or broken down pasterns; too straight in stifle; too long in back.

AUTHORS' COMMENTS—It may be helpful to see the front leg in rough analogy with the human arm. Both have shoulders, upper arms and the canine lower leg takes the place of the human forearm. The joint at the base of these bones, so large and obvious in puppies, is the wrist in man but the pastern joint in dogs. The pastern length is made of bones analogous to the human hand. The dog walks on the last three joints of these bones which, instead of being free as human fingers, are doubled up to form arched toes. The dew claw is a vestigial thumb.

For "great length of foreleg" the bones between elbow and pastern must be noticeable and measurably longer than those of shoulder and upper arm. Forelegs should be well-boned ending in very large feet. These long, broad feet with lengthy and high-arched toes in a heavily furred webbing are strong characteristics of the agile Afghan Hound. English canine anatomist, Dr. R. H. Smythe, says that "The Afghan possesses non-skid brakes, lacking in the Greyhound. That is why Afghans travel much better than Greyhounds over rough or slippery ground." Non-skid factors of thick rough pads, and hairy, semi-retractile long arched toes enable the foot to contract for braking action. Such feet are a requisite for the Afghan and should never be overlooked by judges. No short toed "cat" feet, please!!

It is the authors' opinion that the description of pasterns is the most confusing one in the standard. "Long pastern" readily fits into line with long leg bones and large feet. But "straight" is the puzzler. "Straight" could well mean upright (vertical) as in some breeds, but there are specific anatomical reasons to doubt this. According to McDowell Lyons and other canine experts, the combination of well-sloped shoulders, upper arms set well underneath the dog, long fore-legs and long pasterns—necessitates a somewhat sloping pastern to place the heel pad directly under the center of gravity where it belongs. In England the sloping pastern receives acknowledged preference in the breed.

We can only speculate that the term "straight pastern" might refer to the front view of the dog. The problems of crooked pasterns has been, and still is, thoroughly pertinent to the breed as a continuing serious fault. McDowell Lyons wrote about this in *Popular Dogs*, June, 1956: "Standing facing you, the dog's front pads should turn outward slightly . . . created by a slight rotation of the pastern joint, and not a bend of this joint . . . On the inward swing, this pad comes in line with the direction of motion and action is over the two center toes. Without this slight out-turn, the action is over one center toe and the outside smaller toe, which is not so efficient as the former." Although such compensatory action may preclude the absolute dead-straight front right through the toenails, it in no way excuses east-west feet that crook outward from the pastern joint, as such bent pasterns do anything but advance the cause of straight motion.

The broken-down pastern is quite different from the normal sloping pastern, being also found on the dog originally blessed with upright pasterns, there being more concussion on this type of un-yielding leg. The crooked pastern can also break down in record time. This pastern talk may be academic to those who think of Afghan legs as pillars of flying fur, but firmly muscled and flexible pasterns are absolutely essential in the production of the correct reach-and-spring Afghan gait. Broken down pasterns may be likened to human fallen arches in that most of the foot's strong flexing ability has been lost. Pitiful effects of slack pasterns are quite evident in gait, as symptoms of flopping pasterns (most noticeable on the back stroke) and poor step rebound appears.

As the pastern joint has a certain amount of lateral flexibility, twisted pasterns often indicate leg and trunk faults by compensating for lack of strong columnar leg support. Exhibitors know that some cases of out-turned feet respond to repositioning of the elbows rather than of the feet. The dog with the skimpy rib cage frequently turns his feet outward to form a broader base of balance. This effect is highly undesirable in the Afghan Hound. The barrel-chested hound, with elbows pushed to a stance broader than the point-of-shoulder (juncture of shoulder and upper arm) may tend to toe inward. Invariably, gait faults follow all such pastern deviations.

The width between the points-of-shoulder and between the elbows should be equal. The term "elbows well held in" does not call for narrow elbows, but for a minimum of open space between the upper arm and the brisket, thoroughly dependent on a correctly built rib cage of a gently spread "U" shape rather than of a narrowing "V" shape.

In addition, a well-developed and moderately prominent sternum (breastbone) is an important indicator of proper breadth and length of the front ribs. Insufficient character of these front ribs is generally accompanied by narrow bodies and a crossing-over action of the forelegs, seen far too often in the Afghan rings.

Because the Standard calls for front legs that are set well-beneath the dog, the humerus (upper leg) must be fully as long as the shoulder and well-angled at the juncture. Such a front is more characteristic of the Afghan than of the other gazehounds and adds to his compact appearance. A line dropped perpendicularly from the top of the shoulder should fall directly past the back edge of the elbow. Such a test does not necessarily prove adequate angulation, but it does indicate well-matched lengths of shoulder and upper arm. Hounds with shorter upper arms do not have legs set well-beneath them and also tend to have straighter pasterns and tight "cat" feet. This type of front is common in Greyhounds, but undesirable in the Afghan. The free "reachy" long front quarter stride of a good Afghan is dependent on the existence and proper use of the long upper arm and even longer lower leg. Deviation from this structure frequently produces a "hackney," knee-lifted, show pony type gait, which tends to be quite flashy but highly inefficient, and is too often seen in the rings. Another example of faulty front quarter stride, accepted too frequently without question, is the faking "over-reacher" who throws his front legs well forward, as in correct stride, but is really just pawing a lot of air as he settles his feet on the ground at a point considerably short of the maximum reach potential.

Hind legs, down from the stationary pelvis, are comprised of the upper leg (thigh or femur) and a small kneecap, called in dogs the "stifle joint." Beneath this, the dog's lower leg corresponds to the human calf, called the "second thigh." The second thigh terminates

163

Afghan Hound fronts: Left, poor, pinched chest and toed out; center, excellent front; right, poor, barrel chest and toed in.

in the "hock joint," roughly corresponding to the human ankle, with the uppermost point-of-the-hock analogous to the human heel. The full length of hock replaces the human instep, and again we see that the dog walks on his toes. Gazehounds differ from smaller dogs in the length of their long bones from hip to hock, producing a shorter hock area by contrast. The Standard states that the coat gives the illusion of a somewhat exaggerated bend of stifle; this is true, as the great length of hind leg bones actually reduces the apparent angle of the stifle-joint on uncoated gazehounds. A definite bend at both stifle and hock is absolutely necessary for proper folding and reaching of hind legs in proper hound stride, and the careful judge will not allow profuse coating to blind him to the importance of these angles.

Much that is said of pasterns is also pertinent to hocks in that strong hind leg flexion requires tight springy hocks. Slack or over-long hocks too often lean inward, producing cow hocks, with hind toes turned outward in compensation. Out-turned hocks are also evidence of weakness. In either case poor columnar transmission of drive power results, and the Afghan's typical "high style," driving rear quarter gait will be absent.

The impression of the hind legs being "bowed" slightly from hock to crotch when viewed from the rear, is due to a desirable broad mass of muscles on the upper and lower thighs in conjunction with a rather broad pelvic formation. The leg bones themselves should fall into a perfectly straight line.

Coat—Hindquarters, flanks, ribs, forequarters, and legs well covered with thick, silky hair, very fine in texture; ears and all four feet well feathered; from in front of the shoulders, and also backwards from the shoulders along the saddle from the flanks and ribs upwards, the hair is short and close forming a smooth back in mature hounds—this is a traditional characteristic of the Afghan Hound. The Afghan Hound should be shown in its natural state; the coat is not clipped or trimmed; the head is surmounted (in the full sense of the word) with a topknot of long silky hair—this also an outstanding characteristic of the Afghan Hound. Showing of short hair on cuffs on either front or back legs is permissible.

Faults—Lack of a short-haired saddle in mature dogs.

AUTHORS' COMMENTS—We treat the entire subject of coat with trepidation, because of its wide scope of natural variation. The traditional coat pattern, described in the Standard is that of a mature coated hound. But in coat, as in so many facets of his make-up, the Afghan Hound insists on retaining tremendous individuality, with coat maturity (the development of a smooth-haired saddle) occurring anywhere from 10 months to 3 years of age—a remarkably wide span. For each hound that quietly passes from a puppy coat to the adult pattern shortly after its first birthday, there are other well-coated puppies which will show no true natural saddle until their second birthday. At the other extreme, too many well-patterned yearlings continue to drop coat and go quite bare. Adolescence in the Afghan can be both awkward and misleading. The modern deification of the champion with precocious coat maturity is sadly naive, for such indications are not necessarily signs of lasting quality for either the coat or for the dog that wears it.

A wild increase in the prevalence of the great, dripping-coated Afghan Hound of the last 15 years has contributed to the breed's high standing in the show ring and with a mink-loving public. The modern American Afghan Hound's drape of coat is now more synonymous with lush beauty than with any original utilitarian purposes. In the Afghan Hound's native land, reasonable quantities of such fur had genuine value, furnishing insulation in the great extremes of desert and mountain temperatures in the arid country. It has been said that the topknots "keep the sun off the brain" and prevent sunstroke. While this may be open to scientific skepticism, certainly thick coating does give certain climatic advantages and more importantly buffers the hound's sides and feet from bruising jagged rocks and ridgy upland crags as Afghanistan is primarily stony and arid with seasonal, low sharp grasses as vegetation. Evidence from this country, however, indicate that the sheer quantity of the Afghan Hound's hair played a small part in native evaluation of the dogs. The following quote (*Zafar-nama*, op. cit., p. 25) from the 14th century A.D. states: "A year later Sharifu 'd-Din returned to this vicinity, which apparently had been subjugated from Timur's governor, and again mentioned three hounds, noting that once a year they were shorn as sheep, and the hair was used by the women in making felt of a high quality, which was prized in the markets of Herat."

166

Fanciers deploring excessive coat as "impractical in the Afghanistan mountains" have taken up the wrong cudgel. Afghan natives quickly turn any disadvantages of animal hair to their own ends. At shearing time of their sheep, the addition of a few pounds of hound hair has long been known to enhance their felts and wools. By the next freeze, a practical short mantle of fur has again sprouted from the dogs. Such seasonal clipping is an affront to most Western fanciers, but dog hair that has been combed and brushed (and occasionally cut) from our hounds has been woven, alone or in conjunction with other wool, into charming and durable garments for the owners that like to literally "wear their dogs".

Today a super abundance of coat seems to be blurring some of the hound's other sterling qualities and there is absolutely nothing in the Standard that implies "the more fur the better." Moreover, many of the great coats do not conform to the correct natural pattern and texture and are no longer particularly becoming to the kingly hunter, as they dilute the effect of the sturdy angular hound beneath them. There are several rather important details in the Standard's wording that are being neglected in the rush for great coat and young champions. In addition to the natural short haired saddle, the Standard clearly requests that the hound be shorthaired "from in front of the shoulders" which means on the sides of the neck. This should not be glossed over. Smooth neck sides greatly enhance the effect of lean elegance, as heavily furred necks automatically appear foreshortened. Also, super-coated hounds tend to carry the fault of the bushy tail.

Some of this apparent difficulty stems from the fact that once these hounds have passed their first birthday, they are judged by adult standards which are not always applicable. Consequently, impatient exhibitors strip a little fur here and there, attempting to pass off woolly-fuzz puppy coats as the mature item, despite the fact that with many dogs the draping coat, short-haired saddles and sleek neck-sides may not emerge for many more months. Ignorant judges who penalize quality youngsters garbed in obviously in-between coats without making inquiries as to the dog's age are as much to blame for the current confusion over coat in the breed as are the dishonest exhibitors. The Afghan Hound would benefit from

167

something akin to a "teenager class" of the type seen in many European countries and Mexico where precociousness is not rewarded—but merely tolerated with a "wait and see if it holds" attitude. More understanding of and attention to coat tampering on the part of the judges and less subterfuge by exhibitors would bring about the same purpose.

The Standard clearly states that bare pasterns and hocks in the form of "cuffs" is perfectly acceptable. In fact the "Turkish pants" can be quite attractive, as they lighten the look of a heavy leg with the break at the pastern. However, cuffed hounds demand large heavily-coated feet to avoid a top heavy tiny-footed appearance.

Coat texture is described as "thick, very fine and silky." Any coarseness of coating or lack of the silky effect dulls the coloration and brings about an unbecoming bushiness. The Standard makes no mention as to whether the fur should be flat or wavy, both types being common in Afghanistan.

The ethics of trimming Afghan Hounds cannot be ignored in this book. The emergence of the now common "great coat" with its frequent side effects of long-lasting and excessive facial hair and late developing or non-existent saddles in conjunction with hordes of impatient exhibitors unwilling to wait for the natural pattern of smooth hair to emerge on saddle, cheeks and elsewhere, has evoked widespread sly stripping, clipping, and plucking of the Afghan Hounds. Trimming is especially evident in geographic areas where competition is very keen and often Afghans are professionally groomed. Fully aware of this trend, the Afghan Hound Club of America has consistently reaffirmed its stand against all tampering of the natural coat pattern. The end result has been a double standard that is greatly confusing to the novice who reads the Standard prohibition on trimming, only to reach the show grounds and be told, not only by earnest fanciers, but also by many "helpful" judges, that his dog would look better if "cleaned up" on saddle, shoulders, neck and jaw line. Until the day when judges begin to penalize this flagrant infraction of the standard, decisions to trim or not to trim remain with the conscience of each exhibitor.

Height—Dogs, 27 inches, plus or minus one inch; bitches, 25 inches, plus or minus one inch.
Weight—Dogs, about 60 pounds; bitches, about 50 pounds.

AUTHORS' COMMENTS—As wide variation of height and weight constituted one of the greatest differences in the early Afghan imports, it was especially important that the Standard clearly specify an ideal range for both facets. Weight stipulations are not included in the European standards, giving American fanciers the edge on ascertaining proper substance for a good Afghan Hound. Tests prove that a lean, well-muscled, 27 inch male that makes the 60 pound weight is a fairly heavily boned gazehound, quite in line with breed descriptions dating back before 1900 in which the Afghan Hound was consistently described as similar to the Saluki but more sturdily built. As size advances or diminishes, an accompanying change in weight, at about 5 pounds to the inch, is justifiable. Proper attention to this height-weight ratio should ferret out the truly coarse or weedy Afghan Hound immediately.

The Afghan Hound is best known for his grand versatility. He must be large and powerful enough to pull down a stag gazelle, a cunning jackal, or his legendary foe, the snow leopard which is about 60 pounds of clawing dynamite. He must also be refined and light enough to stick on the heels of the illusive fox or the agile hare. While the best hare hound should not be expected to be the best leopard hunter, extremes of size in the breed should be strongly discouraged lest the dogs sacrifice their versatility and revert to the weirdly dissimilar Bell-Murray and Ghazni types once again. Any acceptance of giantism with its tendencies towards awkwardness, overly refined, skimpy or "weedy" individuals, must be considered as serious steps backwards in the continuation of the best of the breed.

The oversized hound looms as the greater menace as he "stands out" in classes by virtue of size and impresses many judges. It is to be hoped that judges and exhibitors will better familiarize themselves with the actual space encompassed in the ideal size range specified in the Standard in order to accurately gauge which specimens are or are not within its range. (Some judges have been known to make chalk marks at the 27 and 25 inch height on trouser legs, a commendable act.) Once the facts of the matter are established, the importance of the dog's size must be weighed against the appearance of the whole dog and the way he handles his body in action. In the Standard there is no ground for size disqualifications and exceptions to the prescribed range warrant judicial penalties as with any other infringement.

Color—All colors are permissible, but color or color combinations are pleasing; white markings, especially in the head, are undesirable.

AUTHORS' COMMENTS—The Afghan Hound is permitted a rainbow of colors. Partiality for specific coloration has brought many new fanciers into the breed, but the Standard is quite clear in its lack of prejudice. Only white comes in for discrimination, and rightly so, for true white in dogs is not a color, but the lack of it. Afghans that appear totally white are accepted on the grounds that such "whites" are actually very pale cream or gray animals. Signs of white markings, in the form of white feet or tail tips, are undesirable. White marks on the head, in the form of blazes, are most noticeable and specifically criticized in the standard. As the unattractive blazed and white-marked Afghan was accepted in show circles until the 1948 Standard revision, such "spotting" factors are deeply imbedded in the breed and bear careful weeding. (Note: Small white marks on the extremities at birth frequently fade away. See Chapter Seven.) Any evidence of poor pigmentation, be it white marks, less than jet black eye rims and nose leathers, or light eyes, are disapproved of in the Afghan Hound Standard.

Gait—(Discussed after temperament).
Temperament—Aloof and dignified, yet gay.
Faults—Sharpness or shyness.

AUTHORS' COMMENTS—To some, the combination of aloofness and gaiety is unreconcilable. The answer is that they do not necessarily occur simultaneously but both can be an integral and highly developed part of these clownish hounds. The mature Afghan, so devastatingly aloof to some strangers, is still irrepressibly exuberant with family and close friends. A breeder, once queried about the main difference, aside from coat, between her Salukis and Afghans, immediately replied, "The Afghan has a far more robust sense of humor." Here is the breed's charming "gaiety."

Sharpness (biting, snarling and fighting) or shyness (cringing and slinking) are to be penalized as manifestations of possibly neurotic personalities. The aloof Afghan may not make friendly overtures towards strangers, but neither should he panic or behave in a nasty manner. The King is above such behavior.

170

Gait—When running free, the Afghan Hound moves at a gallop, showing great elasticity and spring in his smooth powerful stride. When on a loose lead, the Afghan can trot at a fast pace; stepping along, he has the appearance of placing the hind feet directly in the footprints of the front feet, both thrown straight ahead. Moving with head and tail high, the whole appearance of the Afghan Hound is one of great style and beauty.

AUTHORS' COMMENTS—Very little is actually written about gait in most breed standards, an aggravating fact to the novice who naively expects the intricacies of motion to be spelled-out in a few well-chosen words. It has recently become fashionable to deprecate standards for their lack of detailed descriptions of gait. In some instances, carping is justified; in others, it is not. The dedicated "dog people" who write breed Standards know that good gait in one breed is not too dissimilar from that in other breeds, except where extreme structures demand special effects as in the "rolling gait" accepted in some very heavy-bodied breeds. All breeds are aimed towards facile progress across terra firma. For the interested novice we recommend study of the well-illustrated texts on the subject in McDowell Lyon's *Dog in Action* to be used in conjunction with actual observation of moving dogs. The fascinated student will soon find himself espying gait differences in every street mongrel as well as in pure-breds. An interesting fact soon crystallizes: It is the "in-between dog," not highly angulated, medium sized, moderate in body width and depth, and slightly longer than high, that has the least gait difficulties regardless of lineage. When the middle-of-the-road is left in the interests of specialization, gait problems multiply. The abnormally short-legged, heavy-bodied, long-legged, short-backed, and massive-headed breeds upset canine frame ratios. Yet from such extreme types arises the super-utility that has given rise to breeds such as the squat badger-catching Dachshund or the gigantic Wolfhounds.

The Afghan Standard's stipulation that the dog be able to achieve great length of stride within a framework of more or less "square" proportions, implies a compactness that "long dogs" such as Greyhounds lack. The Afghan's shoulders, firmly attached to the rib cage by muscles which allow slight lateral mobility and cushion the long blade, furnish a fulcrum for all front leg action. Maximum reach of front leg is governed by the angle of shoulder lay-back. The upper arm with its hinge-joint is capable of opening widely enough to permit almost complete diagonal extension from the top of the shoulder to the tip of the fully extended pastern and foot. As a front foot catches the ground at the forepoint of this reach, good forward progression is maintained. On the backstroke, elbow and pastern bend and fold to allow the leg to pass without raking the ground. Powerful rear quarters provide most of the needed propelling force as the hind legs "push off" from the ground, ramming "drive" through the thighs, to the pelvis, and along the vertebrae to the front quarters. Dogs' hind legs are so constructed that in maximum thrusts the rear legs straighten into a practical working extension of the pelvic line. At the forward end of such a stroke, the hind leg is at right angles to the fixed pelvis. A long hind leg, well-bent at stifle and hock, straightens to provide maximum hindquarter reach. Such hind legs must be well-contracted when standing still and capable of full opening and decisive muscular push to function effectively. Any deviation from the correct pelvic angle, poor articulation of joints, unfortunate ratio of hind leg bone lengths or underdeveloped muscles, become obstacles to the desired strong reach action. It is only at a full trot, however, that dogs begin to use all this possible extension of fore and hind limbs. The poor mover, of course, will not even achieve it then.

Basic mechanics of canine motion can be observed in the walking dog, as the legs travel slowly with action staggered in all four of them. At the walk the dog needs and uses only part of his potential extension and reach, but as he begins to put on speed, the legs begin to move further forward, momentum increases, and with the longer steps, an easy-going trotting stride is established. This is the usual cross-town-and-country gait of most dogs. The Afghan Hound is a great exponent of the bounding gallop, but his outstanding characteristics include wisdom as well as endurance and he makes excellent use of an efficient, tireless, ground-covering trot. As general weaknesses and efficiencies of motion are most visible at the trot, this is the usual gait requested by judges in the show rings.

Certain dogs, including Afghans, at some times resort to the "pace" (right and then left sides of the dog moving in unison) instead of the trot (where diagonal front and rear legs move together) especially when the dog is old or fatigued. The pace is about as fast as a trot and evidently less tiring, but frowned upon in the show ring as evidence of weakness.

The hound with strong angulation in oblique shoulders and well-bent stifles must use these advantages for grand diagonal reach, or in practice such a build is no asset to the dog. Faulty frontquarter movers with well-laid shoulders are frequently seen in Afghan rings, among dogs which hold back, moving halfway forward from their elbows instead of swinging out from their lower shoulder joints. Such movers, with driving rear legs, appear to have their back halves trying to get somewhere fast while their front legs are window-shopping. Dogs with moderate but well-used angulation are preferable to such cases. At the other extreme we have the "mincer" taking short stilted steps. As such hounds usually lack sadly in angulation but do move out well from the shoulder, such a stride may appear flashy and fast in the confusion of quick multiple steps, but such a dog is also just "getting nowhere fast." Such movers are at distinct advantages in the small show ring where they appear to be covering much ground, while their long-striding brothers are unable to "get going" in such restricted spaces. The reachy-moving Afghan is at his best in the large variety group rings where his impressive stride can be utilized.

The Afghan Hound should pick up his feet purposefully and cleanly, never shuffling across the ring. This calls for great elastic spring in the lilting stride, but is definitely not to be confused with the faulty "Parade Horse" type of knees-up prance that lacks forward extension. Correct front leg spring arises from strong flexion of the pastern as the foot lands on the ground. In the rear quarter there should be similar good flexion and noticeable "kick-back" of hocks. High-knuckled toes are important, as "splay feet" are commonly found on dogs lacking in springy stride, as is the "broken-down pastern" with its weak and floppy action. With all this springy leg action, the aloof body appears to be "floating," smoothly projected by its own momentum over the shock-absorbing reach-and-lift of the legs.

As it is the muscles that make all this reach and spring possible, a lack of muscular tension will gravely affect correct gait. It is not easy to separate faulty structure from weak musculature, but symptoms that point to the latter are problems of the joints. Elbows that

173

wobble, limp pasterns, "cow hocks" and slack toplines might well improve with invigorated muscle tension.

Gravity has its involvement in canine gait. In motion a dog's legs become a frame of balances working against gravity. Balance must be constantly maintained as the dog's weight is carried by two, or even one, of the legs at faster gaits. As the dog increases speed in the trot, the legs tend to converge under the midpoint of the body as viewed from the front or the rear. The faster the trot, the more pronounced the convergence, as the dog brings his paws under his own center of gravity. This in no way changes the fact that a straight columnar leg should be seen, for "convergence" emanates from the point of the shoulder and the hip joint, not from any visible bends in leg joints. Convergence is not apparent from the side view and, with the thick, swinging coat of the Afghan Hound, it is not readily seen from the front and rear views, occurring underneath the dog as it does, promoting the impression of practically parallel forward motion in the Afghan Hound of thick coat.

In sight of prey, the Afghan Hound adopts the familiar flying gallop, the pursuit gait used by all Greyhounds. As the first century Arabian poet, Abu Nuwass, wrote: "He peels the skin of the earth with his four feet." Regardless of gait faults painfully apparent at the trot, far less error is seen in the extended gallop, not only due to the flashing speed, but because many pitfalls of the trot are minimized or non-existent in the different kind of motion used in the gallop. In the flying gallop, the rear legs push-off almost simultaneously in tremendous thrusts, propelling the dog into the air. It is surprising to see that the "cow hocked" hound with such decided trotting weaknesses will gallop with the best of them until fatigue sets in. Even the strongest hound cannot sustain the top speed gallop for very long periods of time due to the strain on his lungs and muscles.

Timing is far less tricky between front and rear quarters in the gallop, as the dog arches upward and then jackknifes on the ground with his hind legs over-reaching the front legs by nearly a full body length. Back and loin come into strong activity as the body arcs into the air, folds close on landing and then arches upward again. In the bounding gallop, the prime function of the forelegs is to catch a good forward piece of ground and maintain it while the rear legs catch up to surge forward again. Such motions are instantaneous. As

174

one foreleg receives the full weight of the descending body on a certain instant, one can readily appreciate the necessity for strong resilient pasterns. This joint bends almost to the ground on the landing instant before recovery.

Unlike the other gazehounds, the Afghan owes his reputation to his coverage of rough mountainous ground. He may be expected to have shoulder muscles and front quarter strength above that of his flatland brothers, for in uphill surges the forelegs bear a greater portion of the physical burden. His tremendous "monkey-like" leaps necessitate tremendous hind leg thrusts and a front half that is capable of some pull as well as mere reach.

The Afghan's fantastic nimbleness cannot be demonstrated on a flat race track and is not easily perceived at a show ring trot, but must be recognized and protected as his most precious trait of specialization, an almost cat-like sense of balance and maneuverability. This remarkable agility can be sensed by the sharp observer or judge who appreciates the uncommon elasticity of joints and the seemingly weightless stride. On "turns," the Afghan illustrates his fantastic balance regardless of the ground surface.

A head-and-tail-held-high Afghan Hound trot is no less than awe-inspiring. As for the Standard we can only wish that the last sentence under *Gait* might have been expanded to read, "The whole appearance of the Afghan Hound is one of great style, agility, purpose and beauty." The most tragic thing that could happen to this magnificent breed would be if it should degenerate into a race of handsome long-haired statues, perfect when motionless, but awkward and ungainly in action. The fear that this might happen is not utterly without foundation. The fancy might well ponder the significance of Jackson Sanford's comment, "The Breeder will best solve his problem who does not lose sight of the fact that his is a task rather of preservation than of improvement."

175

7

Breeding

"Let us grow careless in breeding and the Afghan will lose his tremendous differences and gently slide back to become like other dogs. We must guard against any tendency to lose top-knot; to coarsen head; to shorten legs; to raise hocks; to lose those picturesque hips; to raise too much coat or not enough; to lose that characteristic high head carriage with its accompanying high tail. To lose any of these characteristics would be disastrous and to lose many would be to lose our dog."

Dr. A. W. Combs,
A.H.C.A. Bulletin 1942

THIS chapter is divided basically into three topics for the convenience of the reader: picking a mate; selecting puppies; and color breeding. As a general dictum, it should be stressed that no breeding of Afghan Hounds should be done without the express intent to produce offspring that conform as closely to the Standard as possible and that will be delightful companions, sound in body and mind. There is not now, nor has there ever been, any large unfulfilled demand for pet Afghan Hounds, but there is a market for top quality show specimens. As a natural by-product of breeding

176

for the "world beaters" there are more than enough second string pups to fill the "companions only" demand. The majority of non-show pets should never be used for breeding for the completely practical reason that there are just not enough suitable homes waiting to accommodate them.

Picking a Mate

The Afghan Hound is not the dog for everybody. Impulsive attraction to their picturesque appearance at shows or elsewhere brings cries of "I wish I owned one of these . . ." from the gallery, but this is no guarantee that the admirer is willing or able to make the personal sacrifice of time required to keep such a hound in his admired state of beauty. Few sights are less attractive than a neglected and matted Afghan Hound, a shamefaced prince in tatters and sores. Many casual admirers cannot cope with the breed's effusive and changeable temperament. Still, fortunately for the preservation of the breed, there are some people who are just right for Afghan Hounds, who on acquiring one, soon could not imagine life without these wonderful creatures which demand so much from their owners in the way of care but which give so much pleasure in return. The Afghan Hound is not an inanimate status symbol to be kept on a shelf, but a very lively bundle of flesh and fur.

Being deliberately negative at the thought of overbreeding and its consequences in puppy mills and dog pounds, we list the following points of when not to breed:

1. Never breed just so that "Scheherezade" can have one experience with motherhood before she is spayed.
2. Never breed with the mistaken idea that it will prevent further false pregnancies in a bitch so inclined. Spaying is the only permanent answer here.
3. Never breed expecting to make a profit on the litter. The Afghan Hound is not that kind of breed. Raising a healthy litter, with the costs of shots, food, advertisements, and expenses such as the stud fee, is expensive.
4. Never breed unless you are in a position to properly feed and house the pups indefinitely, as it may take some time to find suitable owners.
5. Never breed a sickly hound or one with doubtful mental

177

stability. The breeding process improves neither a dog's health nor its mentality, and both problems could be hereditary.

6. Never breed a poor or sub-average specimen of the breed. In reality, it is often far cheaper to go out and buy a quality hound than to work up to one through inferior breeding stock.

In Afghan Hounds, as in all breeds, a number of serious hereditary defects occur with varying frequency. In the "native state", stringent demands of natural rearing culls the puny pup, the faltering adolescent and the mildly disabled adult. In our insulated world of domestic pets, sentimental owners and sympathetic veterinarians apply all the miracles of Love and Science to the saving and raising of the weak and the strong alike. Commendable as this reverence for canine life is, the hereditary aspects of preserving the weak and faulty—to become the basis of future generations—is frightening, especially to those who have seen how quickly serious genetic problems can take over a breed.

Entire books have been written which delve into the wide range of genetically-induced physical (and mental) problems; therefore, we make no attempt to cover them here. Fortunately, the American Kennel Club gives guidance by wisely setting disqualifications covering some of the most glaring troubles. Even the one-time breeder owes it to the breed, and himself, to study these precepts and apply them to any Afghan Hound considered for mating.

AKC "Rules Applying to Registrations and Dog Shows", Chapter 16, Sec. 9 states: "A dog which is blind, deaf, castrated, spayed, or which has been changed in appearance by artificial means except as specified in the standard for its breed, or a male which does not have two normal testicles normally located in the scrotum, may not compete at any show and will be disqualified."

Chapter 16, Sec. 9-A: "A dog that is lame at any show may not compete and shall not receive any award at that show."

Among the less obvious principles, let it be known that—per AKC "Guidelines for Dog Show Judges"—a judge must excuse from the ring any dog that attempts to bite, or that snarls and will not permit a judge to examine him.

It is in these specifically AKC-mentioned areas that "guarantees" are made with promises of refund or replacement should such defects develop on dogs purchased as "show stock". Of even greater

178

importance is the absolute prevention of any dogs and bitches with signs of such defects, whether overt or clinical, from mating. They should be neutered to avoid "accidents". Should an accidental mating occur, a quick trip to the nearest veterinarian for an injection of a canine aborting hormone should prevent the mis-mating from developing into an unwanted litter.

Unfortunately, all of the above conditions can exist in Afghan Hounds, as in all breeds, without owners being really aware of it. Dogs do not complain verbally—in most instances, and have exceptional compensatory facilities. Judges frequently are presented with the embarrassment of such defects in the ring. Veterinarians find a number of dogs to be blind or deaf (partially or completely), or quite "lame" from degenerative joint diseases, to the complete surprise of the owners. Some fanciers don't even know the meaning of "two normal testicles". Entirely too many cases of serious defects are missed, and then passed on to the next generation, due to owner's ignorance, or unwillingness to look for the signs.

Routine physical examinations should be given old breeding stock by a veterinarian. Special investigations should be made for all problems mentioned.

Blindness, in Afghan Hounds, in the form of hereditary lens cataracts, has been reported in young dogs (1 to 5 years of age) with some frequency. Incipient signs of cataracts can be found on clinical examination, with dilation, long before any vision loss. Dogs with cataracts can make amazing adjustments to fading sight and may well live out their lives without owners sensing any problem. Judging from special mass clinical testing in the breed, the incidence of the problem is something near to 1%, but known cases have been seen from such a wide array of diverse backgrounds, including imported stock, that the genetic potential warrants ocular examinations of all breeding stock.

Somewhat the same condition exists with hip dysplasia, a hereditary disease of the hip joints. While less of a problem in Afghan Hounds than in most big dogs, enough documented cases have been seen in a wide variety of show lines to call for X-raying as suggested by the Orthopedic Foundation of America. Compensation can change a clinically serious case of dysplasia to one that is quite undetectible, except through X-ray. Breeds that have ignored the menace of hip dysplasia in its milder stages are now seriously en-

179

meshed in its clutches, to the point of near hopelessness. Let it not happen to the Afghan Hound.

The AKC ban against dogs being "changed in appearance by artificial means" refers to a large body of repairable, but often hereditable defects such as entropic (inturned) eyelids, poor bites, large congenital hernias, and any other superficial change done for medical or cosmetic reasons. This prohibition now includes the pectineotomy, a cutting and tying off of the petineus muscle, to alleviate the degenerative process of hip dysplasia. It would also include cataract repairing, or the surgical improvement of faulty testicle placement. Obviously, many of the "changes" cannot be detected in the ring, or anywhere else, but only a foolish breeder falls for the "out of sight, out of mind" routine, as the gene structure remains as defective as ever. If the "sins of the father" are not visited upon his children, they still may turn up in the grandchildren or someplace else down the line. Conscientious and aware stud owners should not accept bitches that are in the least suspect in the above areas, and should demand proof of examination and clearance where it can be had.

The non-ending controversy over whether specific defects, at any given time, are due to environmental trauma or illness—as opposed to genetic pre-determination (or combination thereof)—provides rationalization fuel. It is far better to err in the direction of not breeding than to take chances. All living Afghan Hounds are entitled to all the love, care and respect they can muster—but many are the unwise roads to the next generation in a world where Humane Societies are hopelessly overburdened with surplus stock. And Afghan Hounds are no strangers to their confines.

A word of caution about breeding contracts. There are no standards for such agreements. Stud owners' concepts range from those who believe a stud fee carries no obligation other than to see that some male services the bitch, regardless of whether a litter materializes or not, to those with a more responsible attitude. Some consider just one pup as a "litter", a special problem when the stud fee is "one puppy". Other owners agree that it takes at least two living whelps to constitute a litter. Stipulations should be made as to the status of pups (or the whole litter) that die within a few days of birth, as well as whelps that are to be culled as surplus, weaklings, defectives, mismarks, etc. All such arrangements should be specific and in writing, signed by both parties—especially when the mating agreement is between "friends", or the result of a forced breeding contract that was a part of the purchase agreement on the bitch in question.

Now that we have forewarned the reader that having one litter may not be a completely profitable and delightful experience, we can try to give a bit of help to the tenacious souls determined to carry on with the game, dreaming of the day when their "baby" takes major points in the Bred-by-Exhibitor class.

Afghan Hounds are difficult to breed with predictable results as the breed is fraught with wide genetic variability, one of its charms to the observer and its curse to the methodical breeder. The historical chapters portrayed a breed of multiform types in Afghanistan arriving in England and America. Early abortive attempts to produce stable balanced types through close breeding of related hounds were made by some breeders. All too frequently, in America these effects faded as the breed was caught up in a constant intermixing with each new import or top show winner of the day. Many early winners would be bypassed in today's competition. It was necessary for ambitious breeders to experiment with available combinations to create flashier specimens as Show Business became progressively tougher. We have only praise for the breeders who brought the King of Dogs to its current magnificence and we are not for bringing back the "good old days" but wish to warn novices that careless missteps in breeding can throw the breed into degeneracy.

Old timers bred Afghans with an educated instinct, unconscious knowledge gleaned from many years' experience in various breeds of dogs. The novice with limited experience wisely supplants this lack of instinct with textbook study of canine anatomy, gait and genetics. When properly applied, such studies may provide shortcuts in the interminable road to successful dog breeding. We urge our readers to avail themselves of these specialized texts. The technical aspects of genetics will not be covered here, as smatterings of this complicated science of life serve only to confuse those who are not familiar with its intricate principles.

The study of genetics illustrates and explains the pitfalls of the

181

ubiquitous hidden recessive and the value of predictable strains that breed reasonably true to type. Textbook breeding of Afghan Hounds must be approached with caution, for in this breed, it is misleading and risky to think that winning strains derive from firm policies of close breeding. Pedigrees in Chapter 5 reveal that many of our most successful and influential modern hounds do not repeat a family in a four-generation pedigree, being as outcrossed as dogs can be and remain of one breed. Kennel names are not necessarily synonymous with set strains, due not only to breeding practices within the home kennel, but to the affixing of such kennel names to purchased hounds and stud fee pups. Casual reliance on kennel names as a short-cut to predictable breeding may prove a costly error. The few really closely-bred hounds in this country can be expected to breed quite true to type in both their assets and their liabilities.

The great hounds of the past deserve accolades. They proved their ability to hold their own with dogs of all breeds in top competition. Nevertheless, many show type and temperament faults were transmitted by these very popular studs. These hounds were fortunate in having overwhelming virtues that outweighed their faults in the eyes of judges. Problems plaguing even some of the greatest Afghan Hounds and certainly not limited to any one breed were general unsoundness of leg with turned-out front feet and cow-hocked rears, often hidden under leg fur. Some heavily-coated bodies sadly lacked the strong bones, deep brisket, or shoulder angulation that the short-haired Greyhound must exhibit to avoid severe penalties. Coarse heads and weak or "plain" muzzles lacking in distinctive chiseling have been transmitted by popular studs, outstanding in other departments. Serious problems of body/leg ratio imbalances have persisted to this day. Surface improvements in temperament have possibly been the greatest gain in the breed, other than the highly coveted coat. Despite the fact that they harbored such "faults," the great ones stood out brightly and were constant challengers for top awards. In explanation, judge "Cissy" Froelich of the Elcoza kennel says, "Many of the old Afghans had that great quality that I call 'dash' that makes you look a second time . . . that 'I'm the grandest tiger in the jungle' look of long ago . . . which few Afghans of today possess. Today there are so many gorgeous animals in the rings. Judges have a much harder time than years ago, when one could easily pick the 'best.' We must breed good ones just to keep going. . . ." But we can only obtain fine Afghan Hounds from sires and dams who, in combination, possess superior qualities themselves. Recognition of these qualities on the part of the breeder is the very first step. Virtues cannot be assumed on the basis of a pedigree full of champions. Almost all modern Afghan Hounds, good or poor, have pedigrees rich in titled ancestry. A mediocre dog or bitch from the most imposing background of royalty is the unfortunate result of the undesirable aspects of the pedigree coming home to roost. Quality must be in hand to be transmitted. Acquiring and maintaining the best in the breed calls for a mixture of unrelenting vigil and the weeding out of inferior specimens (plus the unending generosity of Lady Luck).

Decisive proof that quality begets quality is supplied by our own Afghan champions. Through the years from 83% to 95% of all Afghan champions have come from champion sires. This is a remarkable percentage. The only non-champion sire of great note, with ten champions to his credit, was Westmill Omar. Many of the other early non-champion sires of champions were imported hounds, valued for very special characteristics.

At first glance, the dam's side of the ledger is different. In the 1930s and 1940s, only about 30% of champions boasted champion dams. But, in many cases, such dams were of acknowledged quality, lacking only a point or two of finishing. Seasonal coat drops interrupted many a fine bitch's show career. Some bitches, such as the lovely Far Away Loo, were selected exclusively for their brood bitch potential. Ku Mari Khyaam of Arken had a crippling injury that prevented her from being exhibited, but her quality was obvious. Admittedly, there were many cases of stock improvement breeding of a mediocre bitch to a top sire that did produce some fine specimens.

As competition broadened, the percentage of champion dams also increased. By 1960, 53% of the newly titled dogs were from champion dams. By 1963 only 7% of the champions listed could not show at least one champion parent, with the great majority having two of them. Certainly we do not mean to imply that all pet hounds lack quality, for this is not true. Many successful breedings were made well before one or both promising parents had achieved their titles. We are saying that only the experienced breeder, well aware of

183

what they are doing, has the right to experiment with untested quality.

There are two key words to be used in deciding whether a bitch that is not pleasing the judges at the shows should be used for breeding. These are "sound" and "type." A bitch that is unfashionably small, but within the Standard, with only moderate coat and an indifferent show presence but without any serious structural faults, can be an excellent brood bitch when bred properly *if* she is really sound (meaning that her legs and gait are strong both coming and going) and "typy" (meaning in this instance, that she has a good head shape with an "Afghanish" look). It is preferable that such a bitch should also have a broad loin; an asset to rear quarter gait and the easy carrying and whelping of puppies. A very feminine bitch, short of superficial dramatics, is a far better potential brood bitch than the drippy coated, faultily constructed showgirl that finds favor in the eyes of careless judges.

As a firm rule in breeding, it is absolutely essential that at least one of the two prospective parents excel in soundness and in type or the offspring deserve to be nonentities regardless of their superficial attributes. The assets of both prospective parents must greatly outweigh their liabilities and such liabilities must never be duplicated. The fond owner who foresees fine puppies resulting from two mediocre dogs, on the chance that both hounds will throw only their best qualities, is forgetting the law of averages and indulging in the saddest type of wishful thinking.

The most unforgivable error made in Afghans is in breeding primarily for coat, whether for color or for quantity. Such grievous mistakes are testimony to a lack of knowledge of hound structure and the mesmerizing effect of constant ringside comments on coat and color, promoting a completely false sense of Afghan Hound values. We warn the novice that it is far easier for any loser to alibi that the judge didn't like his hound's color or that his dog didn't have enough coat than to admit that his dog lacks brisket or has poor shoulders and crooked legs.

As the writer of a circulated pamphlet on Afghan color, one of the authors can testify to the horrible emphasis on breeding for certain colors after receiving blueprints of pedigrees projected well into the future to be checked as a basis for setting specific color strains in

Afghans completely irrespective of the suitability and structural quality of the dogs involved.

The great race for coat, begun in the 1920s and never dropping momentum, has plunged many breeders into a frightening trap. In 1931 a champion English bitch of most ungainly proportions was described thusly: "Her marvelous coat makes her an outstanding Afghan." Little else about her could be complimented. While some judges are blinded by such drivel and by great hollow surplus coats, wise and dedicated breeders are not, and it is only through their insistence on retaining Standard ideals and quality beneath the fur that has kept the breed from degeneracy. Knowing that such heavy coat factors have stemmed from their breeding, owners of many full-coated hounds have cried bitterly as the trend to the great coat engulfed the breed. To these dedicated breeders, coats were not ultimate ends but means to more graceful quality hounds. They never wanted to see the "coats wear the dogs." One of the most established breeders, Mrs. Drinkwater, writes, "Regarding coats, some of the early hounds had very little indeed and one would not like to go back to those days, but I think now we have too much and have lost the lovely saddles and angularity of line that was so typical." Impressionable judges and unthinking breeders do not seem to know when enough is enough and are methodically covering the outlines of the Great Hound. Novices must beware of breeding great coat to great coat without deep concentration on the bones beneath them.

Only when information is available on the dogs listed, are pedigrees useful. Almost all breeding represents a certain amount of covering-up of the faults of one parent with the virtues of the other. Awareness of such covered-up areas prevents the next breeder from backsliding into the same pit the former breeder arose from. For this reason even the darkest-eyed dog, a product of a dark eye-light eye complementary breeding in the previous generation, is a poor bet for eye-color improvement when bred with a light-eyed bitch.

Any dog that is double-bred (from both sides of the family) for any specific asset has twice the chance of passing the virtue intact to a large number of offspring. For such clues the novice must rely on opinions from older experienced breeders better acquainted with the dogs listed on the pedigree. It is a wise move to get as many such evaluations as possible. The novice will soon discover that even

185

the great hounds had their gallery of critics seated right across from the rooting sections. A verdict from the detractors leaves them wondering how the poor dog ever won a blue ribbon in a single entry class. In counterpoint, the boosters infer that the dog was just slightly less than perfect on his very worst days. The truth falls in between. Investigation of old photos help and would be more valuable if so many of the hounds were not stacked into their best, but not necessarily natural, positions. Some photographs are retouched, adding qualities not evident on the living model.

To recapitulate, mating Afghan Hounds under optimum conditions, as in any type of livestock, consists of putting together a pair of nearly perfect complementary specimens, from related backgrounds of nearly perfect hounds. But only the naive believe that such optimum conditions are readily available. Most every breeding is an experiment to be carefully planned, executed, and analyzed. To inbreed, outbreed or line-breed depends on the strong and the weak points of the dogs involved and whether a stable and desirable family background for line-breeding can be found. As long as dedicated breeders continue to breed the best to the best with their eyes focused directly on the Standard, chances are that top quality Afghans will continue to emerge.

In addition to structure and the many external niceties required of show dogs, temperament must also be carefully considered. A dull and stupid hound in a handsome, well-coated shell is certainly no more typical of this bright and lively breed than the shy or nasty dog.

Selecting Puppies

The Afghan Hound puppy is a delightful ever-changing creature and a challenge to the most experienced breeders. The younger the pup, the greater the perplexity. The buyer who is determined to have a winning show prospect has no choice but to buy a nearly full-grown pup with proven merit under respected judges and over respectable competition. Even such a hound can suddenly throw his coat or be unresponsive to his new owner. Buyers, not adverse to a bit of a gamble and confident that with the proper upbringing a well-bred pup goes a long way, may prefer to pick a less expensive younger pup who can grow up with the family.

Prices are not a certain guide to the pup's quality. Popularity of

186

the color and the reputation of the parents will make a difference as will the practical desire of the breeder to retain or dispose of the pups. Pups, being the enigmas they are as to future potential, are not easily priced in any from-good-to-bad order. The cheapest pup in a litter of high quality may be a better bargain than the most expensive pick in a mediocre litter. An astute buyer who moves very slowly, learning as much as possible about the breed and the breeders as possible before making a purchase, may well find a bargain.

For the novice, the best guides to the probable adult appearance of the pups, within limits, are the parents of the litter. It is not necessary that they be titled champions if they have proven quality. It certainly is against the law of probabilities to believe that pups will be any better than their combined sire and dam. Beware of pups whose parents are hidden away for any reason. The bitch will not be in her best coat, but this makes it easier for the buyer to see her basic structure and her temperament. It is absolutely necessary to know the Standard before buying puppies, if only to tell whether the parents really pass muster.

All Afghan puppies are born squat-nosed, short-legged and smooth-coated. Signs of differences among siblings, other than in size and color, can be very subtle. In a litter with a wide range of from-poor-to-good pups, even the observant novice with an eye for a dog, can see the better ones at a glance. A uniform litter, either all good or all bad, is more puzzling. The novice must rely heavily on the breeder's word for clues, but would do well to take another experienced breeder with him to view the pups. Whether the visiting breeder cares to pick other people's pups or not matters far less than the fact that his presence may be helpful in giving the buyer an objective view of the whole litter.

Any buyer should be on the lookout for clean surroundings and healthy pups that are lively and friendly when wide-awake. He is also within his rights to ask to see charts of growth gains and evidence of supplemental food consumption in the way of meat. Beware of the large litter of eight or more pups unless positive proof is given that these pups had supplemental rations from the beginning. Few pups can overcome a poor nutritional start. By seven weeks they should be practically or completely weaned and on a good high-protein diet which, incidentally, is expensive and the reason why

Note variety of colors in this three-weeks-old litter. *Arthur L. Child photo*

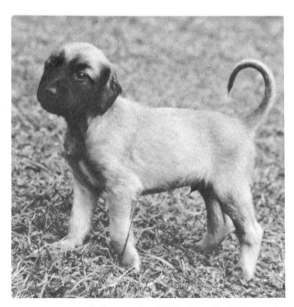

Four-weeks-old black-masked silver male.

pups cannot be sold for pittances. Be suspicious of the pup that does not eagerly eat solid food by seven weeks. This does not refer to the period of adjustment when a pup goes into a new home, often temporarily affecting the appetite.

By seven or eight weeks, the pups should be well up on their feet, not down on their pasterns and hocks. Bodies should feel sturdy, not bony or ridgy, but also not covered in heavy fat. Avoid the pup who shows fear reactions and shakes badly when picked up.

Birth size itself is no gauge to adult size but, coupled with advances on weekly weight charts, may prove a fair indication. There is no size disqualification in the breed but a wide range among individuals does exist. Unduly coarse and puny animals are equally undesirable. A buyer would do well to take clues from the parents here. Avoid the gross bitch or the puny male as possible signs of undesirable extremes.

Check for bright clear eyes of small size. Don't assume that dark-eyed pups will stay that way. Most all young pups are dark-eyed and the few that show early lightness will probably turn yellow.

Heads can be puzzling. First, unless at least one of the parents had a really lovely well-chiseled muzzle, there is little chance of finding one in the litter. Not much can be seen on forefaces at an early age, but they should have good depth, with a pronounced Roman bump across the top or the nose will finish flat or dished. Length means very little and comes with the development of the permanent teeth. Decidedly domed occiputs, well-pointed at the rear of the skull, are good signs as are flat inconspicuous zygomatic arches. To indicate refinement, the skull should have a look of greater depth than breadth to it.

By three months, the deciduous teeth are widely spaced and should be slightly overshot (uppers protruding a bit) at this age for even adult teeth spacing. Any sign of an undershot mouth (lowers protruding ahead of the uppers) usually worsens.

Tails should begin to show some curl by eight weeks, especially at chow time. Some have good rings already. Beware of the really limp tail or the one that flops loosely on the back.

Unfortunately, experiences with specific lines of Afghans cannot be carried confidently over to unrelated breedings. Some "families" tend to early leggy development, filling in breadth later. Others portray early heavy body development in broad chests over temporarily

189

bandy legs, bringing the Bulldog to mind. A few hounds grow slowly and evenly, but even this is a worry to some breeders who, from good experience, fear the perfect miniatiure adult type, as such pups often complete their growth too early and are undersized. The hound that goes through one annoying stage of imbalance after another is usually the large, awkward, fast-growing pup whose parts just can't seem to catch up with each other.

Experienced breeders pick up a seemingly shapeless pup to assess neck and shoulders. The broad, flat shoulder should be oblique and placed well behind the neck. Breastbone and rib cage should be large and well-defined. The lifted head must show early length of neck if it exists. Such long necks thicken with fur and fat and get lost for a while, but usually reappear in adults.

Rear legs should be very wide-spread, well-bent at the stifle and the eight-weeks pup should practically waddle when seen from the rear. As legs lengthen, the tendency is for angulation to decrease. If shoulder and rear quarter angulation is not in hand on a young pup, it never will be. Rear quarters can be forgiven for being slightly higher than the shoulders as the tendency is for rear quarters to drop when the pup is more mature. Loin should be short. Feet must be huge if the puppy is to grow to a respectable size. Joints of the legs must be quite knobby and obvious. Ears should be broad, long and as low-set as possible. There are times when nice ears appear perched on top of the head, later to drift back into place. At three months, the ears should be longer than the muzzle, but will soon be passed by the lengthening snout.

To the experienced eye, style and stride is one of the best evidences of quality in a young puppy of ten to twelve weeks. It is well to find them at least partially leash trained by this age. The most promising Afghan pup will show its fine heritage through a naturally erect body and head carriage, and a free-moving, trotting gait with feet properly lifted and well-placed. The gait should approximate that specified in the Standard, with the rear legs hitting about where the front feet have left. Any interference of the rear feet with the front, causing side-stepping, is an indication of permanent gait problems. We are discussing a highly changeable ratio of body-length to leg-length on stride but, somehow, at about three months they often line up like they will in adulthood.

As the dog is seen coming and going, any deviation from a straight

190

line is to be avoided, unless there is an obvious and temporary reason for such misalignment. The legs are hinged and jointed to reach the ground from their attached positions on the body. Hence the male with the broad rib cage that needs growing into may pass a period where his still short legs are on the bandy side. The narrow-chested pup whose feet turn out will only get worse.

Coat is the first thing breeders and buyers attempt to assess, both as to color and quantity. The heaviest-coated puppy will be well considered, but many a real bargain in Afghans has come with the nicely formed puppy who looked to be short on coat. A shiny appearance is undesirable; coats should have the look of dusty velveteen pile. Each breeder has his own signs of coat prediction. Some check for curling hair along the backs of the front legs. Others look for thickness on the pasterns or across the nape of the neck, by ruffling the hair backwards. There are those that swear by profuse face hair and monkey whiskers. These theories are just great as long as they work. The entire scope of Afghan coat is too variable to fit any one gauge. Some breeders have pups that are practically smooth-coated at six months of age, but are still confident that they will develop fine adult coats as did their parents before them. Other breeders look with horror on such pups, as their line of pups tends to great fuzzy fur jackets at this age, obliterating all but the tip of the nose. But the latter owners know well that these are puppy coats and not positive indications of adult quantity either. Two well-coated parents generally produce reliably coated offspring. If the parents exhibit two different types of coat textures and come from two different growth pattern calendars, the results are far less certain. Some heavy-coated males are strong at producing well-coated sons but poorly-coated daughters. Scanty-coated parents can be expected to produce more of the same but as long hair is known to be recessive to short hair, there is a chance of an occasional well-coated specimen cropping up unexpectedly. Don't rely on it, though.

Breeders prefer not to see the Afghan Hound develop a complete saddle before it is a year old. Precocious development is rarely a good sign in Afghans. The yearling should have a good thick coat, a a mixture of puppy and adult fur, plenty of facial hair, and a ready-to-emerge saddle lurking as coarse short hair beneath the longer fur. It is well to check the extent of such coarse fur by ruffling the fur backwards, for wherever such short hair can be found on sides,

Twelve-weeks-old puppies.

Ten-months-old black-masked red male.

pasterns, and hocks, there is a possibility that the dog will become smooth-coated in these areas, temporarily or permanently. A bitch that does not have her first season until well past her first birthday is also giving a welcome sign, as the largest coat drop often comes with that first real season. To some extent, coat will come and go, rise and fall, all during the hound's life.

The looks of the pup are not all of the story. He must adjust to the world of his owner and other people. The Afghan puppy should be very outgoing as he is certain to gain dignity and reserve in adulthood. He is exceptionally quick to react to stimuli; a necessary trait in the wilds where a split-second delay in reaction can mean sudden death. But beware of the skittery, over-reactive pup who just might be neurotic and untouchable when adult. Much of his future mental attitude will be due to his environment, but some of the germs are planted at birth or in the nest. The big dull sleepy boy may be storing all his energy for growth and should not be ignored.

Finally, never be ashamed to give in to that immediate magnetic rapport that flashes between some people and certain puppies. These instinctive reactions often signal compatible personalities, so important for the enjoyment of the dog as a life-long companion and worth far more than all the blue ribbons in the world.

Color Breeding

The nature of Afghan Hound color is of great fascination to many breeders. Its transmission has long been considered a bit of a puzzle. This is not because it is in any way unique in canine coloring, but because no other long-haired breeds are allowed such wide latitude in coloration. In the surprisingly wide spectrum of Afghan colors and color combinations, somehow ordinary dog colors tend to look very different on this breed with its long sweeping side-coats and contrasting close-haired saddles and muzzles. Long hair tends to diffuse coat colors and allows a noticeable incomplete domination of different genetic factors that produce many subtle unmatchable tones. There is unwarranted stress on Afghan Hound color both inside and out of the rings. The Standard embraces all but white markings. But, as the quiet iridescence of some shadings and the brilliant flash of other hues has lured many fanciers into the tribe, such color concern is understandable.

193

Afghan Hounds occur in greater or lesser numbers in all the common canine colors except liver brown. Actually there are only three primary base colors that concern the breeder. All other tones are merely shades and combinations of the original three. To understand this, breeders must first disregard all the flamboyant sales psychology color names coined by various imaginative breeders. These three base colors are not so much really single colors as they are the basic manifest forms of the red-black pigment conflict. In order of their *dominance* or power over each other, they are:

1. Black
2. Red (this is a sable red, generally found with some black hairs in ear leathers and down the backline of the saddle and tail).
3. Black-and-Tan (B-T). An obvious black-red conflict with the black substituting for the red in the form of a permanent overlay over much of the outer surface of the dog. It ranges from the small black "blanket" seen on many Beagles to an animal that at first glance appears solid black, with red retained only on the underbelly, tips of the feet, and dashes over the brow.

These three base effects are all forms of just one specific gene. Any dog contains in his genetic make-up just two of these forms, one received from each parent. Color in dogs is far from a simple case of dominants and recessives as these three base color forms are subject to drastic changes by the addition of other genetic factors acting alone or in conjunction with each other. This will be seen as we discuss the individual colors and their changed forms.

At birth, most common black-masked red (or black-masked cream and silver) Afghans are some shade of mahogany, due to a temporary overlay of blackish "guard hair" that fades in the ensuing months. Only the experienced breeder can predict the future color of these bronze pups as the very darkest sables may well become the lightest silvers when grown. This dark overlay can also confuse ready identification of brindles and other bi-colors. The pup, born with little or none of this short-lived guard hair, calls out its color immediately. However, puppy color may be far from the dog's permanent tinge. Hairs are constantly growing, aging and replacing themselves. As the side hairs lengthen and mature, they also lighten. Incoming new hair, rich with fresh pigment, counteracts with deepening tones.

The coarse, close saddle and muzzle fur, so different in texture from the side-coat, remains full-colored. Blacks tend to "sunburn" or gray, reds turn creamy, and creams fade to white as the coat ages, until periods of re-growth reverse the fading process. The old adage, "You can't tell the color of an Afghan until the day he dies" covers these ever-changing effects.

At the time of whelping, novice breeders have become alarmed by the appearance of pups with pink noses and footpads. This is very common, indicating incomplete pre-natal development of pigment in the extremities. In most instances, the black color replaces the pink within a few days (some solid creams furnishing exceptions). More perplexing to breeders is the appearance of any white-markings on the feet and muzzle of the newborn. By rights, all such white-markings bring suspicion of the presence of mis-marking genes, but their occurrence is very common and experienced breeders know that white feet and barely visible bits of white above the nostrils will probably fill with color later. The line of demarcation between temporary white tips and true "mis-marks" is a tricky border dispute.

The most important base color in Afghans is the red as it has always been the most widespread color of the breed, giving it the heaviest genetic frequency. In the scale of powers the black is dominant over the red but of less importance as black genes are comparatively rare in total Afghan population. Black, being dominant, requires at least one black parent (see blue or cream also) in order to produce black offspring. The B-T (black-and-tan) pattern is more common than the black, but less than the red, and recessive to both the other base forms, meaning that the B-T must be transmitted by both parents to produce visual B-Ts. Such single B-T genes can be carried recessively for many generations before meeting their match. Hence, the occurrence of B-Ts from any breeding should not be surprising.

The common red in Afghans is well known in the world of dogs, being genetically similar to the shades called sable in Collies or fawn in Great Danes and Boxers. The dark masking found on the muzzle of most red Afghans is the result of a separate additional marking gene of a dominant type. This masking gene is very widespread in the breed, but one parent at least must be masked to produce masked offspring. Invisible masks can be worn by black-masked *black* dogs. The effect of the masking gene may be limited to just a few dark hairs around the lips or extend as dark pigment running well above the eyes. It is interesting in the U.S.A. that the mask factor is uncommon in Borzoi, Greyhounds, Whippets and Saluki.

The tints of cream or silver, with some exceptions (see cream or blue) are merely let-down shades of the common red, whether seen on the black-masked cream, as the pale background of a brindle, or on the ivory feet and underbody of the light-pointed B-Ts. This reduction of red pigment is due to a specific paling gene that, for some strange reason, limits its effects to the base red hairs, having practically no effect on any black hairs in attendance. As the paled forms are recessive to the full darker reds, such genes must be acquired from both parents.

The permanent retention of a goodly number of blackish hairs (sabling) on the various shades of red-creams is not uncommon, producing extremely dark saddles and black tails, often shading over parts of the shoulders and body. This heavy sabling is particularly evident in certain strains of Afghans.

Brindles are base red animals with a superimposed dark striping over the lighter background due to another specific genetic effect, dominant in type. This calls for at least one parent to have the visible brindling phenomenon to produce brindle offspring. (Again, as with masking, brindling may exist but not be visible on a black dog, there being no available light hairs for contrast.) On a B-T patterned dog, the brindle effect can only be viewed on the light points of feet and face. These two overlay features are due to distinctly different genes, but can occur simultaneously on one animal.

Brindle is the most variable of all Afghan colors. The dark striping can be so extensive that the dog is mistaken for a true black hound. Or slight dark markings on a gold dog can be so light as to escape detection and yet blossom out into full stripes in the next generation. Afghan brindles frequently appear more mottled and blotched than clearly striped due to the diffusive effects on long coat. Many so-called Afghan brindles are nothing more than heavily sabled dogs mis-labeled brindle. The base red visible as background between the dark stripes varies as with red found anywhere else according to the paling genes present. The dark overlay is affected

196

by the same factors of dilution that govern any black hairs. (See "blue.")

The true solid dominant black is an uncommon color in the breed, but when present it conceals all other forms of coloring recessive to it. Most black Afghans are heterozygous for the color (have just one gene for black and one gene carried recessively for either red or B-T). Dilute shades of black, called Maltese Blues, are the rarest of all the Afghan colors. The true blue dog (not to be confused with blue-brindles) is genetically black, with a coat that has been diluted from black to gray by means of the Maltese Blue dilution factor (that restricts its effect to black pigment of the coat and ignores the red areas). Such blues occur in shades from deep slate gray to a pale dove gray that can be taken for white. This Maltese Blue dilution gene is recessive to the fuller color and must be supplied by both parents. As this same gene will effect black hairs on any color hound, it is present in a double dose in the gray-masked red hound (when the hound is born gray-masked). It turns the B-T to blue-and-tan. Dark striping on brindles is similarly affected.

While the Maltese Blue gene is detected at birth because of its gray-blue cast, another gene also produces blues of a slightly different type. This graying gene (most common in Kerry Blue Terriers) is a progressive deterioration of black, bringing premature graying to a hound born jet black. Some graying is evident by the dog's first birthday and may continue until the hound is three years old. This graying gene, unlike the Maltese Blue, is a dominant factor and need come from one parent only. Black-masked reds who turn gray very early may well harbor this gene. Both types of blue-grays have been unconsciously selected and often intermixed by breeders striving for the illusive blues. A word of caution for those anxious to dabble in blues in hopes of setting a strain of this color. In Afghans it is a highly frustrating experience. The necessary factors are quite rare and very difficult to control. There is a distinct danger of blindly sacrificing total quality for color as there is in all deliberate color breedings. Even under the most carefully controlled conditions, breeders hoping for blues often find themselves getting poorly pigmented creams and whites instead (see "cream"). Remember also that the blue genes only succeed in making the more common black-masked stock turn gray bearded and ancient before their time. There

197

is great charm and unusual beauty when the blue factors occur on brindles, B-Ts and blacks. Fortunately, they do turn up as natural happy surprises, remaining the rare gems of the Afghan spectrum.

The *cream* Afghan Hound is difficult to discuss and assess, for such hounds genetically may be any one of the three primary base colors, despite not having a single black hair visible in any part of their coat. This phenomenon is due to a "restriction factor" that positively prohibits the appearance of black hairs in the fur. Such animals are born sans dark guard hairs, remaining clear cream to white throughout their lives. They are never black-masked but frequently are reddish on the muzzle and ear fringes. This restriction factor is recessive and must come from both parents. Two such creams, regardless of their true genetic base colors, can produce only more such creams, but when the double restriction factor is broken as in mating with any full-color dog with black hairs in its coat, the true hidden base color of the cream can be released to their offspring. These self-colored creams were once far more common than they are today and responsible for many surprises when bred to black-masked reds, such as the occurrence of black or blue pups when least expected. Such experiences lead to the widely-held belief that there was just no accounting for Afghan colors. These same creams are apt to thwart schemes for blues by cropping up through a re-pairing of recessive restriction factors, so closely woven into much blue and black breeding. The ivory hounds are very lovely in themselves, and show off a good eye and a well-chiseled head to great advantage, but they have a slight problem, sometimes only seasonal ("winter nose") in a lack of jet black nose and eye rim pigment. This may appear as pinkish-grey and is a minor fault in a Standard which calls for a black nose.

The white Afghan is somewhat the same story. Most whites are either pale gray or pale cream animals due to a piling up of paling and dilution factors, plus the aforementioned "restriction factor." But it is certainly conceivable that some of our pure whites are just one big spot caused by the extreme forms of the "spotting genes" known to exist in the breed. White spots (mis-marks) are due to a specific recessive and predictable multiform gene that allows absolutely no pigment into portions of the skin, leaving it transparent (pink) with colorless (white) hairs growing from the areas. These

198

spotting effects increase in intensity from the extremities inward. Going down from the dominant full-color form (with no white on the animal anywhere), the mildest form of spotting consists of white toes and a breast locket, so common in the breed that it attracts no attention. In a stronger dose, there will be one or more white feet, a white tail tip, and possibly a definite "blaze" on the muzzle. A stronger dose of the spotting genes produces white climbing up the legs and circling the neck in the "Collie collar" pattern. The obviously spotted parti-color animal ranges from this stage to a piebald appearance with remaining splotches of color on a large white background. Most of these white-splashed Afghans are mercifully put down at birth or not used for breeding. However, extremely white-spotted animals may reach the other end of the stick in appearing a solid white color. This is frequently seen in Borzoi and the white Collie. Any traces of actual color would be found around the ears and near the base of the tail but, if cream in tone, it would go unnoticed. Such a white lacks proper pigmentation and, together with parti-colors or blazed hounds, constitutes "mis-marks," undesirable according to the Standard. All other colors are perfectly permissible.

Leading Producers

The following lists of Top Producer and Honorable Mention sires in this country has been compiled as carefully as possible from all sources currently available. It is not claimed to be exhaustive. In the case of many fine dogs, the owners were unable to furnish exact production records because none had ever been kept. In the case of some others, correspondence requesting this information went unanswered. No responsibility can be accepted for this. Mr. Leach of National Breeders Registry provided invaluable aid.

If any outstanding producers, sires or dams, have slipped through the screening or have not been credited with a full tally, this serves to point up the need for a centralized file of records kept up-to-date. This is not the function of the A.K.C., but rather of the breeders themselves, ideally through the Parent Club. Any omissions should be brought to the attention of the publisher for future editions.

Under the early Standard the two really top producers were Ch. Rudiki of Prides Hill with thirty-one champions, and Ch. Ali Khyber, his record-holding son, with thirty-five. The producers who deserve honarable mention and the number of champions to their credit are listed below:

Honorable Mention Afghan Stud Dogs—Before 1948

Westmill Omar (10)
*Ch. Tufan of Ainsdart (10)
*Ch. Sardar Khan el Kabul (10)
    (Note: 9 of these were out of Flo Flo of Ghazni)
Ch. Yusseff, C.D. (10)
Ch. Agha-Kush (12)
*Ch. Rana of Chaman of Royal Irish (11)
*Ch. Badshah of Ainsdart (17)
*Ch. Garrymhor Zabardast of Arken (20)
    (Note: 12 of these were out of Ku Mari Khyaam of Arken, see Top Producers—Bitches)

*Imports

Under the revised Standard with many more males available, we consider the great studs to be those with 20 or more champions to their credit. Those with 10 to 19 deserve honorable mention and the number of champions to their credit are listed below:

Honorable Mention Sires—Since 1948

Ch. Akaba's Blue Banner (14)
Akaba's Royal Blue (14)
Ch. Akaba's Sterling Silver (10)
Ch. Ammon Hall Nomad (12)
Ch. Artemus of Province (11)
Ch. Belden Bali Hi (16)
Ch. Coastwind Gazebo (16)
Ch. Crown Crest Dhi-Mond (11)
Ch. Crown Crest Kabul (14)
Ch. Crown Crest Rubi (15)
Ch. Crown Crest Topaz (14)
Ch. Crown Crest Zardonx (15)
Ch. Dahnwood Gabriel (11)
Ch. Desert Chieftain of Mikai, C.D. (11)
Ch. Djandji Radja of Stormhill (10)
Ch. Dureigh's Golden Harvest (15)
Ch. Holly Hill Sultan (10)

Ch. Ammon Hall Nomad (Ch. Holly Hill Desert Wind ex Ch. Holly Hill Lorna Doone), black mask red dog, bred by Jay Ammon and Sue Kauffman, owned by J. Playfair and M. P. Gray.

Ch. Coastwind Gazebo (Akaba's Allah Kazam ex Ch. Shaader's Blajnhe), black mask red dog, bred and owned by Coastwind Kennels (Mike Dunham and Richard Souza).

Ch. Ibn Nekhoro El Khani (16)
Ch. Javelin of Camri (18)
Ch. Karli Ben Ghazi (14)
Ch. Majara Mahabat (14)
Ch. Majara Menelek (15)
Ch. Majara Mihrab (15)
Mecca's Shoe Shine Boy (10)
Ch. Mecca's Tajma Khan of Tajmir (19)
Ch. Moonshyn of Moornistan (12)
Ch. Pamir Storm Ho (10)
Ch. Patrician's Sherwood (12)
Ch. Sahadi Sessu (10)
Ch. Shahmir's Sampson (18)
Ch. Stormhill Silver Dream (11)
Ch. Turkuman Nissims Laurel (14)

The great producing bitches in the breed are listed under Top Producers—Bitches. Many of these bitches are included on the lists of great sires. It certainly takes two to make quality. A careful look at the Top Producers—Sires list will show that some of these bitches have produced well with several of the top studs. The following list contains the Honorable Mention Bitches, those with 5 to 9 Champions to their credit:

Honorable Mention Bitches

Ch. Akaba's Brass Bangle (6)
Akaba's Brass N'Soot of Camri, C.D. (7)
Ch. Akaba's Daphne-Lin (5)
Akaba's Gigi in White (5)
Ch. Akaba's Glacier Blue (5)
Ch. Alcara's Aida Alif (5)
Ch. Alde-Barbe's Tabu (9)
Asra of Ghazni (7)
B-Egypt's Echo of Belden (8)
Belden Blue Angel (5)
Ch. Bellvicta Sheba Jiratch'Mir (5)
Ben Ghazi's Jaman (5)
Ch. Bey Bombay of Five Mile (5)
Ch. Bletchingley Sahari of Scheherezade (8)
Crown Crest Kuchi (9)
Ch. Crown Crest Safari Sand-Star (6)
Crown Crest Sharizade (5)
Ch. Crown Crest Taejhanne (6)
Ch. Delhi Downs Bathsheri (6)

Ch. Delhi Downs Bathsheri (Ch. Dureigh's Golden Harvest ex Delhi Downs Koh-I-Nana), black masked red bitch, bred by Elsie S. and Jack L. Roth, Jr., owned by Delhi Downs Kennels (Norman Kattleman and Bernard W. Mansfield).

Ch. Bletchingley Sahari of Scheherezade (Eng. Ch. Horningsea Sheer Khan ex Eng. Ch. Bletchingley Zelda), black mask golden bitch, bred by Mrs. Peggy Riley (England), owned by Lt. Col. and Mrs. Wallace H. Pede.

Ch. Dureigh's Fai of Hillbanks (6)
Echo of La Paloma (5)
Ch. Elru's Sae-Zah-Hni (5)
Ch. Estahla of Estioc (7)
Ch. Faith, C.D. (7)
Far Away Loo (9)
Flo Flo of Ghazni (9)
Ch. Gran Ellen Sheba (5)
Ch. Holly Hill Bon Voyage (8)
Ch. Holly Hill Hex (7)
Ch. Holly Hill Lorna Doone (7)
Ch. Holly Hill Vanity Fair (7)
Ch. Kabul's Carol of Patrician (5)
Ch. Kabul's Tjani of Naranjal (6)
Ch. Karan of Khanhasset (6)
Ch. Kashmoira Marzar-I-Sharif (7)
Ch. Khanhasset Ginger of Grandeur (5)
Ch. Khayam's Kism of Scheherezade (8)
Ch. Kismet's Little Egypt (5)
Laineux Dolly De Lux (5)
Ch. Laineux Kara Koh (6)
Ch. Longlesson Ophelia (5)
Longlesson Summer Shadow (5)
Ch. Majara Munshi (5)
Ch. Mandith Miranda (5)
Ch. Marsinah of Moornistan (5)
Ch. Maymun of Moornistan (6)
Ch. Mirasia of Moornistan (9)
Ch. Pamir Sali (6)
Patrician's Sheila (5)
Ch. Patrician's Victoria (8)
Rani El Kabul (5)
Ch. Rhana Dei Zenga (5)
Rudari of Arken (6)
Ch. Rudika of Blakeen (6)
Ch. Sashay El Sayyad (5)
Ch. Scarlhett O' Scharlau (6)
Ch. Shaadar's Blanje of Karlyle (6)
Ch. Shahmir's Khalua (6)
Ch. Shibergam of Dunrobin (8)
Ch. Siva Ben Ghazi (5)
Ch. Soroya Khieba (6)
Ch. Stormhill San-Dhal (6)

Ch. Sultan's Cuttingadido, C.D. (6)
Ch. Tahida of Arthea (5)
Taj Mahal Kenya (5)
Ch. Wendiblu's Soraya of Taralane (6)
Winonie of Ghazni (5)
Zahera of Prides Hill (7)
Ch. Zumurrud of Five Mile (6)

The following list is divided into two major sections, Top Producers—Sires, and Top Producers—Dams. In the Top Producers—Sires list, the first column of names are champions sired by the Top Producers and the second column lists the Champions' dams. In the Top Producers—Dams list, the first column of names are Champions and the second column lists the Champion's sires. These lists are based on the records contained in *Pure-Bred Dogs American Kennel Gazette* through the December 1974 issue.

Top Producers—Sires

CH. ALI KHYBER (Ch. Rudiki of Prides Hill ex Pommel Rock Kashan)

Khanhasset Kush of Five Mile	Far Away Loo
Khanhasset Kairouan	Far Away Loo
Khanhasset Ginger of Grandeur	Far Away Loo
Zenana of Elcoza	Ch. Zannette of Elcoza
Zevadne of Elcoza	Ch. Zannette of Elcoza
Sikula of Havenshare	Ch. Shibergam of Dunrobin
Shiwoh of Havenshare	Ch. Shibergam of Dunrobin
Karach of Khanhasset	Ch. Shibergam of Dunrobin
Karan of Khanhasset	Ch. Shibergam of Dunrobin
Scheherezade VI	Ch. Shibergam of Dunrobin
Sayjah of Havenshare	Ch. Shibergam of Dunrobin
Sange of Havenshare	Ch. Shibergam of Dunrobin
Kahlua of Khanhasset	Ch. Shibergam of Dunrobin
Kho-Kho	Khosan
Yeghis Shan el Khalif	Ch. Beharah Malki of Ghazni
Khyber Kim, C.D.	Ch. Beharah Malki of Ghazni
Hamadan	Ch. Beharah Malki of Ghazni
Amanullah Ibn Ali II	Ch. Beharah Malki of Ghazni
Khyber's Arora of Gramur	Five Mile Kismet Chandra
Ali Kismet	Five Mile Kismet Chandra

—continued

CH. ALI KHYBER (Continued)

Windtryst's d'Numtu	Ch. Windtryst's Ba-Midji
Windtryst's d'Erbab	Ch. Windtryst's Ba-Midji
Windtryst's d'Bomi	Ch. Windtryst's Ba-Midji
Majara Mardan-I-Ghayb	Ch. Majara Mustapha
Majara Malihah	Ch. Majara Mustapha
Majara Mamrak	Ch. Majara Mustapha
Majara Mundarris	Ch. Majara Mustapha
Gambula of Iradell	Ch. Karan of Khanhasset
Gishku of Iradell	Ch. Karan of Khanhasset
Gyges of Iradell	Ch. Karan of Khanhasset
Alcara's Azimur Alif	Ch. Alcara's Alif
Alcara's Aida Alif	Ch. Alcara's Alif
Alcara's Ahab Alif	Ch. Alcara's Alif
Tahrkifa of Indarra	Ch. Kismet of Tuffi of Grandeur
Alla Habad of Karikal	Ch. Kiam Jonel of Karikal

CH. RUDIKI OF PRIDES HILL (Ch. Badshah of Ainsdart ex Ch. Shireen of Prides Hill)

Rudika of Blakeen	Lasca Klana
Far Away Kuh-i-Besman	Far Away Dash-I-Margo
Ali Khyber	Pommel Rock Kashan
Maharanee Kohibaba, C.D.	Pommel Rock Kashan
Khanhasset's Kanda	Pommel Rock Kashan
Blakeen Odessa of Laineux	Ch. Babec of Blakeen
Bradwood Mata of Shajehan	Ch. Bul Bul of Arken
Sahib of Sutton Place	Ch. Bul Bul of Arken
Mo-Qua-Hee's Remus	Mo-Qua-Hee's Fantasy
El Mio Bambi of Chamee	Ch. Kerrin Fachamis
El Mio Shelah of Chamee	Ch. Kerrin Fachamis
El Mio Zabu of Five Mile	Ch. Kerrin Fachamis
Conjo of Bevero Downs	Rudari of Arken
G.I. Joe of Bevero Downs	Rudari of Arken
Gungo Ho of Bevero Downs	Rudari of Arken
Kurley Kares of Bevero Downs	Rudari of Arken
My Ideal of Bevero Downs	Rudari of Arken
Asta of Altoun	Rudari of Arken
Arthea Bathsheba of Five Mile	Ch. Zudiki of Arthea
Arthea King Thut of Five Mile	Ch. Zudiki of Arthea
Sita Zurudika of Arthea	Ch. Zudiki of Arthea
Five Mile's Tachi	Tachi of Prides Hill
Rudiki's Medhi-Yama o'Five Mile	Rani of Altoun
Rudiki's Beni of Five Mile	Rani of Altoun
Casanova of Five Mile	Shireen of Ainsdart
Bey Bombey of Five Mile	Shireen of Ainsdart
Zabul Khan of Elcoza	Ch. Zannette of Elcoza
Zanya of Elcoza	Ch. Zannette of Elcoza
Talacavia's Tandar	Ch. Kandar of Riverside
Rudiki's Sultan of Brucemik	Ch. Nenar-es-Sena of Barukara
Tamassar Chaman of Parkway	Tulla of Chaman

CH. AKABA'S ROYAL FLUSH (Akaba's Royal Blue ex Ch. Akaba's Brass Bangle)

Charaj Cassandra	Ch. Charaj El Samantha
Charaj Summer Storm	Ch. Charaj El Samantha
Charaj Shabah	Ch. Charaj El Samantha
Dynasty's Marked Card	Beldon Blue Angel
Dynasty's Lady Dealer	Beldon Blue Angel
Dynasty's Midnight Cowboy	Beldon Blue Angel
Dynasty's Wild Card	Beldon Blue Angel
Esfahan Apache Tear	Ch. Akaba's Brass Ariel of Esfahan
Esfahan Echohawk of Apache	Ch. Akaba's Brass Ariel of Esfahan
Keva's Allegra	Ch. Charaj El Jasmine, C.D.
Keva's Akela	Ch. Charaj El Jasmine, C.D.
Ibn Rah Ishtar	Akaba's Dustee Trayl
Riptide Vodka of Holly Hill	Ch. Holly Hill Dolphin
Akaba's Stacked Deck	Ch. Rhana Dei Zenga
Dea Zenga Smoke Signals	Ch. Rhana Dei Zenga
Blu-Belle of Stormhill	Ch. Sakti Sighra of Stormhill
Pele of Stormhill	Ch. Sakti Sighra of Stormhill
Tinker-Belle of Stormhill	Ch. Sakti Sighra of Stormhill
Mafreeka's Johia of Stormhill	Ch. Sakti Sighra of Stormhill
Akaba's Stone Flower of Karima	Ch. Akaba's Devilish Tinker Toy
Akaba Alice Blue Gown of Miraj	Ch. Akaba's Devilish Tinker Toy
Arabi's Dark Secret	Al Quahid's Moon Mist
Witchall Cygnet	Tallaway Persian Sunset

CH. AKABA'S TOP BRASS (Ch. Shirkhan of Grandeur ex Genii Al Peraa)

Akaba's Kharma of Torrekesh	Akaba's Gigi in White
Shalimar's Sable Sparkler	Ch. Athena of Windswept
Shalimar's Sweet Surprise	Ch. Athena of Windswept
Akaba's Brass Bandit	Thais of La Paloma
Djandji Radja of Stormhill	Ch. Stormhill San-Dhal
Smoke-Dream of Stormhill	Ch. Stormhill San-Dhal
The Kicapukid of Stormhill	Ch. Stormhill San-Dhal
Tarina Brass Charm of Akaba	Tarina Whispering Sands
Akaba's Brass Bangle	Lightfoot's Tahnee of Kamir
Gold Coast's Brass Spangle	Lgihtfoot's Tahnee of Kamir
Akaba's Brass Bonanza	Lightfoot's Tahnee of Kamir
Donna-Shmain El Sayyad	Tangye El Sayyad
Valair Brass Knuckles	Bombay's Ebony Escapade, C.D.
Akaba's Brass Filagree	Akaba's Brass Brocade
Akaba's Brass Ariel of Esfahan	Capuchina of Khayyam
Khayyam's Brass Jezebel	Capuchina of Khayyam
Akaba's Persian Lilac	Ch. Akaba's Glacier Blue
Akaba's Brass Cinder-Fella	Ch. Akaba's Glacier Blue
Akaba's Brass Cinder Smoke	Ch. Akaba's Glacier Blue
Sanallah's Topflight	Esther El Prydemahr
Sanallah's Quicksilver	Esther El Prydemahr
Shaughnessy's Dante of Kobi	Ch. Holly Hill Evening
Akaba's Yankee Doodle Brass	Saba's Chim Chim Chaba
Shangrila's Pharaoh Uhuru	Pharoah Princess Scheherezade
Tallaway Lord of the Rings	Kazah Asshra

Ch. Crown Crest Sancy (Ch. Crown Crest Dhi-Mond ex Ch. Hope), black mask silver bitch, and Ch. C.C. Vegas Ghamblr of Belden (Ch. Crown Crest Khanazad ex Ch. Crown Crest Safari Sand-Star), black mask silver dog, both bred by Kay Finch and owned by Leo D. Goodman.

CH. C.C. VEGAS GHAMBLR OF BELDEN (Ch. Crown Crest Khanazad ex Ch. Crown Crest Safari Sand-Star)

Sardar's Sardi of Arkendale	Ch. Sardar's Sarlana, C.D.
Belden Bajara	Ch. Crown Crest Sancy
Belden Bali Hi	Ch. Crown Crest Sancy
Belden Bazana	Ch. Crown Crest Sancy
Belden Borghana	Ch. Crown Crest Sancy
Belden Cleopatra	Ch. Crown Crest Sancy
Belden La Cover Girl	Ch. Crown Crest Sancy
Belden Creation	Ch. Crown Crest Sancy
Belden Dhi-Mond	Ch. Crown Crest Sancy
Belden Debrah	Ch. Crown Crest Sancy
Belden Eve Queen	Ch. Crown Crest Sancy
Belden Fortune Hunter	Ch. Crown Crest Sancy

—continued

CH. C.C. VEGAS GHAMBLR OF BELDEN (*Continued*)

Belden Bengalion	Ch. Crown Crest Safari Sand-Star
Belden Brab	Ch. Crown Crest Safari Sand-Star
Humble Acre Heirloom O'Belden	Ch. Crown Crest Safari Sand-Star
Kashmoira Mazar-I-Sharif	Shalimar A Chandni
Continental Kharam	Shalimar A Chandni
Marshes Omar Sharif	Shalimar A Chandni
Loubelle's Zadia of Belden	Shalimar A Chandni
Cleo of Fleetwing	Shalimar A Chandni
Alif's Naveh El Kandahar, C.D.	Winsome Nadire
Tajmir's Desert Dream	Ch. Crown Crest Khittiku, C.D.
Krishna	Jalalabad Ariana Karakum

CH. CROWN CREST MR. UNIVERSE (Ch. Ophaal of Crown Crest ex Ch. Hope)

Crown Crest Mr. Vanguard	Crown Crest Kuchi (14 pts.)
Crown Crest Miss Venus	Crown Crest Kuchi
Crown Crest Miss Universe	Crown Crest Kuchi
Crown Crest Mr. Mars	Crown Crest Kuchi
Crown Crest Miss Nike	Crown Crest Kuchi
Crown Crest Miss Peggi	Crown Crest Kuchi
Ravenwood's Bronze Star	Ch. Crown Crest Zarzanya
Ravenwood's Miss Venus	Ch. Crown Crest Zarzanya
Ravenwood's Sundance	Ch. Crown Crest Zarzanya
Khanda-Jhar of Ravenwood	Ch. Crown Crest Zarzanya
Crown Crest Miss Tiara	Ch. Crown Crest Khoronah
Crown Crest Xakliliku	Ch. Crown Crest Khoronah
Mali of Kumar	Crown Crest Crown of India
Kabu of Desertaire	Ch. Zar-Kari of Shamalan
Abu Kazi of Desertaire	Ch. Zar-Kari of Shamalan
Tarazah of Desertaire	Ch. Zar-Kari of Shamalan
Khaijhao Kawn Al Shaarq	Estioc El Abahdan
High Life Destiny's Tot	Ch. Sultan's Cuttingadido, C.D.
High Life Sheba's Fortune	Ch. Sultan's Cuttingadido, C.D.
Crown Crest Miss California	Ch. Hope
Crown Crest Mr. Jhan Jhan	Ch. Hope
Crown Crest Mr. California	Ch. Crown Crest Eve Queen
Crown Crest Miss Lhiberti	Stardust of Kashmir
Crown Crest Jiss Jwandai	Crown Crest Sharizade
Rubicon Nubian Star	Holly Hill Monsoon
Aladin's Torch of Ahab's Tent	Fatima fo Ahab's Tent
Crown Crest Miss Levade	Crown Crest Cleopatra
Crown Crest Mr. Mariner	Bakaar Kin of Zabul
Crown Crest Miss Dhali	Bakaar Kin of Zabul
Crown Crest Mr. Taejhon	Bakaar Kin of Zabul
Glen Gary of Royal Thistle	Black Magic

CH. HASSAN-BEN OF MOORNISTAN (Ch. Zaamarakuri of Ghazni ex Ch. Maymum of Moornistan)

Shaker Dawa of Kubera	Ch. Majara Munshi
Babur-Ben of Kubera	Ch. Majara Munshi
Bacha Khiva of Kubera	Ch. Majara Munshi
Lakshima of Kubera	Ch. Majara Munshi
Poobah of Kubera	Ch. Majara Munshi
Talomies of Province	Dutch Lane's Kim Zara
Tajmir's Desert Sheik	Ch. Crown Crest Jasmine, C.D.
Tajmir's Redstone Rocket	Ch. Crown Crest Jasmine, C.D.
Ammon Hall Misdeal	Ch. Holly Hill Lorna Doone
Ammon Hall Dealer's Choice	Ch. Holly Hill Lorna Doone
Simon of Moornistan	Ch. Mirasia of Moornistan
Beuschan of Moornistan	Ch. Mirasia of Moornistan
Tangerine of Moornistan	Ch. Mirasia of Moornistan
Amos of Moornistan	Ch. Mirasia of Moornistan
Noah of Moornistan	Ch. Mirasia of Moornistan
Khajah's Taska	Green's Shara
Tamora Shara Ginger	Green's Shara
Little Acres Ahab the Arab	Green's Shara
Alde Barbe's T-Bird	Ch. Holly Hill Forever Amber
Alde' Barbe's Ferraro	Ch. Holly Hill Forever Amber
Basti Girl	Harashid's Kham
Kauno Lavas	Harashid's Kham
Step's Kauno Girl	Harashid's Kham
Mohrlunds Thunder Boy	Tajmir's Desert Song

CH. HOLLY HILL BLACK MAGIC (Ch. Sahadi Sessu ex Ch. Samaris of Moornistan)

Ammon Hall Barfly	Ammon Hall Jezebel
Ammon Hall Hundred Proof	Ammon Hall Jezebel
Gemel's Shadrach of Poodaf	Come Back Little Sheba
Princess Indira of Poodaf	Come Back Little Sheba
Tanner's Maharani of Xanadu	Come Back Little Sheba
Panjhet of Stormhill	Ch. Pandora of Stormhill
Panorama of Stormhill	Ch. Pandora of Stormhill
Panthor of Stormhill	Ch. Pandora of Stormhill
Pantomine of Stormhill	Ch. Pandora of Stormhill
Sakti Sahadeva of Stormhill	Ch. Pandora of Stormhill
Sakti Sighra of Stormhill	Ch. Pandora of Stormhill
Andarab of Aida of Lynncrest	Ch. Alde-Barbe's Tabu
Andarab Othello of Lynncrest	Ch. Alde-Barbe's Tabu
Lynncrest Lakme of Andarab	Ch. Alde-Barbe's Tabu
Lynncrest Fidelio of Andarab	Ch. Alde-Barbe's Tabu
Lynncrest Mahjong of Andarab	Ch. Alde-Barbe's Tabu
Andarab Bacarat of Lynncrest	Ch. Alde-Barbe's Tabu
Lynncrest Manon of Andarab	Ch. Alde-Barbe's Tabu
Hi-Lu's Magic Dahle Diddit	Sanallah's Gypsy of Keva
Majal Nomad's Rhubi	Nomad's Arlah
Majal Mahisha	Nomad's Arlah

CH. HOLLY HILL DESERT WIND (Ch. Khabiri of Grandeur ex Ch. Samaris of Moornistan)

Juno's Sampson of Forest Hills	Holly Hill Sweet Stuff
Malandra's Nantucket	Ch. Barrister's Portia
Ammon Hall Nomad	Ch. Holly Hill Lorna Doone
Holly Hill Hobo	Ch. Holly Hill Lorna Doone
Holly Hill Bon Voyage	Ch. Holly Hill Lorna Doone
Holly Hill Safari	Ch. Holly Hill Lorna Doone
Holly Hill Shane of Lynncrest	Barrister's Miss Feasance
Lynncrest Lawrence of Arabia	Barrister's Miss Feasance
Lynncrest National Velvet	Barrister's Miss Feasance
Excalibur Wind Symphony	Holly Hill Dusk
Holly Hill Gust of Excalibur	Holly Hill Dusk
Holly Hill Fallen Angel	Holly Hill Indus
Holly Hill War Hawk	Holly Hill Indus
Holly Hill Genii of Lyncrest	Ammon Hall Delilah
Lynncrest Suez	Ammon Hall Delilah
Tradewinds Golden Dawn	Ch. Holly Hill Treasure Island
Tradewinds Thunder	Ch. Holly Hill Treasure Island
Jinni of Bedside Manor	Ch. Holly Hill Treasure Island
Excalibur Desert Dream	Ch. Lynncrest Saki of Excalibur
Jaune's April Dancer	Ch. Jaune Myasia
Jaune's Aristocrat	Ch. Jaune Myasia
Shenn's Czardawn	Keptah of Grandeur

CH. OPHAAL OF CROWN CREST (*Import from Holland*) (Nereus VDOM ex Pythia VDOM)

Crown Crest Topaz	Ch. Crown Crest TaeJoan
Crown Crest Rubi	Ch. Crown Crest TaeJoan
Crown Crest Zardonx	Ch. Crown Crest TaeJoan
Crown Crest Dhi-Mond	Ch. Crown Crest TaeJoan
Crown Crest Onyx	Ch. Crown Crest TaeJoan
Crown Crest Carnelian	Ch. Crown Crest TaeJoan
Crown Crest Kristal	Ch. Crown Crest TaeJoan
Crown Crest Kabul	Ch. Crown Crest TaeJoan
Crown Crest Khanazad	Ch. Crown Crest TaeJoan
Crown Crest Khayti	Ch. Crown Crest TaeJoan
Crown Crest Khittiku	Ch. Crown Crest TaeJoan
Crown Crest Kesu	Ch. Crown Crest TaeJoan
Crown Crest Khalifah	Ch. Crown Crest TaeJoan
Crown Crest Khoronah	Ch. Crown Crest TaeJoan
Little Oaks Lakme	Crown Crest Dardanella
Crown Crest Babaloo	Ch. Crown Crest Egypt's Echo
Crown Crest Bokkarah	Ch. Crown Crest Egypt's Echo
Crown Crest Baydho	Ch. Crown Crest Egypt's Echo
Crown Crest Bhojangles	Ch. Crown Crest Egypt's Echo
Crown Crest Bhoti	Ch. Crown Crest Egypt's Echo

—continued

Ch. Sasha of Scheherezade (Ch. Alibaba of Scheherezade, C.D. ex Benihaar Autumn Heather), black masked golden dog, bred by Bonita Visser and owned by Lt. Col. and Mrs. Wallace H. Pede.

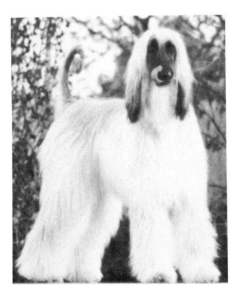

Ch. Akaba's Royal Gold (Akaba's Royal Blue ex Ch. Akaba's Brass Bangle), black mask cream bitch, bred by Lois Boardman, owned by Dr. Gerda Maria Kennedy.

CH. OPHAAL OF CROWN CREST (continued)

Crown Crest Mr. Universe	Ch. Hope
Crown Crest Hi-Dhal	Ch. Hope
Crown Crest Hi-Bhayb	Ch. Hope
Crown Crest Hi-Bhutiphaal	Ch. Hope
Crown Crest Hi-Hopephaal	Ch. Hope
Crown Crest Hi-Dhiri	Ch. Hope
Crown Crest Jasmine, C.D.	Ch. Crown Crest Taejblu Minx

CH. SASHA OF SCHEHEREZADE (Ch. Alibaba of Scheherezade, C.D. ex Benihaar Autumn Heather)

Harmony's Bandit	Harmony's Phuma of Bellvicta
Khali's Khem of Scheherezade	Harmony's Phuma of Bellvicta
Shamall of Jhabhul	Sha's Heen of Shai-Taj
Khan Dar Khan of Scheherezade	Ch. Bletchingley Sahari of Scheherezade
Khayam's Kism of Scheherezade	Ch. Bletchingley Sahari of Scheherezade
Alfandias Ke of Scheherezade	Ch. Bletchingley Sahari of Scheherezade
Kameera of Scheherezade	Ch. Bletchingley Sahari of Scheherezade
Kleopatra of Scheherezade	Ch. Bletchingley Sahari of Scheherezade
La Sabre of Scheherezade	Ch. Bletchingley Sahari of Scheherezade
Nativ Dancer of Scheherezade	Ch. Bletchingley Sahari of Scheherezade
Shangrila Pharahna Tara	Ch. Akaba's Royal Gold
Shangrila Pharaoh Bhima	Ch. Akaba's Royal Gold
Shangrila Pharahna of Xanadu	Ch. Akaba's Royal Gold
Shangrila Pharahna Sujara	Ch. Akaba's Royal Gold
Shangrila Pharahna Uvasa	Ch. Akaba's Royal Gold
Raja of Scheherezade	Ch. Akaba's Royal Gold
Shangrila Pharahna Tessah	Ch. Akaba's Royal Gold
Shangrila Pharaoh Anavadya	Ch. Akaba's Royal Gold
Shangrila Pharaoh Sandharra	Ch. Akaba's Royal Gold
Shangrila Pharaoh Saranym	Ch. Akaba's Royal Gold
Pasha of Scheherezade II	Ch. Kameera of Scheherezade
Qishon of Scheherezade	Ch. Kameera of Scheherezade

CH. SHIRKHAN OF GRANDEUR (Ch. Blue Boy of Grandeur ex Mahdi of Grandeur)

Sahadi Shikari	Ch. Crown Crest Khalifah
Sahadi Sessu	Ch. Crown Crest Khalifah
Sahadi Sinbad	Ch. Crown Crest Khalifah
Sahadi Scaramouche	Ch. Crown Crest Khalifah
Sahadi Sequin	Ch. Crown Crest Khalifah
Moonshyn of Moornistan	Ch. Maymun of Moornistan
Mirasia of Moornistan	Ch. Maymun of Moornistan
Mazur-I-Sherief of Moornistan	Ch. Maymun of Moornistan
Akaba's Top Brass	Genii Al Peraa
Akaba's Shara of Grandeur	Genii Al Peraa
Akaba's Know It All	Genii Al Peraa
Cammar's Pa'Yunga of Grandeur	Ch. Silver Pearl of Grandeur
Spartan of Grandeur	Ch. Silver Pearl of Grandeur
Akaba's Faust of La Scala	Akaba's Gigi in White
Akaba's Glacier Blue	Akaba's Gigi in White
Akaba's Kobalt Khan of Sarai	Akaba's Gigi in White
Akaba's Kobalt Kommander	Akaba's Gigi in White
Juli of Grandeur	Kragcha of Interhill
Rhyn Tayl Rhasputyn	Ch. Jo-Fran's Ranee
Shiraz Angyl Blue	Nah Neen's Kara Bas
Le Gran Salaam de Grandeur	Amberlea's Sabel of Grandeur
Infashia of Grandeur	Khishna of Grandeur
Taj Arru of Grandeur	Khishna of Grandeur
Chinah of Grandeur	Saadia of Grandeur
Pandora of Stormhill	Ch. Stormhill San-Dahl
The Millionaire of Stormhill	Ch. Stormhill San-Dahl
Khyam's Simat-I-Mashriqi	Hilltop Troy
Patrician's Sherwood	Ch. Crown Crest Taejhanne
Amir Kazan of Timbala	Ben-Ghazi's Jaman
Timbala's Jambala of Grandeur	Ben-Ghazi's Jaman
Timbala's Dracula of Shahana	Ben-Ghazi's Jaman
Tiger Khan of Grandeur	Suki of Grandeur
Chi Chi Sharaz of Tabriz	Suki of Grandeur
Blue Hawk of Grandeur	Sabreya of Grandeur
Ben Ghazi Mandith Bagheera	Ben Ghazi Alsi
Khaibara Khan of Grandeur	Sheba of Grandeur
Herkhan of Grandeur	Kalakhum of Kubera
Scaramouch of Gray Dawn	Kalakhum of Kubera
Karistan's Shirka of Grandeur	Monarco's Durrani
Prince Igor of Kashmiri	Tajmir's Stardust of Kashmiri
Kaftan Khan of Grandeur	Black Pearl of Grandeur
Westwind's Dorian of Grandeur	Sharakhana of Grandeur
Khan Shah of Grandeur	Sharakhana of Grandeur

CH. TAEJON OF CROWN CREST (Ch. Elcoza's Ponder ex Ch. Winomana of Rreks)

Crown Crest Persian Prince	Ch. Egypt's Eudora of Crown Crest
Crown Crest Arabian Knight	Ch. Egypt's Eudora of Crown Crest
Crown Crest Gymkhana	Ch. Egypt's Eudora of Crown Crest
Crown Crest Tae-Joan	Ch. Egypt's Eudora of Crown Crest
Crown Crest Taejallah	Ch. Egypt's Eudora of Crown Crest
Crown Crest Taejblu Minx	Ch. Egypt's Eudora of Crown Crest
Crown Crest Taejhanne	Ch. Egypt's Eudora of Crown Crest
Ibn Nekhoro el Khani	Nekha el Khani, C.D.
Crown Crest Kob-I-Baba, C.D.	Asuma Sands
Mumtaz Mahal of Manterra	Nara of Manterra
Desert Chieftain of Mikai, C.D.	Kismi Khan of Crown Crest
Shaitan's Lucky Chance	Tina
Hope	Ch. Kandorissa of Aldachar
Faith	Ch. Kandorissa of Aldachar
Candace	Ch. Kandorissa of Aldachar
Stormhill Silver Dream	Ch. Kandorissa of Aldachar
Crown Crest Jesi Jhaimz	Ch. Breezealong of Kandabar
Crown Crest Devikkarokit	Ch. Breezealong of Kandabar
Crown Crest Taejkati Dhali	Crown Crest Dardanella
Hamra of Mustagata	Princess Kousha of Patah's Pride
Hamads Polanise	Ch. Black Lyn of Donde
Crown Crest Rain Willow, C.D.	Ch. Crown Crest Taejblu Minx
Sahadi Saan	Ch. Crown Crest Khalifah
Sahadi Sabrina	Ch. Crown Crest Khalifah
Sahadi Sadruddin	Ch. Crown Crest Khalifah
Crown Crest Taejakbar Khan	Ch. Crown Crest Khalifah
Khan Koochek	Belhana
Khandi Khane of Kaitu	Ch. Crown Crest Khayti
Crown Crest Kaejon	Ch. Crown Crest Kristal
Crown Crest Kaejoan	Ch. Crown Crest Kristal

215

Holly Hill Indus (Ch. Moonshyn of Moornistan ex Ch. Samaris of Moornistan), bitch, bred and owned by Sue A. Kauffman.

Ch. Crown Crest Tae-Joan (Ch. Taejon of Crown Crest ex Ch. Egypt's Echo of Crown Crest), bitch, bred and owned by Kay Finch.

CH. AKABA's ROYAL GOLD (Akaba's Royal Blue ex Ch. Akaba's Brass Bangle)

Ten champions on list of Ch. Sasha of Scheherezade

CH. CROWN CREST KHALIFAH (Ch. Ophaal of Crown Crest ex Ch. Crown Crest Tae-Joan)

Five champions on list of Ch. Shirkhan of Grandeur
Four champions on list of Ch. Taejon of Crown Crest
Sahadi Comanche Brave Eagle   Ch. Crown Crest Jesi Jhaimz

CH. CROWN CREST SANCY (Ch. Crown Crest Dhi-Mond ex Ch. Hope)

Eleven champions on list of Ch. C. C. Vegas Ghamblr of Belden

CH. CROWN CREST TAE-JOAN (Ch. Taejon of Crown Crest ex Ch. Egypt's Echo of Crown Crest)

Fifteen champions on list of Ch. Ophaal of Crown Crest
Crown Chest Zarjonx   Ch. Crown Crest Zardonx

CH. EGYPT's ECHO OF CROWN CREST (Ch. Felt's Thief of Bagdad ex Big Carmelita)

Four champions on list of Ch. Taejon of Crown Crest
Five champions on list of Ch. Ophaal of Crown Crest
Kisu Khan of Crown Crest   Ch. Felt's Allah Baba

HOLLY HILL INDUS (Ch. Moonshyn of Moornistan ex Ch. Samaris of Moornistan)

Holly Hill Evening	Ch. Tajmir's Redstone Rocket
Holly Hill Midnight	Ch. Tajmir's Redstone Rocket
Holly Hill Twilight of Tajmir	Ch. Tajmir's Redstone Rocket
Holly Hill Golden Doubloon	Bletchingley Draughtsman
Holly Hill Pirate	Bletchingley Draughtsman
Holly Hill Sultan	Bletchingley Draughtsman
Holly Hill Treasure Island	Bletchingley Draughtsman
Holly Hill Sin Badd	Bletchingley Draughtsman
Cranny Blak Nite of Holly Hill	Bletchingley Draughtsman
Holly Hill Coho	Ch. Akaba's Blue Banner
Holly Hill Dolphin	Ch. Akaba's Blue Banner
Holly Hill Rip Tide	Ch. Akaba's Blue Banner
Holly Hill Davey Jones	Ch. Akaba's Blue Banner
Holly Hill War Hawk	Ch. Holly Hill Desert Wind
Holly Hill Fallen Angel	Ch. Holly Hill Desert Wind
Holly Hill Ebb Tide	Ch. Djandji Radja of Stormhill

217

Ch. Hope (Ch. Taejon of Crown Crest ex Ch. Kandorissa of Aldachar), bitch, bred by Kay Finch, owned by Charles Costabile and Kay Finch.

CH. HOPE (Ch. Taejon of Crown Crest ex Ch. Kandorissa of Aldachar)

Six champions on list of Ch. Ophaal of Crown Crest
Two champions on list of Ch. Crown Crest Mr. Universe

Crown Crest Hope Dhi-Mond	Ch. Crown Crest Dhi-Mond
Crown Crest Great Mogul	Ch. Crown Crest Dhi-Mond
Crown Crest Sancy	Ch. Crown Crest Dhi-Mond
Crown Crest Eve Queen	Ch. Crown Crest Dhi-Mond
Crown Crest Pasha	Ch. Crown Crest Dhi-Mond

KU MARI KHYAAM OF ARKEN (Ch. Badshah of Ainsdart ex Zahera of Prides Hill)

Bul Bul of Arken	Ch. Garrymhor Zabardast of Arken
Mogul of Arken, C. D.	Ch. Garrymhor Zabardast of Arken
Sultan of Arken	Ch. Garrymhor Zabardast of Arken
Rajah of Arken	Ch. Garrymhor Zabardast of Arken
Maharanee of Arken, C.D.X.	Ch. Garrymhor Zabardast of Arken
Pocono Persica of Arken	Ch. Garrymhor Zabardast of Arken
Much Ado of Arken	Ch. Garrymhor Zabardast of Arken
Ya Hak of Arken	Ch. Garrymhor Zabardast of Arken
Jadaan of Arken	Ch. Garrymhor Zabardast of Arken
Roxana of Arken	Ch. Garrymhor Zabardast of Arken
Babar of Arken II	Ch. Garrymhor Zabardast of Arken
Kashan of Arken II	Ch. Garrymhor Zabardast of Arken

CH. PANDORA OF STORMHILL (Ch. Shirkhan of Grandeur ex Ch. Stormhill San-Dahl)

Six champions on list of Ch. Holly Hill Black Magic

Pandora's Pride of Stormhill	Ch. Mecca Tajma Khan of Tajmir
Pandora's Image of Stormhill	Ch. Mecca Tajma Khan of Tajmir
Pandora's Xotica of Stormhill	Ch. Mecca Tajma Khan of Tajmir
Pandora's Sheik of Stormhill	Ch. Mecca Tajma Khan of Tajmir
Pandora's Rullah of Stormhill	Ch. Mecca Tajma Khan of Tajmir

CH. SAMARIS OF MOORNISTAN (Ch. Zaamarakuri of Ghazni ex Ch. Maymun of Moornistan)

Holly Hill King Lear	Ch. Dureigh's Golden Harvest
Holly Hill Lorna Doone	Ch. Dureigh's Golden Harvest
Holly Hill Vanity Fair	Ch. Dureigh's Golden Harvest
Holly Hill Forever Amber	Ch. Dureigh's Golden Harvest
Holly Hill Talisman of Kismet	Ch. Dureigh's Golden Harvest
Holy Hill Draco	Ch. Moonshyn of Moornistan
Holly Hill Ara of Moornistan	Ch. Moonshyn of Moornistan
Holly Hill Desert Wind	Ch. Khabiri of Grandeur
Holly Hill Night Breeze	Ch. Khabiri of Grandeur
Holly Hill Sorceress	Ch. Sahadi Sessu
Holly Hill Hex	Ch. Sahadi Sessu
Holly Hill Vampire	Ch. Sahadi Sessu
Holly Hill Witch Hazel	Ch. Sahadi Sessu
Holly Hill Zombie	Ch. Sahadi Sessu
Holly Hill Voodoo	Ch. Sahadi Sessu
Holly Hill Black Magic	Ch. Sahadi Sessu
Gran Salaam Echo of Holly Hill	Ch. Le Gran Salaam De Grandeur

SHALIMAR A CHANDNI (El Mari C'est La Vie ex Hil Lane Camille)

Five champions on list of Ch. C C. Vegas Ghambir of Belden

Continental Blue Falcon	Ch. Mecca Tajma Khan of Tajmir
Mahabbi's Continental Sytar	Ch. Mecca Tajma Khan of Tajmir
Continental Bahia	Ch. Mecca Tajma Khan of Tajmir
Continental Saddrudin	Ch. Mecca Tajma Khan of Tajmir
Continental Blue Hamaad	Ch. Mecca Tajma Khan of Tajmir
Continental Kalu Bataka	Ch. Mecca Tajma Khan of Tajmir

219

8

Care

THERE are excellent pamphlets and books devoted entirely to the care, breeding, and raising of dogs. These belong in every dog owner's library and we shall not attempt to abbreviate them here except in regards to the peculiar needs of the Afghan Hound.

Written material concerning the acts of mating and whelping is necessarily averaged from the reproductive cycles of all breeds. Such mid-point charts cannot be expected to fit precisely all Afghan Hounds. In reproductive activity there is considerable, perfectly normal variation. Owners, determined to rigidly follow the "book," rather than observe and keep notes on the cycles of their own bitches, may find themselves unable to gain issue from their hounds.

The majority of Afghan bitches commence their first season between 9 to 12 months of age, but variation, ranging from 6 to as late as 18 months remains within the normal range. Bitches should not be bred at their first season, particularly if they are less than a year old at the time.

A fair number of Afghan bitches do follow the book, coming into season regularly every six months, being ready to be bred on the

10th to the 12th day, and completing their season in approximately 21 days, but many more do not. Once-a-year seasons are not unusual, harking back to the primitive dog habits, nor are cycles of 9 to 10 month intervals. A few bitches really confuse the issue by flaming into season more than twice a year. By making notations on the backs of pedigrees or on health charts as to the exact onset and duration of each season, fairly regular cycle intervals for each bitch should reveal themselves.

Lengths of heats also vary. At the extreme, a rare bitch may have to be mated before the end of the first week; others have produced issue from breedings on as late as the 21st day. Such tendencies may be familial. Obviously this variation brings confusion in ascertaining the precise day for conception, and such bitches must be watched extra carefully to prevent unwanted matings.

The actual behavior of the dog and bitch remains the most reliable sign for optimum mating periods. The male will certainly coax the female long before she is "ready" and she may tease him in return, but she will not stand still nor hold her tail aside. During such test runs, the hounds must have room for wide maneuvering as a resentful harried bitch will snap at the male.

The physical signs are quite reliable when properly read. The bitch's vulva swells noticeably, emitting a bright red discharge at the onset of the season. Fastidious bitches, however, clean themselves constantly, often hiding early traces from unwary owners. The discharge continues and the bitch's changing scent will attract the males but she will repel any serious advances. At the time of acceptance by the bitch, there is a definite lightening of the discharge to a pinkish-yellow; and the vulva will be somewhat softened. The bitch can be assumed to have passed her season only when all discharge has completely stopped and the swelling disappears whether she has been bred or not. The owner who is unable to interpret the signs of the estrus cycle may wish to have a veterinarian make smear tests for advancing ovulation. The smear test is an aid in deciding whether to force the issue if either mate is known to be a somewhat reluctant breeder.

In breeding, as elsewhere, the Afghan retains an independent spirit, occasionally determined to choose their own mates by refusing to have anything to do with the suitor offered by their owners. It is certainly advisable to put a maiden bitch to an experienced

221

stud, and allow them ample courting time well before the day of mating. Conversely, a calm matron is always an asset to an over-anxious untried male.

At mating time, a non-slippery ground surface should be provided (not linoleum). If the bitch is frightened or the male unpracticed, seek help from an experienced dog breeder. Breeding plans have been thwarted and potential brood stock ruined by human bungling. Forcing a bitch to be bred before she is physically and psychologically ready, just because it is the 12th day can do long-lasting harm. If the bitch is fractious, but not utterly unwilling, she can be held for the male by competent persons. A soft bandage should be tied about the muzzle of the bitch to prevent fear-biting. She will also need lavish reassurance in words and pats to calm her maiden fears.

The breeding of persistently unwilling bitches is not to be encouraged. They frequently make indifferent mothers, and may possibly be illustrating an innate reproductive weakness. We might warn novice owners that Afghan bitches are quite inclined to scream at the time of actual mating, shattering the nerves of the unprepared and sending the neighbors dashing for help. It is a blood-chilling, semi-human scream, unmistakable to the experienced. Once the animals are "tied," the cry simmers to a moan or mutter, and fades away entirely.

The "tie" lasts for a few minutes or as long as an hour. Fertile breedings can occur without a tie but are very rare. During the tie the male may wish help in lifting his hind leg over the rear of the bitch until the two are standing back to back. The bitch should be held and soothed until the tie is naturally broken. If she tries to dash off, the helpless male can suffer real injury. Bitches are not vindictive during the tie and can be unmuzzled at this time. Offer water to both parties.

Afghan bitches usually settle down and follow the book along the usual pattern of embryo development. Jot down the date (or dates) of mating to gauge the expected whelping time. Weigh the bitch at mating time and measure her circumference just past the last rib. The first definite signs of pregnancy appear about the fifth week after mating in the form of a sudden and definite jump in weight and girth. Keep weekly records of measurements.

Top physical condition of the bitch-mother cannot be over-stressed. The poorest start on any breeding program is an unfit dam.

A sickly bitch, one that is infested with parasites, or one that is weak-muscled from lack of exercise should not be used for breeding. Any bitch, seven years or older (five years if she has never had a litter) is a breeding risk and breeding should be under a veterinarian's supervision. Overweight bitches should be trimmed to normal weight before breeding, as obesity contributes to infertility as well as whelping time difficulties. Thin bitches should be medically checked for predisposing causes. Any brood bitch benefits from a complete physical check-up before the mating time. If not done before the breeding, it should be done right afterwards (this is too late to call it off should complications be diagnosed). Infestations of parasites, even mild ones that do not normally bother the bitch, will interfere with optimum embryo development. A firm program of exercise and weight control should be instituted and carried to the wire. Only walking exercise is advised as the bitch grows heavy with whelp the last three weeks.

Only normal quantities of food are required by the bitch for the first four weeks of pregnancy—assuming that the bitch consumes a highly nutritional diet, including real meat and vitamin supplements regularly. From the fourth week onward, the diet should be bolstered gradually in both quantity and quality. The need for added assimilable calcium rises greatly in the pregnant bitch as puppy bones are being formed. Veterinarian-prescribed special prenatal supplements, rich in calcium and iron, should be given to all in-whelp Afghan bitches. The gradually increasing food amounts should contain, in addition to added kibble, concentrated proteins and minerals as found in meat, eggs, fish, cottage cheese, and powdered milk.

During the last four weeks the bitch usually gains in girth rapidly with an average litter (five or six pups). The embryos can sometimes be felt, like soft walnut-sized balls, moving in the abdomen. However, the Afghan bitch has a deep and cavernous chest and can be rather difficult to follow through pregnancy if she has a small litter tucked well under the ribs.

Full-term puppies emerge from the 58th to the 65th day as well as on the celebrated 63rd. General signs and needs of whelping time are well covered in the books. One often observed sign is when the Afghan bitch, who has eaten ravenously for the last few weeks, suddenly loses either her appetite or her dinner. Another reported indication is the bitch who *shivers* uncontrollably for several hours. When any suspicious signs appear, rectal temperature can be taken. The normal temperature is 101°; the bitch's temperature will usually fall below 100° within 12 to 24 hours before the litter arrives.

From the first sign of straining or labor, the bitch should be watched unobtrusively by an attendant who is prepared to call a nearby veterinarian for help if necessary. The most common source of trouble is *uterine inertia* whereby the bitch is unable to properly contract the uterus and expel all the puppies. We do not want to be alarmists but this problem is to be anticipated in out-of-condition bitches and has complicated what appeared to be healthy situations. Today's bitches lead entirely too sedentary lives for their own good. More than two hours between pups can be an unwelcome sign of possible difficulties, especially if there is straining by the bitch. When the litter has finally arrived, we advocate calling the veterinarian to give the dam a post-natal injection containing pituitrin to contract the uterus and expel any remaining afterbirths or late puppies and anti-biotics to ward off infections. In this breed it is not easy to be certain that the last pup and afterbirth have arrived, and late-comers are not at all unusual.

Most Afghan dams do a creditable job of bringing pups into the world once the initial fright of having the first-born subsides. An age-old instinct tells them what mothers of all mammals have known since the advent of the species, but these messages are not spelled out in great detail and can get slightly garbled in translation. A bewildered dam might spend so much time cleaning the rear end of the pup that she neglects to bite the sack off the head and start the breathing. This is especially true with breech births, where the dam is not sure which end is which. If pups arrive in too quick a succession, a harried mother may not finish cleaning one pup properly before the arrival of another. There is a question as to whether to allow the bitch to eat the afterbirths or not, and it really does not matter greatly. They no longer furnish the only available nourishment for the bitch as they did in the wilds but it is believed that they do stimulate the flow of milk into the nipples and the bitch should be allowed to have at least one if she desires it.

A bowl of milk and a nutritional concentrate such as meat soup should be offered to the bitch during the whelping hours. When all the puppies have arrived, the bitch may have to be led, forcibly, outside to relieve herself, as she will regret leaving her newborns for even a few seconds. Ignore the loud protestations and hope the neighbors know you are not torturing her.

A word of caution at whelping time concerns umbilical hernias which occur in Afghans frequently enough to deserve mention. Some experts claim they are inherited. Others blame predisposing causes such as inept dams and short umbilical cords. A few bitches insist on pushing newborns around by their cords, and other dams draw their pups close to the side of their teeth and bite the cord right next to the pup's tender navel. In such cases hernias are quite apt to develop. Many owners try to sever the cords for the dam to reduce this problem. These hernias are more of a nuisance than a serious injury. Inconspicuous bumps can be left indefinitely, but large bulges should eventually be surgically repaired. Most veterinarians do this for a modest fee.

The number of puppies born to one Afghan dam can be a problem. Litters of up to 12 pups are not uncommon. This is entirely too many pups for one dam to feed without seriously tearing herself down. She will manage for the first week or so, but pups grow at an amazing rate, ever expanding their capacity and needs for milk. If such demands are not fully met, the pups' growth will be retarded. In large kennels "foster mothers" (bitches of any breed that are giving milk) are used, but foster mothers are not easily located for the home-bred litter. As the usual number of good milk-producing faucets is 7 or 8, this is as many pups as the dam should be expected to handle. Unless the owner is actually in a position to take over the arduous task of "foster mother" on a 24 hour basis, large litters should be culled to a reasonable size. It is very difficult to cull litters and no one likes the idea very much but breeders that refuse to cull on the grounds that they may be putting down the "best one" are particularly short-sighted, for in a small litter, better fed and cared for, several pups may become outstanding. In the large poorly fed litter, none may reach their potential. Culling litters is not only accepted but mandatory in many European countries where dog raising is such a fine art. In America, the decision is left to the individual owner.

A word on false pregnancies: Afghan bitches are notorious for these false alarms. They occur as frequently in bitches who never see a male during their seasons as in females who are bred but do not "take." Such bitches insist on going the full route of preparing for whelping, milk production, etc., but do not produce any pups. False pregnancies cause some bitches to eat as if they were supplying a brood, gain weight, have milk in badly swollen nipples, and sustain an emotional crisis that we human beings cannot possibly appreciate as time arrives for the birth of the imaginary pups. These bitches take to mothering small animals or stuffed toys and produce enough milk to function as a foster mother. Injections may be required to relieve the milk congestion. The mild false pregnancy brings a short period of moping and slight nipple distention, but others are truly heart-rending. As it is the nature of the Afghan bitch to drop large quantities of coat towards the end of the nursing period, the bitch with the false pregnancy will do the same, to the consternation of the owner who deliberately refrains from breeding in favor of exhibition at the shows. Allowing such a bitch the privilege of one litter will not necessarily correct the false pregnancy tendency. Spaying is the only positive answer, and in the case of bitches not being exhibited nor part of any planned breeding program, such surgical action should be considered. The coat, which is greatly affected by the reproductive cycle, improves in stability and quantity with spaying. However, spayed bitches are not eligible for conformation exhibition.

The new-born Afghan Hound generally weighs about one pound. Large pups of one and one half pounds are not really uncommon. Pups from small litters tend to be larger at birth than those from the more crowded groups. For the first three weeks, the average gain is about a pound (or a little more) per week. By the 21st day, the pup's eyes are well open and unclouded, and the puppy senses are responding in a decisive manner. This is the time to introduce some solid foods. From this point onward, with the inclusion of some solid food in the diet, the weight gain jumps to about 2 pounds per week until weaning time. A range of approximately 13 pounds (bitches) to 16 pounds (males) constitutes good weight for the eight to nine week old pup. From weaning onward, if fed properly, the rate of gain is astonishing, with pups often weighing 25 and 30 pounds at the 12th week. Forty pounds for a good sized four to five months old male Afghan is not unusual. The weights given are from actual litters of Afghans but are only indications as different pups from different bloodlines and backgrounds develop at decidedly different growth rates.

The average Afghan reaches full height by his 11th month, but a few continue to inch slowly upward for a few more months. Full height certainly does not mean either full weight or full frame development which, in the Afghan, frequently comes quite slowly. Some yearlings are built much like the 12 year old boy who shot up to six feet while away at summer camp. The "fill-out" comes later.

The diet of the Afghan Hound never ceases to be of tremendous importance to his welfare, but it is more important in puppyhood than in adolescence. The Afghan, with his large, raw-boned frame only lightly covered with fat, requires a fantastic production of bone, sinew and muscle to support and construct his sprouting structure.

During the first three weeks of life, there is little that the owner can do to nourish the pups excepting to keep the bitch-mother stuffed with high quality foods, calcium supplements and plenty of fluids. The bitch-mother will eat from two to five times her normal amount while nursing. The owner can, however, clip the tiny razor sharp toe-nails of the pups on the second or third day after birth, and again every few days as they become repointed. The dam who is gouged by puppy talons soon becomes reluctant to expose herself to nursing pain. The Standard says nothing about dew claws, but it is wise to have them removed on the second or third day; it is a simple surgical procedure and will cause little pain or bleeding. They become a nuisance when left to grow and are far more difficult to remove at maturity.

Supplemental feeding of solids is best begun during the third week. As in the pediatrics wards, there is some question about the nutritional value at such an early age, but the consensus of opinion is that while not much more than milk is easily assimilated at this tender age, the body is becoming prepared for advancing textures and tastes. If no adverse reactions are seen, continue to expand the quantities. The very act of offering food to pups at this age sets up an important rapport between puppy and human, of greater value than its use in the digestive tract. The emphatic importance of this early man-dog relationship is discussed in *The New Knowledge of Dog Behavior* by C. J. Pfaffanberger; one of the truly important dog books of the decade.

With bitches' milk being the nutritional mainstay of pups until they are six weeks old, first supplemental foods should be a mixture of scraped meat (canned baby meats are good) or lean hamburger, warmed to room temperature and mixed with equal parts of cottage cheese. To this, add a bit of powdered vitamin supplement and some form of calcium. Let the pups lick bits of the mixture off the ends of your fingers. Soon they will eagerly lick it out of the bowls.

Not all forms of calcium are equally assimilable by the dog. The preferred form is *dicalcium phosphate* with added viosteral. This can be purchased as a complete mixture in pill form or as less expensive dibasic calcium phosphate power (obtainable by the pound from the druggist) used with any brand of cod liver oil. Those who are able to find a fine steamed bone meal (in feed and grain stores) have an even cheaper substitute for the dicalcium phosphate. The addition of cod liver oil is of special value for winter litters or in areas where pups cannot readily soak up quantities of daily sunshine. When using the handy bulk dibasic calcium phosphate powder, begin with one half teaspoon per pup, with a scant one quarter to one half teaspoon cod liver oil. As the pups readily accept the solid foods and consume ever increasing quantities, raise supplements gradually to a maximum of one rounded teaspoon of calcium and one teaspoon of cod liver oil (by about 12 weeks) plus some all-purpose vitamin of the pet type.

We do not recommend pablum or any cooked cereals for early supplementary feedings as they are primarily carbohydrates and do not fill the puppy needs for bone-building materials. Only when pups are taking copious amounts of milk from the dam, plus a good quantity of meat and cottage cheese ration is it time to add any additional "filler" foods. A commercial "puppy kibble" or whole grain unsweetened cereal, such as shredded wheat softened with warm water or milk, can then be added to the meat mixture.

Young pups should be offered solid foods two or three times a day until they are weaned. These feeding times are marvelous opportunities to discover and note individual personalities in the pups. The dam must be watched carefully as she may think the food pans are for her rather than for her kids. She may be getting multiple rations but will try to steal the pups' food if not discouraged.

It is acceptable to allow the pups to sample some of the dam's food if she does not object. Such activity should be supervised to prevent the bitch being cheated of her food or irritated with the presumptuous youngsters. A sense of adventure and enthusiasm for various foods should be encouraged in young Afghan Hounds to prevent them from becoming excessively finicky or demanding at a later date.

Attempts at weaning the pups should be made by the sixth week, through offerings of milk (whole, canned or powdered) between each meal of solids. Pups should be gaining weight rapidly at this point and eating ever-increasing amounts.

There are several systems of feeding growing and grown dogs, and we immediately state that if it works for you and your dog, don't change it. However, proper feeding of the Afghan Hound, especially the finicky small eater, is a loudly sung problem of many owners, warranting a few words over and above that listed on the backs of the kibble sacks.

Some misguided new owners decide to feed their hounds those wonderfully convenient, but expensive, cans of dog food that need only be opened and spooned into a pan to be eagerly gobbled by their tail-waggers. We must say, emphatically, that canned food is absolutely wrong for Afghans. Such foods are up to 80% water, actually starving the Afghan with the small stomach, by filling him with water-expanded food when he needs concentrated nourishment. Afghans, erroneously fed in this manner by well-meaning owners, can be seriously malnourished. When taken off the canned food diet and given a good grade of concentrated kibble, they soon consume far less in volume, are much less expensive to feed, and rapidly prosper in condition. An exception to the canned food ban is the canned meats (horsemeat, chicken, liver, and beef) which can be used in place of fresh meat as an additive to the kibble.

Self-feeding, a much talked about method, consists of making dry kibble available for dogs to eat at will. A drawback to self-feeding among Afghan Hounds is that long-eared hounds chew their ear fringes to pieces if not fitted with "snoods" to hold back ears at meal time. An additional disadvantage is that added meat, cottage cheese, supplementary vitamins or fats cannot be left out for fear of spoilage. A Combination system, with the dogs having one wet meal including all additives, combined with self-feeding for the remainder of the diet, has been found useful by some owners, primarily for puppies and non-show dogs. With liquid absent from self-fed

229

kibble, it is of the utmost importance that water bowls be constantly refilled, or be of the automatic waterer type.

A good grade of kibble will make up the majority of the dog's diet. Do not be misled by amounts suggested on the package. Few Afghan Hounds eat anything like such quantities (except growing pups that pass a stage of seeming bottomlessness). The quality commercial kibbles have been scientifically improved and tested in recent years, but do not claim some definite variation from brand to brand in protein type and amount, fat content, added vitamins and minerals. Ingredient analysis appears on each package. Due to individual reactions among dogs (and owners), it is reasonable to experiment with several quality brands before settling on one. Take careful notice of the different levels of palatability, signs of weight loss or gain, amounts of kibble the dog eats before slowing down and becoming indifferent to the feed, and both the quantity and quality (firmness) of the residual fecal material formed.

Most Afghan Hound breeders find that some additional protein source, such as meat (up to 20% of the total meal) is often beneficial to the Afghan Hound. Substitutes for meat, where added protein or taste-tempting additives are desired, are cottage cheese, egg yolks, fish or poultry. In the last two, all splintery bones must be removed or the food should be pressure cooked.

The "semi-soft" package foods are exceptionally palatable to most Afghan Hounds, and are a quality product, but expensive to use as a diet mainstay. Their greatest value is that of a "pick-up" meal to be used in travelling, for show purposes or vacationing. Not only are they easily obtained at any market, but their taste appeal keeps dogs from going "off their feed" away from home. Remarkable benefit comes from minimal residual "stools" resulting from change in water, environment or excitement. As some adult Afghan Hounds reject all unfamiliar food in periods of stress (such as travel or being at strange kennels), many owners introduce semi-moist foods in the form of "tidbits"—on occasion—to puppies and young dogs at home.

As substitutions for meat (or in addition to it) other excellent sources of the needed protein are egg *yolks,* cottage cheese, fish and poultry. In the latter two foods, all splintery bones must be removed.

A life-long use of a vitamin supplement is well-considered by

230

most Afghan owners. Such all-purpose pet vitamins plus the afore-mentioned dicalcium phosphate mixture and cod liver oil are especially essential during the growth period of the dog's life, up to 18 months of age. Although the hound may have gained full height by the tenth month, considerable cartilage will fill into solid bone long afterwards.

Afghans prefer their food slightly on the dry side rather than mushy. It is difficult to get them to eat more than one meal a day past 10 months of age, but try to keep them on two meals per day for as long as possible.

Fats are very important to the diet and the Afghan with so much coat to nourish needs as much or more than average breeds, calling for additives of suet, bacon grease, or special oils. One is as good as another. The use of a fatty hamburger cuts down the need for additional fats.

In cases of serious weight problems, a veterinarian should be consulted immediately. Not only is he prepared to find the underlying causes, but he has specially prepared diets to recommend. Veterinarians, however, admittedly have far more success with the overweight dog than the underweight ones.

If simple excess weight is the problem, the most obvious solution is less calories and more exercise. Caloric reduction is accomplished by cutting back on the kibble, and substituting some added lean meat. Bitches tend to fat far more often than males. For the ravenous hound, cottage cheese can also be added. Raw carrots are a marvelous edible that allows chewing but does not turn to fat. We heartily recommend giving raw carrot pieces to young pups as chew-toys. They aid in teething problems, supply roughage and are a good substitute for real bones, so taboo to the show Afghan Hound whose leg coat must be protected from accidental gnawing.

The underweight dog must be considered from several different angles. First, an accurate diagnosis must be made as to whether the hound is seriously thin or not. A healthy, active pup, growing very rapidly, in the all-legs stage, appears terribly slender in a normal developmental stage. Before becoming distressed, owners should check the weight and appearance with a knowledgeable breeder who can give an opinion on the dog's gangliness.

If the dog is a good eater, an ordinary diet, enriched with extra fats and a highly concentrated type of kibble should suffice. Two or

231

three small meals a day rather than just one large one is a help if the dog will eat them. A bedtime bowl of milk adds calories.

Most underweight Afghans are that way because they use up a great deal of nervous energy and are finicky eaters, somewhat of a curse in the breed. The first step here is to make certain that the dog is not ill or wormy. It is then absolutely necessary that the owner take over the diet planning for the dog and not be tricked into letting the dog make the decisions. Finicky dogs quickly learn that their small appetites distress their anxious owners and take advantage of this by refusing to eat anything but table scraps and favorite cuts of meat. Any meat fed to such spoiled dogs must be so very well-mixed into the kibble that it cannot possibly be picked out independently.

There are meats other than steaks that tempt the appetite. Chicken is one of the best. Poultry bones must be removed or pressure cooked to a soft state. The vertebrae bones in a young chicken, however, are not dangerous. Some dogs show a decided preference for liver or heart; both being very nutritious but lacking in necessary fats. A palatable meat, very high in fat, is lamb breast, which combines well with the liver and heart. Broth from cooked meats should be mixed with the kibble for added flavor. Hamburger is excellent as is all fish. "Pet mixes" usually trimmings and meat cuts not used for humans vary greatly with the meat cutter and some are far more appetizing than others. It pays to shop around for these. Add spices and salt to cooking meats. Onion, garlic and tomato juice are great flavor enhancers. Raw meat is fine (if the dog likes it), but the difficulties of storage makes frozen meat, cooked or baked as needed, more practical.

The occasional use of fish or the addition of powdered kelp to the diet may help ward off possible mineral deficiencies in the growing hound. Owners must investigate to find the most practical nutritional foods within their own areas.

For the ill or convalescent dog, there is nothing more appealing than an easily digested mixture of chicken broth and rice. Cubes of chicken or beef bouillon are fortifiers for any meal, as in any meat gravy. Cottage cheese and canned baby foods are well assimilated by the below par system. Pork, with the exception of bacon, should never be fed to hounds.

There is always a fear of rickets in any fast growing dog who does not get the optimum diet or does not properly assimilate his food. Diagnosis of rickets is a professional matter—but spying the pup that should be checked professionally must be done in the home kennel. Pups of all ages should be bright-eyed and, by three months of age, well up on their own feet, off the back of pasterns and hocks, carrying sturdy straight leg bones and a fairly strong topline. Danger signals are any signs of dull coat, lethargy, bent bones, and slack pasterns or hocks. Large knobby pasterns and knots like small marbles at the base of the ribs where the cartilage begins, when found in conjunction with spindly bones, may well be a sign of incipient rickets, especially if these areas are tender and sensitive to the touch. Yet, on the other hand, such knobbiness on otherwise healthy, well-developed large pups indicates desirable centers of future growth, disappearing with maturity. Strangely enough, such knobs are most often found on poor growers and the best growers, and less often on the even-growing, in-between sized pups.

Feeding the Afghan Hound should not be a slipshod arrangement. Curs can exist on any scraps and digestible diggings, but such dogs rarely achieve full size and inherited potentials. Extra thought and pennies spent on diet repay the owner in the production of a healthy, relatively disease-resistant, gorgeous Afghan Hound.

Check with your veterinarian regularly for dates to have the dogs tested for worms (a must that varies with the common parasites in specific localities) as well as inoculations for distemper, hepatitis, and, in many areas, rabies. All records of such treatments should be noted on the back of the pedigree and given with the dog if sold.

Grooming

Concerning fur alone, a young puppy needs practically no grooming. The plush puppy coat grows thickly and quietly, standing well off the body, seldom tangling. Do not be misled by this! It is of the utmost importance that the Afghan puppy, from the age of three months onward, be groomed weekly and regularly. The prime function of such attention is to train the lively pup to submit to necessary restraints when he is still mentally flexible and physically lightweight enough to be easily managed by the owner. Regardless of coat length, the wriggling youngster must be patiently taught to stand or lie still for grooming with a stiff bristle brush. Begin by restraining him for a moment only, and, to stimulate good hair growth, give him a good brush-rubbing both with and against the grain of the fur. Most pups soon enjoy these ministrations from gentle owners but do insist on chewing brushes and being silly.

As thick woolly fur lengthens, it soon becomes evident that the brush cannot get through to the skin, necessitating a change in tools. For fast growing puppy-coats, most fanciers prefer the slicker (a wood-backed brush with numerous bent-angled metal pins set into a rubber base). When the fluff is long enough to require a slicker, it is high time that the owner learn the correct techniques of grooming in the layering method.

It is well to accustom the pup to grooming from both prone and standing positions. Finishing touches and quick maintenance brush-ups are best accomplished with the dog standing, but the under-parts that snag and mat quickly are more accessible with the dog lying quietly on his side. The key words to Afghan grooming are "from the bottom up and from the skin out." Mats form near the skin at the base of the fur and surface brushing merely brushes more fur into the clumping mats. We will briefly describe the technique of grooming the dog in a prone position. With the dog lying quietly on its side, begin with the front feet. Most all Afghan Hounds are touchy about their feet and must become accustomed to having them handled. Inspect and brush the fur between the toes carefully. Brush the fur backwards from the foot upward. Cover the back-brushed fur with the holding hand and rake down small layers with the slicker. In this manner, continue to brush back the hair working up the leg, slickering bits back into place. A large cloth placed between upper and lower leg helps the groomer keep his place on the leg and also catches loose dirt and fur. When the upper leg is completed except for the inside piece that cannot be easily reached, groom the corresponding inside section of the leg nearest to the floor. Pay special close attention to the tender skin right beneath the elbows as mats form there quickly due to the gait friction of leg rubbing against the body. This is also true of the breastbone area lying in front of and between the forelegs. Such mats, not easily seen, must be felt by probing fingers but will damage both coat and gait if left unattended. Clean captured hair out of grooming tools frequently. Young pups lose very little hair, but the brushes fill quickly on older dogs.

234

Follow similar layering procedures with rear feet and legs, closely inspecting the inside of the groin and thighs, these spots tending to friction matting as with the elbows. In grooming the sides of the dog, begin with the base of the brisket. Pampering this lower chest fur enhances the apparent depth of chest. The fidgety pup, who is impatient with leg grooming, welcomes having body fur smoothed. Layer side fur as with the legs. If the body fur is not as dense as the legs, the less harsh bristle brush will work very well.

When tangles are encountered that resist the grooming tools, do not yank them out! Gently tease the knot apart with the fingers. Here is the successful Afghan owner's art, a skill that should be acquired as early as possible. Most felted mats found on reasonably well-kept hounds are easily pulled apart. A wide-toothed comb will find any such mats if they are missed by the brushes, and the same comb works well with fingers for separating the hairs when the mats have been reduced to narrow clumps.

Never use the scissors or any cutting tool except as a last resort. The dog that is impossibly matted should be clipped completely (and allowed to grow out evenly—which takes quite some time) or tranquilized so that he can be groomed at length without suffering. If it seems that a few cuts would save the coat, *snip with the grain of the fur but never across the hairs.* Such clips separate the fur into smaller knots that can be worked apart with the fingers.

The Afghan Hound should never be allowed to get into this condition. This generally happens when one is left in a kennel with no care, or improper care. Every attempt should be made to break felt mats, or knotted balls with the fingers. If this cannot be done, cut into the knotted balls with the grain of the coat. Do not cut them out! Then continue to tease them apart with the fingers and a wide-tooth comb.

Most pups adore having their ears, topknots and throats brushed. Fluff the topknot in every direction. Tenderly comb the earflaps and valuable ear fringes. Slicker thoroughly behind and underneath the ears, a prime spot for undetected mats to form during the change of coat.

For even the heaviest puppy plush the slicker plus a wide toothed comb, both used in the layering technique, are the only tools needed —until the puppy-fluff has fully developed and begins to loosen. By 10 to 18 months of age there should be some intermixture of puppy and adult coat, turning some youngsters into animated brier bushes and others, with the more draping texture, into walking dust mops.

The era of the dropping puppy coat is undoubtedly the most horrible of all grooming periods in most Afghan Hounds' lives. The owner who lives through this phase with a really heavy coated hound can take it easy from then on. Handfuls of fur come out with each combing. If this loosening fur is not brushed out immediately (daily) and faithfully, it will tangle and form felted mats and then hard knotted balls that cannot be removed except surgically. However, it is for this reason that it is said "the Afghan does not shed." He loses hair like any animal, but it stays near the body, clumping with other hairs, rarely falling on furniture or clothing. The red alert is up when the slicker becomes plugged with hair unusually often or when the short-haired saddle begins to emerge. Grooming must be intensified. During the emergency period, the slicker is the preferred tool but get a new one as bent-over out-of-line pins do more harm than good.

This crucial coat-change period varies greatly from dog to dog. It may be passed in a month or linger for a half-year or more. Daily exploratory checks with the fingers, in the guise of petting, find fresh mats in lieu of full groomings. Habitual behind-the-ear scratches, which the dogs love, and chest attentions between the front legs will find the felting hair knots before damage is great. On the rear of the dog, check loins and inside of thighs. Thick quantities of fur often drop from feet, pasterns and hock fronts during coat-changes, requiring localized extra brushing. When the smooth short-haired saddle has cleared the full length of the back, the worst is over. There will be intermittent periods of coat growth spurts and drops but once the puppy coat is out, a thorough weekly grooming keeps most hounds in handsome condition (barring jaunts in weed laden fields).

Do not shave a saddle onto an Afghan Hound. Use your natural bristle brush to brush out the loose long hairs. This hair can be easily brushed out when the short saddle coat is underneath. Some dogs have produced a clean saddle at six months; others wait until they are two years old. Remember what the Standard says: "The Afghan Hound should be shown in its natural state; the coat is not clipped or trimmed . . ."

The adult coat, longer and usually far silkier than puppy fuzz, is

236

less suited to the slicker as the sharp pins can rake the skin and tangle the fur if not handled expertly. Different thicknesses and textures of Afghan coats do necessitate individual tools and some grooming experimentation with each dog. The awesome kit of combs and brushes carried by the seasoned exhibitor is bewildering to the novice but is a case of the right tool for each dog. As a general rule, for most adult coats, a good stiff bristle brush and a wide-toothed comb are recommended. The same "from the bottom up" technique is an absolute necessity. All brushings must be done with long smooth strokes, layer by layer, with no flicking motions that cause the hair to twist and tangle on itself.

For the exceedingly heavy, long, durable coat that defies bristle penetration, a Poodle pin brush can be substituted. This good-sized oval brush contains long straight metal pins set into a rubber base. The pin brush does not give the smooth finish that many owners desire, but is efficient and relatively quick for home maintenance. A final surface touch-up with bristles or slicker gives polish.

During grooming, close attention should be paid to the skin beneath the fur. Check ears for any form of matter and clean them with baby oil or alcohol only if dirty. Long eared dogs such as the Afghan Hound are especially susceptible to ear infection. Do not use any liquids in the ear such as the commercial dog ear cleaning fluids. Whenever the ear gets wet inside, dry it out. If ears have a dark red exudation especially with a foul odor, get veterinarian aid immediately. When brushing feet, check for small mats that cause sore spots between the toes as well as burrs that might be caught under the foot between the pads. If toenails appear long and sharp, have them trimmed before the quick grows out too far. Neglected toenails cause the toe-arches to break down, a problem with old or very lazy dogs and those with no access to rough hard ground surfaces.

If rashes are seen on the skin, get help immediately. Many fanciers have home remedies for mild skin eruptions, alcohol, antiseptic powders, etc., but the novice should not experiment with skin symptoms as the Afghan Hound can ruin his coat with frantic chewing and scratching in an unbelievably short time. An injection from the veterinarian will put a quick end to the inflammatory state, and professional treatment will seek the roots of the trouble, be it diet, allergy, or parasites (the most common being fleas, often difficult to detect on this thick-furred breed).

Bitches are prone to lose coat with each season regardless of the loving care given to their fur. Some drop much more than others due most probably to hereditary factors. The large coat drop that comes with the very first season, usually timed to occur with the puppy-coat fallout, is generally the worst that will be experienced. When bitch-coats are at low ebb, brush frequently to stimulate the regrowth. Most unspayed bitches tend to be in or out of coat all their lives.

Males have less extreme ups and downs, but do have lusher coats in some parts of the year than others (not necessarily coordinated with the weather). An adolescent male coat of some skimpiness is not unusual, following the puppy-drop. Those that expect a full-length drape to magically supersede the puppy fuzz are in for a disappointment. The magnificent draping of a full-blown champion takes time. Ear fringes, for instance, may take years to gain reputable length despite protective "snoods" and tender grooming care. Illnesses that include periods of fever or the use of anesthetics may cause a coat drop of a temporary nature.

Caring for the Afghan's coat is not really such a chore if a particular person, place, and time are designated for the job. No Show Coat or even handsome pet coat will last on hounds that suffer through spasmodic slap-dash attentions. Such neglect only results in stubborn dogs who detest being groomed and cut-up, jagged, ugly coats, ripe for immediate re-tangling. The fancier who is unable or unwilling to give constant attention to the Afghan coat has taken on the wrong breed.

There are tricks-of-the-trade used by professionals that give coats an extra brilliance at the shows, arousing the curiosity of the novice. Much of this sparkle comes from pure undiluted cleanliness. Show dogs are bathed from one to three days before the show, depending on the type of fur and the color of the dog. For the best-behaved coat, many show dogs are constantly brushed while drying after the bath. A gentle human shampoo that gives a glossy sheen is used or special pet mixtures that are a far cry from cheap flea soaps. Liquid shampoos are diluted with water and placed into a squeeze bottle for easy application. Fly away coats are given creme rinses. All soaps or detergents are scrupulously rinsed off the dog.

At the shows commercial spray conditioners help last-minute smoothenings, and are doubly important as cleaners when shows occur too frequently for in-between baths. Baby powder which tends to separate the hairs is used on some light-colored coats that tangle quickly. Such powder is brushed out before the dog enters the ring and is of little value on dark colored dogs as it dulls the coat color. Dogs with extremely dry coats are occasionally oiled, but all such oil must be washed out completely before the show date as the oily or dirty coat will hang in lank strings.

The professional applies know-how to moulding the coat, through controlled brushing, to enhance the best possible lines of the hound. The heavier dog benefits by being brushed smooth to minimize bulk, while the refined hound takes a bit of extra fluffing. Some hounds are flattered by topknots that hang forward, while others are enriched with full sweep of clear muzzle. Brisket hairs should be carefully combed to emphasize depth of chest. The bend of stifle on rear leg is accentuated with forward brushing, but at the hock the fur should flow backwards to indicate low hock-points and large feet. Wide fluffing of foot fur to the front and sides increases apparent size. Skimpy hair under brisket and on feet detracts from the line of a well-endowed hound.

From the front of the Afghan there should be a columnar look from leg to floor. If the coat is scanty or bunchy at the elbow line, careful brushing might prevent the coat from indicating a fault that does not exist under the fur.

Such tricks can never make a poor dog into a good one (and will not last in the wind or high motion) but can easily make a small point difference between two dogs of similar quality. Cleanliness and careful grooming have tipped many scales in producing greater visual impact on the judge's eye.

9

Exhibiting

"A Show Dog is essentially a production to delight the eye, a presentation, as is a piece of theatre . . . The stars in the heavens are not more numerous than good prospective Show Dogs that have been ruined by poor management."

C. Bede Maxwell

OF the annual crowd of Afghan Hounds which enter the show rings, only a few fill the judge's eye, outstanding with power and pride, sparkling in a well-kept, immaculate coat that accentuates the hound's courtly manner. Too many others, often of no less basic structural quality, are practically ignored by the judges. Their puzzled owners are blind to the obvious, unaware that their hounds fail sadly in coat condition, musculature, or ring demeanor. To a marked extent, the difference between the "eye-catcher" and the "also-ran" is a man-made commodity known as conditioning. Proper conditioning of the show dog allows him to take his starring role as a proud and able color bearer for his breed.

An early decision faced by many a novice giving the Show Game a whirl, is whether to hire a professional handler or go the route him-

Ch. Khayam's Kism of Scheherezade (Ch. Sasha of Scheherezade ex Ch. Bletchingley Sahari of Scheherezade), black masked red bitch, bred by Lt. Col. and Mrs. Wallace Pede, owned by Dr. and Mrs. Doyle N. Rogers.

Ch. Khayam's Apollo (Ch. Ammon Hall Nomad ex Ch. Khayam's Kism of Scheherezade), black and tan dog, bred and owned by Dr. and Mrs. Doyle N. Rogers.

self. The amateur owner may well make a few bumbling efforts at showing his own dog, only to have a kindly onlooker, sensing greater potential in the dog than the handler, suggest a professional be hired.

This decision hinges on clear-cut practical principles. Undoubtedly, the pro can take a dog of reasonable quality and present it with the skill of many years' experience to quicker success than the shaky novice. If the owner's primary aim is to boast of one quick champion—hiring a competent handler is probably the most practical solution, but the owner with a yen to be a part of the breed, do some breeding and exhibiting of offspring after offspring, must weigh the expense of the hired professional against future aims. And there is as much knowledge of the breed to be gained in the ring as from without. As in most sports, the thrill of competition keeps the owner-handler going. The smart handler knows that the judge cannot fully disassociate the dog from the handler. Therefore, he must always keep his team sharp.

The challenged, able-bodied fancier concludes that the pro had to learn once, and while the training period may cost their dogs a few wins (and it probably will), they are making an investment in skills for the future. This trend of thought is bolstered by the knowledge that most of the top-winning Afghan Hounds have been owner-escorted past the best that the Professional Handlers' Association offers.

The rivalry between professional and amateur is in the main synthetic, too often a sham excuse for being beaten. Confident owner-handlers take no part in this type of buck-passing. It is the contrast between awkward bumbling and skilled guidance that is real and painfully apparent in many classes. The thoughtful owner will neither curse the pro nor use him as a whipping boy but, instead, courts and learns from these dedicated people who have made showing and winning their vocation.

Showing dogs has different implications in different sectors of the United States. On the heavily-populated coastal regions, exhibiting dogs is a semi-regular weekend diversion for those who have dogs and will travel, but in the interior, show day is long-anticipated with breath held for fear the dogs will be out of coat or the bitch will be in season. At the highly competitive coastal shows, exhibitors are forced into greater awareness of maintaining hounds in peak condition and become sensitive to when they are or are not ready to win. In all cases there are times when the owner knows full well that the hound should be left home temporarily, but succumbs to Entry Blank Fever. As such dogs are actually being exhibited for fun and experience, the owner should never resent losing to dogs obviously more ready on that day.

Novices should contact the local show-giving superintendent, obtain a copy of the AKC Rules Applying to Registration and Dog Shows, and request that their name be placed on mailing lists for the coming shows. The ambitious fancier would also do well to join the nearest regional club devoted to his breed and the nearby All-Breed Club. In this manner, he can become informed of Sanction Matches and Training Classes.

Preparing the Afghan Hound for exhibition begins in early puppyhood. The first steps consist of raising healthy, outgoing puppies. Diet and early socialization have been covered elsewhere in this book. Refer to *The New Knowledge of Dog Behavior* by Clarence Pfaffenberger for information on the importance of early socialization.

Leash training is commenced by the ninth week of puppyhood. Not a severe routine of heeling calculated to win obedience degrees, but a simple accustoming the puppy to leash restraints. This can be a trying period for both the puppy and the inexperienced owner. Most Afghan Hounds stubbornly consider freedom one of their inalienable rights. The timid owner who encounters frantic resistance to such early training is usually conned into dropping the subject, with the misconception that it will go easier in a few months. He is in for a rude shock. Afghan puppies only grow larger, stronger, more determined, and voice louder protests. It is better to carry it through when the pup is young.

Occasionally some pups adapt to the leash without protest, but they are the exception and are usually bitches. Most pups, finding themselves on the end of a leash for the first time, will do one of several things. They will scream in anguish. This convinces the neighbors that they are being brutally attacked. It is calculated to shrink the handler into invisibility and force the matter to be dropped. Puppies use this trick to the hilt. The youngster may buck like a rodeo stallion, hurl himself into the air, head over tail, always fighting the lead. This is an encouraging sign. Most will lie down

243

and positively refuse to budge, screaming at each touch of the lead.

Individual pups demand individual attention and solutions. A few general solutions follow. Use suitable equipment. A light-weight, puppy-sized chokechain (about four inches longer than the circumference of the pup's neck) and a ribbon-weight leather lead. Some pups respond best to the gentler show lead.

Ignore the screaming completely, with a word of explanation to the neighbors, and trade brute force for a little canine psychology. Leash training is an understandably frightening experience for a tiny pup. Not only is his precious liberty being challenged, but he is being dragged away from his siblings, his home and security. For this reason, try carrying the pup to the far end of the yard and work back towards the house and kennel. Tidbits may help as encouragements, but are usually ignored in the early days of stress.

Standard obedience methods of giving small jerks that tighten the collar and the immediate release of tension are called for. Never use steady strangling pulls. This only makes for a bull-necked, uncontrollable hound. Keep training lessons very short, a minute or two for the first few days, and for every inch of progress give liberal praise.

A basic method is to train the dog to come to the handler as a first step. When the pup, finding himself on a leash, lies down with resolute immobility, walk in front of him, stoop or sit a few inches from his face, and call his name while accentuating the call with a positive jerk on the leash. The pup comes, or is dragged, those few inches to lavish praise and sympathy in the trainer's arms. Repeat the performance. Always use an encouraging tone and positive jerks. Move slightly further back from the pup each time, forcing him to advance. This method keeps the pup on his feet a good bit of the time, half the training battle. Some pups respond far quicker than others. This is not seemingly correlated to either intelligence or obedience aptitude.

When the pup unhesitatingly and gaily runs to the handler at the sound of his name and a slight jerk of the leash, it is time to begin to encourage the dog to heel at the handler's side. At this point, specialized show-training comes into play.

The successful show dog moves with great style, unafraid, head and tail high and proud. The style of the dog's heeling is far more important than how close he hugs to the handler's knee. The show dog must be discouraged from sniffing the ground, a great natural temptation. This is best achieved by the handler who sets a brisk pace, with "come-along" jerks. Do not give the pup time to stray towards nearby bushes or ground scents. Encouraging words and, perhaps tidbits, help alert the pup and keep him prancing near the handler's side. Animation and even silliness, such as the pup taking the leash in his mouth, is welcome at this age. Do not attempt to correct the puppy lunging with any severe methods. The very young pup soon learns where the end of the leash is. Most handlers use the obedience trick of making swift turns of directions, away from the puppy, to subtly correct puppy lunges. Such turns, with attendant jerks of the leash, inform the pup that if he doesn't keep an eye on his master, he just ends up facing the wrong direction and no one gets anywhere on these fascinating walks. Lunging is a serious problem on the powerful untrained *older* dog, and must be corrected drastically and immediately. Some breeders have success in taking an older well-trained dog along on these walks to give example and assurance to the pup. It is worth a try if the older dog approves the plan.

Pups are always kept at a *trot* when leash trained. A leisurely stroll with pup ambling along, nose to the ground, neck hauling on the leash, can be harmful to show dog posture. A spirited gait, with flickings of the chokechain under the chin, promotes high head carriage, and glimpses of objects in the distance keep it there. Any dog, properly trained with love and patience, delights in these educational walks.

A word of warning to the novice who has observed Afghan Hounds being "strung up" in the ring (with taut leash held overhead). This is not for most Afghan Hounds. It is a method of forcing the dog to hold its head high, a cruel restraint that pulls the front legs off the ground, preventing the natural free-swinging gait of the breed. Most Afghan Hounds, once well trained to the leash, move far better and with a natural, proud head carriage on a loose lead. A professional handler, given an ill-trained hound to show, has little choice but to employ such high-handed methods. It is definitely not to be emulated by the novice! When the pup has agreed to accept reasonable leash controls in exchange for the enjoyable training jaunts, he is ready to widen his circle of friends.

The normal Afghan puppy illustrates great gaiety and friendliness. But, in adulthood, a very real sense of reserve and aloofness comes over these hounds. Most mature Afghan Hounds give overwhelming demonstrations of affection just to their owners and special chosen friends. The unwary owner who presumes the puppy personality to be a permanent part of the dog's nature, may be in for quite a shock at the later date. Suddenly, at a show or circumstance where the owner expects to show off his gay inimitable puppy, the hound may show a new and frightening face. Such reactions vary from a frantic reticence at being touched, to cringing panic or aggressive uncontrollability. This dog is only demonstrating his awareness of being in strange surroundings. While such reactions cannot be considered actually abnormal, they most certainly are undesirable and have been the ruination of many a show dog.

To understand or to cope with such reactions, it must be realized that Afghan Hounds in their natural semi-wild state must have an aggressive curiosity. But this curiosity must be well-tempered, connected to a trigger-quick, glandular mechanism that controls the dog's lightning fast advances and retreats. This is the essential life-saving and life-taking device of the guard-and-hunter hound. In urban surroundings, the hound may suffer from a glandular over-secretion and frustration. He no longer has a natural channel for such defense and attack impulses, and is given no program to help him identify friend or foe, although he strongly senses that both exist. Undirected glandular impulses confuse the dog to the consternation of his perplexed owner. Owners tend to ascribe such unreasonable reactions to the hound which has been mistreated or over-disciplined in the past. Strangely enough, the very opposite is more often true. Hounds that are victims of over-protection by zealous owners tend to associate owner with "friend" and everyone else is suspect. Certainly there is great temperamental variation among the hounds, but the Afghan Hound as a breed is noted for its marked aloofness and tendency to be a "one-family dog." Controversy as to whether really unstable temperament is inherited points up the fact that we are dealing with a bundle of precious instincts in an unnatural environment of fences and forbidden temptations. Some hounds are far more adaptable than others. Those that cannot cope with their environment may be breeding risks, and pass on their own neurosis.

Canine tendencies can frequently be rechanneled. The owner can deliberately widen the hound's circle of accepted friends in this civilized world by exposing the hounds, from puppyhood onward, to people who are kind to them. Trips to the veterinarian for shots should be counteracted by joyful excursions elsewhere, or the dog is to be forgiven for suspecting that all men have needles behind their backs.

In the home situation, the pup does not show these symptoms, appearing bold and fearless until something disrupts his secure routine such as a trip into the world of men and dogs. The longer such hidden symptoms are unsuspected and undetected, the slimmer the chances of cure. Afghan Hounds are quite capable of changing personalities well past their second birthdays. It is an interesting fact that the Afghan Hound who has led a somewhat more nearly natural existence, having been allowed a certain amount of field hunting experience, often gains a quicker differentiation of safety and danger, friend and foe, than his hot-house brothers.

It is not unusual for the Afghan Hound to have an inherent dislike of being touched by strangers and instinctively draw back from the offered hand. But the show dog is required to allow strangers to examine teeth, body, ever-touchy paws and rear quarters. Under training conditions, the show dog learns to suffer such touches without question. Hounds prosper from trips around shopping centers, or from Sunday afternoons in the park. People are always curious about the breed, wanting to feel the soft hair and the aristocratic snout. The owner will welcome these attentions from strangers and kindly insist that the pup stand for them. A long dry spell between such early social training and adulthood can bring renewed reluctance at being handled as this instinct is not far beneath the surface in many Afghan Hounds.

Dogs learn through imitation of other dogs. Hounds brought up near a suspicious older dog which tolerates advances from no one but his owner often behave in like manner. This goes on for generations. A friendly brood-bitch is a great asset to a show kennel, teaching her pups to view the human race kindly. The matron that gives even a small portion of the soul-bursting welcome, generally reserved for loved ones, to visiting people-friends in sight of the imitative young pups does her owner an invaluable service.

Having older hounds as instructors is a mixture of assets and liabilities. A jealous stud may bully the youngsters. Caste systems are

247

quickly assumed in dogs. Some pups are intimidated into subservient roles. Such attitudes carry over into the show ring. The underdog may act defeated before he begins, or take out his frustrations on small dogs. If two or more hounds vie for attention, the solution is to take them out independently whenever possible. It is also helpful to have individual cages or quarters as a sanctuary for the antagonists. The youngster who accepts the background, or wants to be alone, is demanding special attention away from the pack.

Car sickness is a by-product of fear and nervous reactions. The happy hound, taken on regular rides from early puppyhood, is rarely bothered by the malady. The usual reaction to the dog who upchucks on rides is to leave him home. This is precisely the wrong approach. Car sickness can be cured by the owner who takes time to acclimatize the hound to car riding. Begin with no more than one city block and gradually increase the riding a block at a time to trip status.

There are some who may not connect all this talk of training and re-training with blue ribbons for their dog. It can only be said that bold natural assurance, the basis of a true King of Dogs attitude, is the essence of showmanship and is a commodity most winners have in rich supply.

The importance of powerful musculature on a show dog is often overlooked. Many hounds that look like first place winners when standing still, drop right out of contention after being gaited across the ring. Without engaging in a prolonged discussion of type versus soundness, our working definition of soundness follows: A sound dog is one that strides forward with obvious purpose and strength, without wavering or weaving, shuffling or slipping; a dog in full command of his muscles, able to change directions in a split instant without being thrown off balance, illustrating absolute coordination between all moving parts. Admittedly, there are anatomical faults that prevent such achievements. But many more hounds are unsound in gait due to underdevelopment or incorrect development of musculature because of their sedentary life, so different from the natural routine of the hounds in Afghanistan.

Muscle development is a continuous process beginning the moment the pup stirs in the embryo, continuing throughout the life of the animal. As soon as pups are able to stand on their wobbly feet, they spend their waking time in rough-house push and shove play

248

with their siblings. From their owners, they ask only a little attention to their diet and increasing space as they double and triple in size. As soon as one pup leaves the nest for a new home, often becoming an only pup, opportunity and desire for the important muscle building play is greatly diminished. Some hounds, naturally more excitable than others, compensate for a lack of sparring partners with wild dashes over the furniture at the sound of the postman, milkman, or a cat next door. Such jousting lacks in enduring intensity and is understandably discouraged by the lady of the house. The foolish owner who attempts to rear Afghan Hounds in crates or tiny pens must make very definite provisions to counteract the effect of such a restrained unnatural life. An Afghan Hound is not necessarily unhappy in a limited space as long as he is with loved ones (proven by those raised in garden apartments), but rarely are such dogs well-muscled and good movers.

Deliberate muscle formation can be implemented by owners in several ways. When possible, run two dogs together of a companionable age. Have sufficient space for reasonable romps. A long narrow run is better than a short square section. Uneven terrain or hillsides are marvelous. These hounds are remarkable at turning, dodging, and climbing, but need some length of ground in order to stretch their legs and work up full tilt speed. On flat ground, stairs to leap or man-fashioned obstacles are beneficial. Large wooden crates, tractor tires, etc., make fine doggy jungle gyms. The one-dog owner must contrive play periods for his pet. Balls can be thrown for the dog. Most Afghan Hounds will chase a ball but, unfortunately, few will retrieve it. The game is worth the try and good for the owner's waistline. Tug-of-war is marvelous for developing a strong cord of muscles from jaws to paws. Pieces of tough leather, rug, or towel remnants are lasting. Tugging games are doubly valuable as they can be played indoors with a minimum of furniture interference. The only dog owner will wisely visit other dog-owning friends with his pup as often as possible for invigorating romps with canine pals.

The growing dog does not play every minute; in fact, most of the daylight hours are napped away. Until the puppy is well over six months old, a few minutes of controlled trotting on a leash plus a bit of full-tilt running and dodging once or twice a day, is sufficient for average muscle-building activity.

Lagging muscle development is the curse of all large breeds. The

249

largest, longest legged, and most highly angulated hounds go through prolonged periods of unsteadiness. Some never learn how to stand properly on their underpinnings. While young, immature hounds can be expected to have loose muscles, the judge and ring-side jury rightly penalize hounds of all ages until such weaknesses have been overcome. Mother Nature would be no kinder. In her realm, only the fittest can survive. Some highly excitable hounds do have a muscular self-stimulation that keeps them constantly tense and fit, while the relaxed lazy ones need special encouragement to get them moving.

As the growing hound approaches his first birthday, his demands for muscle-building mileage increases, and the wise owner begins to seek ways to give the hound roadwork with a bicycle or automobile. Few owners on foot can keep up with the requirements of a trotting dog. Hounds can be run alongside the car, being controlled by the driver or, from the back of a stationwagon, controlled by an accomplice. Finding safe roads for such work is the big problem. Possibilities include park drives, lonely roads, fairgrounds, large parking lots, and school driveways.

All roadwork is done at a trot or a fast walk, never at a gallop. Trotting is to dogs as swimming is to people, coordinating muscles from one end of the frame to the other. Greyhound trainers often walk their hounds for miles, but the Afghan Hound seems to prefer a good trot, rarely hitting an even stride at a fast walk.

The young dog must become accustomed to running alongside the car or bicycle without lunging after every bird he sees. This means several slow-moving experimental runs to teach the dog his limitations and the danger of the side of the car. Pups should be trotted for no more than one-half mile for the first few weeks. This can be increased a tenth of a mile per day as the pup gets into the stride of the game. If the hound shows fatigue before the end of the allotted mileage, permit him to slow down to a walk for the remaining distance. It is likely the lack of lung power rather than tired legs that is exhausting him. Convalescent dogs are worked at a walk until positively up to trotting any distance.

The strong yearling can trot continuously for a mile and a half to two miles. This can be gradually increased to three miles a day or more. Some ambitious trainers work hounds five miles a day but this is more than necessary for the average case. The vital point is to take the hounds out for three miles every day. Longer trots inter-mittently are a very dangerous procedure for any dog. It is the con-sistent push, like push-ups every morning, that develops power in lungs, legs, and back.

The proper speed is dependent on each dog and more on the front quarter than the rear section. Adjust speed for a reaching outstride in the front legs. Begin with a low trot and slowly increase speed, hoping to entice the front legs into a more ambitious stride. This rarely exceeds 10–12 MPH, and is usually 3–5 MPH. Watch for a regular gait. We are not discussing optimum structure here, but moving efficiency, as the straight-shouldered hound that uses every bit of his stride capabilities is a more efficient mover than the well-angulated hound with restricted use of his reaching mechanism.

Roadwork is an education for the person in charge. As the dog trots regularly and as he begins to tire, the nature and possible weak-nesses of canine gait become magnified. The crabber can be studied in the dog which swings one hind leg to the inside to sidestep the front legs. Tired rear quarters often stagger or step out of time with front legs. The weak hind leg shuffles along, without clean pick-up of paws or kick-back of hocks. Limp forehands exemplify poor elbow extension, moving almost more from side to side than from forward to back, often accompanied by floppy sprung pasterns. Watch the pasterns and feet very carefully.

In the great reach and spring lilting gait of the Afghan Hound, the front paws should reach as far as possible, contacting the ground at the utmost point of the extension. The knees-up prance of the show pony is pretty, but all wrong for the Afghan Hound despite its being seen frequently in the rings. So is the gait in which the dog kicks his front feet forward and then settles them back at something less than the point of utmost extension. Such wasted motion gaits will probably not improve with roadwork as they are structural rather than muscular, but perhaps the owner will begin to observe the liabilities of such flashy muscular action and no longer accept them as being correct and desirable.

Study shoulders and toplines carefully. They tell volumes. The tired weak back sags between the shoulders, rolls over, or may even "roach," literally dragging the hind limbs forward. The neck may drop low and surge like a draft horse pulling a heavy load. The strong, well-muscled Afghan's back remains practically level and

251

seemingly weightless, floating in momentum with the steady shock-absorbing spring of the legs and paws.

Improvement in erratic, limp or awkward gaits will not appear to the naked eye in a matter of days or even weeks. Movies of the dog taken at full trot at the instigation of the roadwork program, and then repeated every few months best provide evidence of the dog's improvement. There are some dogs with naturally strong gaits which do not need this extra work. But beware of complacency as many dogs slow down and become looser with advancing years.

The dog whose rear quarters need an extra bit of tightening may benefit from trotting up hills or over uneven ground. Some owners swear by the therapeutic value of letting dogs run and romp in the water, claiming this tightens muscles also.

A word of caution. Never work dogs during the heat of warm days. Take advantage of cool mornings and sundown. Do not allow overheated dogs to become chilled, nor let them have more than a couple of swallows of water for at least an hour after the run. Check feet carefully for stones, burrs, cuts, or sores.

It is possible to take a fully mature dog and greatly improve his muscular condition and gait. Wonders have been accomplished in this department by new owners with great faith in the dog's basic structure, who took the time and trouble to build up the musculature surrounding the frame.

Not all exercise is good exercise. Some postures are detrimental to proper muscle development, especially in the long rear quarters. Pups should not be encouraged to stand on their immature hind legs for any length of time. Jumping is also taboo. The upright position puts undue strain and the young dog's full weight on cartilaginous bones and joints, promoting cow hocks as the dog turns his hocks in for better balance of the weight. The pup who loves to stand on hind legs, jumping up and down with excitement, front feet propped against the fence for a better view of the outside world is doing his legs a great disservice. Another form of damaging play is that resorted to by Afghan Hounds reared in confined spaces such as small pens or on balconies. To get exercise in such limited areas, hounds will take to wheeling and spinning around on their hind legs from a crouched position. This does the rear legs no favor, and can produce a semi-crouched gait as well as cow hocks.

No owner need become frantic everytime he sees the dog standing other than squarely on all fours but, if the dangers are in mind, the pup can be discouraged from turning harmless intermittent acts into firm damaging habits. A change of yard shape or fence type may get to the trouble. Roadwork, as outlined previously, is the antidote to such poor posture. The well-muscled hound who has learned to stretch his muscles full and long can throw off the effects of temporary pressures.

The show dog must learn to stand in a show stance calmly and without slouching, while the judge examines him. For every breed there is a specific stance dictated by custom and the natural character of the breed. The Afghan Hound stance is uncontroversial except in the matter of "tails." Since the disapproval of Venita Vardon Oakie in 1940, breeder-judges have deplored the lunacy of handlers propping up the Afghan Hound tail. Judge Cy Rickel has stated, "Basically, an Afghan Hound can show tails if it is a good Afghan Hound, far better than any handler can pose it . . . I do not know where or when this procedure started but, if it continues, it is certainly going to ruin tail carriage in Afghan Hounds . . ." Nevertheless, other judges and the majority of modern handlers have insisted on perpetuating this silly custom. The Standard says nothing about the tail being raised except "in action." There are grounds for suspecting that some handlers have used this trick to slyly foreshorten a long backline, which it does, or to minimize other unflattering effects. One owner freely confessed to holding an Afghan's tail "to keep the darn thing from wagging all the time." But, in the main, it is a frightening case of follow-the-leader. The tail that is flagging naturally at any point from the level of the back upward should most certainly be left alone! The low tail, or the unfortunate, tucked tail, must be left to the handler's discretion. If the tail must be propped, the handler does well to keep a wary eye on it, for unhappy tails can do some weird humping from the point of contact to the tip. A tail pushed too high can spoil a good topline.

The very young puppy should be introduced to the word "stay." This is best taught under home conditions with a minimum of distractions. "Stay" lessons work well when the dog is being groomed in a standing position. Increase the demand of the "stay" from a few seconds for puppies to several minutes for yearlings. It is also important to use the same word, such as "okay" at all times to dismiss the dog from the "stay." Give liberal praise with every bit of success. The dogs may appear not to notice the praise, but Afghan Hounds respond negatively to constant disapproval.

Once the pup knows the stay in quiet home surroundings, the lesson must be extended to new terrain, at which time it will undoubtedly have to be patiently relearned. Mock judging situations with the dog on the stay should be arranged with cooperation of neighbors and friends who are willing to run their hands over the dog's bite, paws, body, and legs. If the dog is jumpy about any specifics such as muzzle, paws, tail, then special attention should be paid to these spots daily.

Bearing in mind the desirability of maintaining good show posture at all times, the novice might do well to remember some of the old training tricks. Always pet the dog by scratching him under the chin or behind the ears, making the dog lift his head for attention. Patting the dog on the top of the skull gives him the idea of approaching his owner with head down for more convenient pats. Most Afghan Hounds adore having their chin and neck brushed or scratched and will stretch their head sky high in appreciation of the act. Handlers use this trick in the ring.

Placing the dog into the proper show stance is called "stacking." See drawing. Front legs are parallel and straight from elbow to ground as viewed from front or side. Feet point straight ahead. If dog stops in a naturally correct stance, do not fiddle with him. The most obvious mark of the amateur is the constant over-setting of the dog. If the dog stands with front legs out of line, correct them with a minimum of motions. Foot and leg adjustments are done most inconspicuously from the elbow level. Frequently, just a small repositioning of one foot will correct the stance. Some handlers place one hand under the brisket and between the elbows, gently lift the feet off the ground to let the dog drop true and even. For the front that is not quite straight and true, pushing the elbows out slightly will turn in the feet, and vice versa. Really faulty stance cannot be corrected past a point, and will bar the dog from winning at the shows. The off-balance dog will soon put his feet right back where they were comfortable, albeit crooked. Regardless of the leg fault, the dog will in someway compensate to retain his prime point of balance. Most fanciers have seen the faulty front stance manually corrected by an optimistic owner only to have the dog give the secret away the moment the judge lifts one front foot off the ground

254

and lets it drop—right back to its natural faulty position. The quickest way to make a judge suspect such a fault is the obvious amateurish twisting of feet and legs into alignment. When the front quarter has been checked and set, many handlers keep one hand under the dog's chin, or hold the leash taut over-head, while checking the topline and rear quarters for proper alignment. Reassuring finger-scratchings under the neck will help relax the figidity hound.

Back (topline) should be as level as possible from withers to hip-bones. As the top of a table is governed by the length of its legs, toplines are adjusted primarily through positioning of the feet. If topline tends to flow uphill towards the croup, hind legs may not be placed either back far enough or spread as widely as they should be. The downsloped topline calls for the reverse procedure. A badly sagging back, resulting from loose musculature, is a dead give-away the moment a dog moves and has no real camouflage in the ring, although some handlers surreptitiously try sticking a thumb under the loin to bolster the sag. Some dogs with a straight moving back often stand with a dippy topline from boredom in a slumped relaxation. A firm loving scratch on the tummy or a brisk turn around the handler may help to stiffen the profile.

Hind legs are correct when hocks are perpendicular to the ground and parallel to each other from all views. The pro frequently walks his dog into a perfect stance without laying a finger on the dog's legs. The less adept handler, with less powerfully muscled dogs will be making hock adjustments and hope the legs can hold the repositionings. Lift the foot lightly from the point of the hock to reset. Feet are to face directly ahead. Here again, as the hocks are twisted outward as with the elbows, the toes will turn in for compensation. In all large breeds, and especially in the more angulated specimens (which have potential magnificence when the musculature is strong), it is difficult for immature hounds to hold a really strong rear quarter stance. It is better to stack these hounds wider, rather than stretching the legs too far back of the point of easy balance. In backyard play, great change of posture of the adolescent well-angulated Afghan Hound can be seen as with maturity he will take to standing with his legs well behind a line dropped from the seat, and the high croup will drop as a result. The dog who is stacked back too far will only roll back from the front legs, which gains his handler nothing but a completely out-of-line hound.

Afghan Hounds stack best with calm adjustments and the fewer the better. It is not uncommon to see a good hound stop in a natural stacked pose, only to have its over-eager handler pick up every leg and soon have the entire dog unstrung. Uncertain figidity actions affect these sensitive hounds quickly. The best rule for the novice is to never make a change on the dog without a good reason for it.

In both gaiting and stacking, every hound will vary in its individual needs. The true secret of properly presenting a dog is in knowing the dog's assets and liabilities—knowing just where the dog does or does not come up to the ideal Afghan Hound image. Remember, the ideal image is presented in the Standard. Know it. The judge has less than three minutes per dog; therefore, it is a case of accentuating the positive and never drawing attention to the negative.

The beautiful movement of the Afghan Hound can only be shown to advantage in an adequately sized ring. It is felt that an indoor or outdoor ring should be at least 30 feet wide and 50 feet long, and under no circumstances be less than 30 feet wide and 40 feet long. Smaller rings can make a good Afghan with good movement look bad because he can't hit his stride. All show-giving clubs should provide rings of this minimum size for the Afghans. If they do not, Afghan judges and exhibitors should insist on it.

There are two distinctly different phases to gaiting, that done in a circle in which the judge is watching the side gait and the overall balanced picture of the hound, and the coming-and-going gait done with the individual examinations. There are different stories to be read here. In the circle, the length of stride, power of drive, and lack of interference is most easily viewed. The skillful handler, long before entering the ring, will have ascertained the most flattering speed for his dog in the big circle. The handler, with the ground-swallowing gaited hound, would be foolish to allow a "mincer" set the pace for his dog. There is no rule that says the fast dogs must stay behind the slower ones. But such maneuvering must be done with courtesy, not in rude drives that force other dogs against the fence or by allowing a fast dog to trod on the heels, or nip the rump, of the dog in front of him.

This large circling is vitally important in the initial impression the judge gets of the hounds and, right then and there, some of these dogs will be mentally picked as winners. The remainder of the

Stacked Afghan Hound.

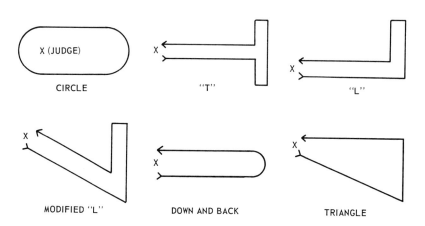

Gait patterns.

judging is a comparison of these dogs against the others. The novice, unless finding himself in the position of leader, should follow the pace set for him without trying any tricks and concentrate on alerting the dog to run gaily with head and tail high.

Once the judge has signaled the line to stop, he will examine each dog individually. This is the second of the elimination rounds taking place in the judicial brain, the first being the impression gained in the circling. The wise handler will not permit his dog to slump while the judge is examining other dogs before him or after him, for the judge constantly looks back and forth, making mental comparisons of this and that. Don't spoil a first impression by letting down in the line. The dog which will not stand still can be quietly moved around the handler from time to time and reset. The bored handler, gazing off into space while his dog takes on a sloppy stance, is throwing away his chances.

As the judge approaches the dog, step back, but do not drop the leash. The judge may ask, "How old is the dog?" or "Does he bite?" and should be listened to carefully. He may want to inspect the dog's teeth personally, or prefer to have the handler show the bite to him.

As a general rule, handlers always keep the dog on the left side, but the paramount rule is to see that the dog is invariably between the judge and handler. The owner pays his fee to have the judge look at the dog, not at legs or trousers. This takes a bit of maneuvering around the dog on the part of the handler at all times. In this matter, the novice would do well to study the methods of the professional handler.

When the judge has checked the dog's structure to his satisfaction, he will send dog and handler to the far end of the ring to see the dog's gait, this time with the emphasis on the coming-and-going aspects. Judges vary in their opinions of how best to view the gait and the size and shape of the ring must also be taken into account. There are several standard patterns, and attention to the dogs gaited previously gives the handler a fair idea of what will be expected of him. Follow the judge's instructions carefully. Some of the common gait patterns are shown in the drawing. These should be practiced with the dog always between the handler and the judge, entailing a bit of hand-switching and dog-turning for smoothness. As a breed

Ch. Egypt's Echo of Crown Crest (Ch. Felt's Thief of Bagdad ex Big Carmelita), silver blue bitch, dam of 7 champions, bred and owned by Kay Finch, Crown Crest. Shown as a puppy at top, and as a champion below.

noted for surefootedness, the hound that makes the smoothest turns wins the merit points. The fumbling owner who throws his dog off stride on the same turns earns demerits.

Take the dog back and forth in his best gait speed unless instructed by the judge differently. On returning to the judge, the dog may be sent out again with instructions to go faster, slower, or perhaps in a different pattern. The judge is usually not trying to find faults at this point, but looking for a special factor in the gait, or possibly giving the dog a second chance to get its tail up or move in a straighter line. Judges usually sense when a dog is not in his best stride and, if time permits, will often give the exhibitor a second chance.

A precious moment of great importance occurs when the dog returns from gaiting and stops in front of the judge. Here is the instant that the pro takes full advantage of. He will stop his hound and immediately alert the dog, knowing that the judge is carefully taking in the hound's natural "expression" at this moment. The Afghan Hound who stops dead true and looks the judge firmly in the eye improves his odds considerably. Such dogs are "asking for the win."

Once all the dogs in the class have been examined and the necessary comparisons and re-gaitings accomplished, the judge may have all the dogs make one final great circling while he makes his final selections and marks them in the Judges' Book.

Ribbons will be given the first four placings and the other dogs are excused from the ring. Recipients of the ribbons customarily thank the judge, and all first and second place winners are to stand by for possible further judging.

Training for show requires regular training sessions at home or in a handling class. Handling technique can be improved by having a friend take movies of your handling. Run the film slowly and study your technique. Improve your weak points.

Exhibitors frequently stand around to ask the judge about his placings after the breed has been judged. There is no rule against this, and occasionally really useful information emerges. Many judges prefer not to be put on the spot. Others have been embittered by quarrelsome losers to the point where they doubt the innocent intention of any questions. Some just do not remember the dog in question. This is a great pity in our breed where helpful and honest comment is golden treasure for the sincere but bewildered novices. The breed would stand to benefit immeasurably from extra time and effort donated by the breeder-judge in helping the novice better understand the breed and the dog beneath the fur coat.

While we are in no position to help the novice see his dog precisely as the judges see him, we do hope that we have convinced him that the properly presented and well-conditioned hound has fully deserved advantages in the ring, as such a dog pointedly puts his best aspects right under the judge's nose, rather than forcing the judge to come and search for his glories. It is not a case of which has the least faults as much as which has the brighter greatness.

Ch. Chinah of Grandeur (Ch. Shirkhan of Grandeur ex Saadia of Grandeur), silver brindle dog, owned by Mrs. Harley Miller and Sunny Shay.

Ch. Holly Hill Desert Wind (Ch. Kabiri of Grandeur ex Ch. Samaris of Moornistan), black mask apricot dog, owned by Mrs. Cheever Porter. *William P. Gilbert photo*

The following is a list of the Afghan Hounds that have won all-breed Bests in Show at shows reported in *Pure-Bred Dogs/American Kennel Gazette* through issues of December 1974. Every attempt has been made to assure an accurate listing. If, however, any omissions or errors are noted, please advise the publisher.

1934	Ch. Badshah of Ainsdart* (Ch. Sirdar of Ghazni ex Ku Mari of Kaf)	dog	
1935	Ch. Amanullah of Kandahar (Ch. Badshah of Ainsdart ex Zahera of Prides Hill)	dog	Multiple BIS
1937	Ch. Barberryhill Charlie (Ch. Badshah of Ainsdart ex Barberryhill Illusive)	dog	Multiple BIS
1939	Ch. Kerrin Fachamo (Ch. Badshah of Ainsdart ex Zahera of Prides Hill)	dog	
1940	Ch. Lakshmi of Geufron-Catawba* (Yudhajit of Geufron ex Tarawali of Geufron)	bitch	Multiple BIS
1940	Ch. Rudiki of Prides Hill (Ch. Badshah of Ainsdart ex Ch. Shireen of Prides Hill)	dog	Multiple BIS
1940	Ch. Barberryhill Dolly (Ch. Badshah of Ainsdart ex Barberryhill Illusive)	bitch	Multiple BIS
1940	Ch. Westmill Natanz* (Mukhlis Samarand ex Illima of Geufron)	bitch	Multiple BIS
1941	Ch. Hazar (Ch. Agha Kush ex Westmill Taree)	bitch	
1941	Ch. Kerrin Fachamur (Ch. Kerrin Fachamo ex Kali of Kushan)	dog	Multiple BIS
1941	Ch. Mogul of Arken, C.D. (Ch. Garrymhor Zabardast of Arken ex Ku Mari Khyaam of Arken)	dog	
1941	Ch. Umberto* (Amanullah ex Sheila Beg)	dog	
1942	Ch. Rana of Chaman of Royal Irish* (Ch. Westmill Bayezid Ansari ex Safiya)	dog	Multiple BIS

* Import

263

1944	Ch. Ali Khyber (Ch. Rudiki of Prides Hill ex Pommel Rock Kashan)	dog	Multiple BIS
1944	Ch. Yenghiz-Khan of Five Mile (Ch. Rana of Chaman of Royal Irish ex Ch. Rudika of Blakeen)	dog	Multiple BIS
1946	Ch. Zannette of Elcoza (Ch. Yusseff, C.D., ex Rani el Kabul)	bitch	Multiple BIS
1946	Ch. Asri-Havid of Five Mile (Ch. Rana of Chaman of Royal Irish ex Ch. Rudika of Blakeen)	dog	
1946	Ch. Rudika of Blakeen (Ch. Rudiki of Prides Hill ex Lasca Klana)	bitch	Multiple BIS
1946	Ch. Khanhasset's Kanda (Ch. Rudiki of Prides Hill ex Pommel Rock Kashan)	dog	Multiple BIS
1946	Ch. Karach of Khanhasset (Ch. Ali Khyber ex Ch. Shibergam of Dunrobin)	dog	Multiple BIS
1947	Ch. Five Mile of Smeich Diamond (Ch. Asri Havid of Five Mile ex Ch. El Mio Shellah of Chamee)	dog	
1948	Ch. Karan of Khanhasset (Ch. Ali Khyber ex Ch. Shibergam of Dunrobin)	bitch	Multiple BIS
1948	Ch. Felt's Thief of Bagdad (Ch. Sinbad the Sailor ex Kara She-Ba)	dog	Multiple BIS
1949	Ch. Majara Mahabat (Ch. Karach of Khanhasset ex Far Away Loo)	dog	Multiple BIS
1949	Ch. Maharanee Kohibaba, C.D. (Ch. Rudiki of Prides Hill ex Pommel Rock Kashan)	bitch	
1950	Ch. Tamerlane II (Ch. Oakvardon Charon ex Ch. Riverside Tuck of Pocono)	dog	Multiple BIS
1950	Ch. Turkuman Nissim's Laurel* (Chota Nissim of Ringbank ex Ch. Turkuman Camelthorn)	dog	
1951	Ch. Majara Mirza (Zombie of Dunrobin ex Ch. Majara Mihri)	bitch	Multiple BIS
1951	Ch. Yusseff Roylat of Rozeclyde (Ch. Yusseff, C.D., ex Zarice of Elcoza)	dog	
1952	Ch. Taejon of Crown Crest (Ch. Elcoza's Ponder ex Ch. Winomana of Rreks)	dog	Multiple BIS
1953	Ch. Majara Mihrab (Ch. Majara Mahabat ex Zaritza of Elcoza)	dog	Multiple BIS
1953	Ch. Majara Mardan-I-Ghayb (Ch. Ali Khyber ex Ch. Majara Mustapha)	dog	
1954	Ch. Karli Ben Ghazi (Ch. Five Miles Punjab ben Ghazi ex Trina Kush of Hazarat)	dog	

* Import

Ch. Kismet's Red Baron (Ch. Sirocco of Camri ex Ch. Kismet's Little Egypt), black mask red dog, bred and owned by John and Shirley Handley.

Ch. Shahmir's Sampson (Crown Crest Zorro ex Ch. Holly Hill Vanity Fair), black mask red dog, bred by Carol Murphy, owned by Galen Outhier (handler).

Ch. Artemus of Province (Ch. Zeno of Province ex Ch. Salima of Province), red dog, bred by Eugene Jantos, owned by Jane Jantos.

Ch. Benvikki's A-Bit of Harmony (Ch. Harmony's Bandit ex Kuh-I-Baba), black mask apricot dog, bred by Benson P. Lee, owned by Vicki Parker Lee.

1954	Ch. Ophaal of Crown Crest*	dog	
	(Ch. Nereus V.D.O.M. ex Pythia V.D.O.M.)		
1955	Ch. Majara Menelek	dog	
	(Ch. Majara Mahabat ex Ch. Karan of Khanhasset)		
1955	Ch. Zaamarakuri of Ghazni	dog	
	(Ch. Zaadulla of Arthea ex Winonie of Ghazni)		
1956	Ch. Crown Crest Zardonx	dog	Multiple BIS
	(Ch. Ophaal of Crown Crest ex Ch. Crown Crest TaeJoan)		
1956	Ch. Desert Chieftain of Mikai, C.D.	dog	
	(Ch. Taejon of Crown Crest ex Kismi Khan of Crown Crest)		
1956	Ch. Alla Habad of Karikal	dog	
	(Ch. Ali Khyber ex Ch. Kiam Jonel of Karikal)		
1957	Ch. Shirkhan of Grandeur	dog	Multiple BIS
	(Ch. Blue Boy of Grandeur ex Mahdi of Grandeur)		
1957	Ch. Crown Crest Rubi	dog	
	(Ch. Ophaal of Crown Crest ex Ch. Crown Crest TaeJoan)		
1957	Ch. Shahzenan of Moornistan	dog	
	(Ch. Majara Mihrab ex Djadji vom Falkenwalde)		
1958	Ch. Connors Mill Jeffara	dog	
	(Ch. Zaadulla of Arthea ex Kenya of Westgham)		
1958	Ch. Horningsea Salim Dar*	dog	
	(Horningsea Majid ex Tressilda of Tamara)		
1959	Ch. Crown Crest Mr. Universe	dog	Multiple BIS
	(Ch. Ophaal of Crown Crest ex Ch. Hope)		
1959	Ch. Hassan Ben of Moornistan	dog	Multiple BIS
	(Ch. Zaamarakuri of Ghazni ex Ch. Maymun of Moornistan)		
1959	Ch. Crown Crest Kabul	dog	
	(Ch. Ophaal of Crown Crest ex Ch. Crown Crest TaeJoan)		
1959	Ch. Kys Sheik	dog	Multiple BIS
	(Ch. Caliph el Kevir ex Pharaoh's Little Sheba)		
1960	Ch. Pamir Storm Ho	dog	Multiple BIS
	(Ch. Stormhill Silver Dream ex Ch. Patrician's Victoria)		
1961	Ch. Holly Hill Draco	dog	Multiple BIS
	(Ch. Moonshyn of Moornistan ex Ch. Samaris of Moornistan)		
1961	Ch. Javelin of Camri	dog	Multiple BIS
	(Jonte of Stri-Mar ex Karma's Jamil Khanum)		
1961	Ch. Tajmir Bhijupiter, C.D.	dog	
	(Ch. Karli ben-Ghazi ex Ch. Crown Crest Khittiku, C.D.)		
1961	Ch. Bacha Khiva of Kubera	dog	
	(Ch. Hassan-Ben of Moornistan ex Ch. Majara Munshi)		

* Import

1961	Ch. Crown Crest Taejakbar Khan (Ch. Taejon of Crown Crest ex Ch. Crown Crest Khalifah)	dog	
1961	Ch. High Life Hi Bibbi (Ch. Crown Crest Topaz ex Ch. Sultan's Cuttingadido)	dog	
1962	Ch. Kabul's Crown Crest Kachmi (Ch. Crown Crest Kabul ex Crown Crest Hi-Honi)	dog	
1962	Ch. Holly Hill Desert Wind (Ch. Khabiri of Grandeur ex Ch. Samaris of Moornistan)	dog	Multiple BIS
1962	Ch. Akaba's Top Brass (Ch. Shirkhan of Grandeur ex Genii Al Peraa)	dog	Multiple BIS
1962	Ch. Khabiri of Grandeur (Ch. Blue Boy of Grandeur ex Kushani of Grandeur)	dog	Multiple BIS
1962	Ch. Akaba's Kharma of Torrekesh (Ch. Akaba's Top Brass ex Akaba's Gigi in White)	dog	
1962	Ch. Chinah of Grandeur (Ch. Shirkhan of Grandeur ex Saadia of Grandeur)	dog	
1963	Ch. Crown Crest Mr. California (Ch. Crown Crest Mr. Universe ex Ch. Crown Crest Eve Queen)	dog	
1963	Ch. El Kevir Gallant Man El Mari (Ch. Ibn Nekhoro El Khani ex Ch. Laineux Kara Koh)	dog	
1963	Ch. Pandora of Stormhill (Ch. Shirkhan of Grandeur ex Ch. Stormhill San-Dhal)	bitch	Multiple BIS
1963	Ch. Sahadi Shikari (Ch. Shirkhan of Grandeur ex Ch. Crown Crest Khalifah)	dog	Multiple BIS
1964	Ch. Shahmir's Sampson (Crown Crest Zorro ex Ch. Holly Hill Vanity Fair)	dog	Multiple BIS
1964	Ch. Wendiblu's Bhi Ghana (Ch. Crown Crest Taejakbar Khan ex Ch. Wendiblu's Soraya of Taralane)	dog	Multiple BIS
1964	Ch. Starlight Knight (Ch. Akaba's Kharma of Torrekesh ex Hi Lane Camille)	dog	
1964	Ch. Cammars Pa'Yunga of Grandeur (Ch. Shirkhan of Grandeur ex Ch. Silver Pearl of Grandeur)	dog	
1964	Ch. Crown Crest Mr. Vanguard (Ch. Crown Crest Mr. Universe ex Crown Crest Kuchi)	dog	
1964	Ch. Harleanas Mukhalla El Wahid (Ch. Chinah of Grandeur ex Rhea of Grandeur)	dog	
1965	Ch. Ammon Hall Judas (Ch. Holly Hill Draco ex Ch. Holly Hill Lorna Doone)	dog	Multiple BIS
1965	Ch. Mandith Alexander The Great (Ch. Longlesson Jason ex Ch. Longlesson Ophelia)	dog	
1965	Ch. Cha Cha Cha of Shamalan (Ch. Crown Crest Zardonx ex Kara-Bash of Shamalan)	dog	
1965	Ch. Smoke Dream of Stormhill (Ch. Akaba's Top Brass ex Ch. Stormhill San-Dhal)	dog	Multiple BIS
1965	Ch. Dahnwood Gabriel (Ch. Crown Crest Zardoni ex El Amron Tarquin)	dog	Multiple BIS
1965	Ch. Kabu of Desertaire (Ch. Crown Crest Mr. Universe ex Ch. Zar-Kari of Shamalan)	dog	
1965	Ch. Balkhwoods Colonel Mosby (Ch. Infashia of Grandeur ex Shamask's Bakchi Sarai)	dog	

Ch. Dahnwood Gabriel (Ch. Crown Crest Zardani ex El Amron Tarquin), black mask golden dog, bred by Forrest Hansen and Donald McIlvain, owned by Mandith Kennels (Herman L. and Judith S. Fellton).

Ch. Mandith Salute (Ch. Dahnwood Gabriel ex Mandith Circe), black mask red dog, bred and owned by Mandith Kennels (Mr. and Mrs. Herman L. Fellton). Yes, it sometimes rains at shows.

1966	Ch. Sandhihi Joh-Cyn Taija Baba (Ch. San-Dhi's Hatim Tai of San-Dhihi, C.D. ex Ch. Dominja Joh-Cyn	dog	Multiple BIS
1966	Ch. Mahabbi's Continental Sytar (Ch. Mecca Tajma Khan of Tajmir ex Shalimar A. Chandni)	dog	
1966	Ch. Tajmir Gunsmoke of Mecca (Ch. Infashia of Grandeur ex Ch. Tajmir's Desert Dream)	dog	
1967	Ch. Rujha's Windman of Grandeur (Ch. Rujha's Rigoletto De Concert ex Rujha's Susahra)	dog	
1967	Ch. Holly Hill Gust of Excalibur (Ch. Holly Hill Desert Wind ex Holly Hill Dusk)	dog	
1968	Ch. Balkhwood Bank Note (Ch. Balkhwood Colonel Mosby ex Balkhwood Miss Sugar)	dog	
1968	Ch. Abashagh's Mr. Tambourine Man (Mecca's Shoe Shine Boy ex Amira Fatima of Abashagh)	dog	
1968	Ch. Altai Ataturk (Catom's Firdausi of Altai ex Ch. Holly Hill Hex)	dog	Multiple BIS
1968	Ch. Artemus of Province (Ch. Zeno of Province ex Ch. Salima of Province)	dog	
1968	Ch. El Grande Rojha (Ch. The Baron of Hide Away Hill ex Estioc El Scheherezade)	dog	
1968	Ch. Tully's Big John (Ch. Patrician's Sherwood ex Patrician's Sheila)	dog	Multiple BIS
1969	Ch. Coastwind Gazebo (Akaba's Allah Kazam ex Ch. Shaadar's Blajnhe of Karlyle)	dog	Multiple BIS
1969	Ch. Dahnwood Season of Bluemarc (Ch. Crown Crest Mr. California ex Ch. Wind Lass of Windswept)	dog	Multiple BIS
1969	Ch. Kismet's Red Baron (Ch. Sirocco of Camri ex Kismet's Little Egypt)		
1969	Ch. Taralane's Carpetbagger (Ch. Musket Fire of Cobb's Web ex Longlesson Summer Shadow)	dog	Multiple BIS
1969	Ch. Shangrila Pharahna Phaedra (Ch. Sandhihi Joh-Cyn Taija Baba ex Ch. Shangrila Pharahna Cleopara)	bitch	Multiple BIS

Ch. Shangrila Pharahna Phaedra (Ch. Sandhihi Joh-Cyn Taija Baba ex Ch. Shangrila Pharahna Cleopara), black and tan bitch, bred and owned by Dr. Gerda Maria Kennedy.

Ch. Sandhihi Joh-Cyn Taija Baba, originally shown as Joh-Cyn Taija Baba of San-Dhihi, (Ch. San-Dhi's Hatim Tai of San-Dhihi, C.D. ex Ch. Sandhihi Dominja Joh-Cyn), black mask red dog, bred and owned by Brandt and Dorothy Houtsma.

1969	Ch. Khan Dar Khan of Scheherezade (Ch. Sasha of Scheherezade ex Ch. Bletchingley Sahari of Scheherezade)	dog	
1969	Ch. Akaba's Royal Flush (Akaba's Royal Blue ex Ch. Akaba's Brass Bangle)	dog	
1970	Ch. Harleana's Arahbezk Del Wahid (Ch. Harleana's Mukhalla El Wahid ex Harleana's La Yanirah)	bitch	Multiple BIS
1970	Ch. Ammon Hall Nomad (Ch. Holly Hill Desert Wind ex Ch. Holly Hill Lorna Doone)	dog	Multiple BIS
1970	Ch. Pamir Ho Chester (Ch. Pamir Storm Ho ex Ch. Kabul's Carol of Patrician)	dog	Multiple BIS
1970	Ch. Mandith Salute (Ch. Dahnwood Gabriel ex Mandith Circe)	dog	Multiple BIS
1970	Ch. Belamir's High Tide (Ch. Holly Hill Rip Tide ex Ch. Lynncrest National Velvet)	dog	
1971	Ch. Ammon Hall Ter-Caj of Tajmir (Ch. Holly Hill Sultan ex Ch. Holly Hill Hex)	dog	Multiple BIS
1971	Ch. Ammon Hall Guru of Ter-Caj (Ch. Holly Hill Sultan ex Ch. Holly Hill Hex)	dog	
1971	Ch. Coastwind Jubilan Tiger Paw (Ch. Akaba's Sterling Silver ex Ch. Shaadar's Blajnhe of Karlyle)	dog	Multiple BIS
1971	Ch. Shangrila Pharaoh Bhima (Ch. Sasha of Scheherezade ex Ch. Akaba's Royal Gold)	dog	Multiple BIS
1971	Ch. Mecca's Mission Impossible (Ch. Mecca's Blue Silks Karu ex Mecca's Evening Song)	dog	Multiple BIS
1971	Ch. Kings Royal Ra-Bul (Ch. Keni's Shadrack of Scharlau ex A-Dar Zulinde)	dog	
1972	Ch. Tajma's Lluvva Bhoi of Zardonx (Ch. Taj Ma of Zardonx ex Sheba of Zardonx)	dog	
1972	Ch. Holly Hill Genie Ace of Spades (Ch. Akaba's Blue Banner ex Ch. Holly Hill Genii of Lynncrest)	dog	Multiple BIS
1972	Ch. Khayam's Apollo (Ch. Ammon Hall Nomad ex Ch. Khayam's Kism of Scheherezade)	dog	Multiple BIS

Ch. Ambrosia Bon-Nanza (Ch. Holly Hill Sultan ex Ch. Holly Hill Bon Voyage), black masked red dog, bred by Dann O. Maly, owned by Phil and Andrea Peck.

Ch. Caravan's Blue Passion (Ch. Akaba's Blue Banner ex Akaba's Moonlight Sonata), light silver blue bitch, bred by Elizabeth and Vincent Leap, owned by Glorvina R. Schwartz.

1972	Ch. Caravan's Blue Passion (Ch. Akaba's Blue Banner ex Akaba's Moonlight Sonata)	bitch	
1972	Ch. Kabik's Suna Dan'l (Ch. Kabik's Rodan ex Ronnee's Enchantress)	dog	Multiple BIS
1973	Ch. Ambrosia Bon-Nanza (Ch. Holly Hill Sultan ex Ch. Holly Hill Bon Voyage)	dog	
1973	Ch. Shangrila's Akabas Daredevil (Ch. Akaba's Blue Devil ex Akaba's Brass Taffy of Khayyam)	dog	
1973	Ch. Benvikkis A-Bit of Harmony (Ch. Harmony's Bandit ex Kuh-I-Baba	dog	Multiple BIS
1973	Ch. Geym Shades of Bou (Ch. Khahah's Abou Ben of Khayyam ex Akaba's Regalia Ruffles)	dog	
1974	Ch. Kalamazoo El-Achmed (Ch. Ammon Hall Nomad ex Ch. Windsor Way's Liana Von Kahl-K	dog	
1974	Ben Haasin's Czar Illya (Zari Pashnadiv-i-Zandik ex Ch. Ta Ala's Shodarrah)	dog	
1974	Ch. King's Royal Kaluku (Ch. King's Royal Ra-Bul ex Cinnamon of Bhambi)	dog	Multiple BIS
1974	Ch. Ninth Turn Argus (Ben Ghazi's The Silver Shadow ex Ninth Turn Black Market)	dog	
1974	Ch. Shiloh Addis Abeda Superstar (Ch. Shangrila Pharaoh Bhima ex Leah Khamara of Tamboran)	dog	
1974	Ch. Sandina Starstream (Ch. Coastwind Gezebo ex Ch. Akaba's Blue Bonnet of Sandina)	dog	Multiple BIS
1974	Ch. Amulet's Pinball Wizard (Mecca's Show Shine Boy ex Amulet's Honky Tonk Woman)	dog	Multiple BIS
1974	Kabik's Cosmo (Mecca's Sahib Karu of Ronnee ex Coastwind Grr-u of Kabik)	dog	

10

Coursing, Racing, and Obedience

DOWN through the centuries the Afghan Hound's existence was fostered by man's need to obtain game for sustenance, to protect his flocks from marauders, and eventually by his more sophisticated activity, the sport of coursing. Westerners entering Afghanistan stumbled onto a professional hound breed highly revered for its successful labors. In *Hounds and Dogs* Mary Amps reported: "They (the hounds) are both trained to hunt deer and wolves and also to course hares and foxes. In fact anything that will bring grist to their owner's mill. Incidentally they act as watchdogs also . . . In Afghanistan the hounds never show the slightest tendency to chase the innumerable sheep, cattle, camels and donkeys scattered over the countryside. They are thoroughly trained from puppyhood what to hunt and what to leave alone." Present day notes on training the Afghan Greyhound from a Middle East newspaper give a seldom-read story:

". . . They are trained for coursing and hunting from the age of two months; the 'prey' used for training is generally the 'Jerboa'

275

or 'Khanay' as it is called. With spades and picks in hand, the trainers take out the budding hunters early in the morning and proceed toward a line of 'Karez' wells, where the Jerboas commonly congregate and have their warren or holes. Soon after reaching the selected spot, the spades and picks begin to fly and, lo, a jerboa pops out like a kangaroo, which it resembles. The excited puppies tumble over each other in an attempt to catch the leaping rodent, but generally fail to do so and return after a few moments with tongues lolling and sides heaving. This is kept up day after day until the pup is one year old, when it is 'matched' with a more mature and 'seasoned' dog to chase the real game, i.e., wild hares . . . It is comparatively easy to catch hares in summer because they feed on green grass and plants and, therefore, are 'heavy,' but few dogs can grapple with the 'autumn' or 'winter' hares which, by feeding on dry grass, are as lean as a fine thoroughbred in racing 'form.' The owners fear most the hare with one ear standing and the other lopping down; such a hare is called, in Afghan parlance, a 'Chot-Khafi.' This is considered to be a 'mean' hare, which may break a young Greyhound for good. The 'break' occurs when a Greyhound pursues the hare or gazelle with intense concentration and uses every ounce of strength in its body; a time comes when the dog has had enough and something snaps inside him. He gives up the chase and lies down, but cannot get up; in other words, it is crippled forever and is ruined as a hunter . . ."

Afghan Hounds have hunted a fantastic variety of game if all reports can be believed. An incredible experience of big-game hunters with Sikh Indians and Afghan Hounds on a safari in the African bush country of Tanganyika in search of the fierce East African leopard was reported by Bob Wales in a letter published in *Kennel Review* magazine, September 1948. He observed that the Sikhs ran a brace of males after the leopards, males being of superior strength. The men and dogs hunt the beast using native drum corps to unnerve the leopard, forcing him from his refuge in the trees. As he forsakes the protective branches the hounds take over: "While moving under full speed, one of the dogs lunges and seizes the leopard's neck on one side while on the opposite side the other hound streaks in, slashing with flashing fangs, ripping and tearing out the

276

leopard's jugular vein." Mr. Wales mentions that the hound's hunting methods are instinctive rather than the product of any human training. The dogs are not held on leashes while hunting, but permitted to range free, ". . . ever alert and ready to pursue and bring their prey to earth." In the past few years there have been reports of the farmers of Kenya, Africa using the Afghan Hound to hunt predatory jackals. (This practice has been deplored by the English Dog Press as jackals are considered to be dangerous spreaders of hydrophobia.)

The Afghan Hound's reputation as a canny and powerful hunter followed him out of the East, but direct purebred associations with the chase have not been well established in the Western world. In England and elsewhere, where hunting or coursing was permitted, the desirability of obtaining "a little bit of the Afghan" was readily accepted. In 1911, with the great Zardin's memory still bright, Mr. Dunn put his red Afghan Hound, Baz, to Capt. Ellis' purebred Greyhound bitch, Explosion, in an honest effort to improve stamina and soundness in competition Greyhounds. In describing Baz, which was a sturdy 26 inches tall and weighed 62½ pounds (having a 32-inch girth), Capt. Ellis wrote: "(Baz) has a strong back, short coupled with splendid legs and feet . . . The dog himself has a peculiar look. He has a hairy coat, long face and ears, and a peculiarly gentle expression which made Mr. Dent remark, '. . . All you want is an organ to make you complete.' " The bitch, Experimental, resulting from the mating was most handsome but utterly smooth-coated, easily taken for a prize-winning Greyhound except for droopy ears and a trace of ring tail.

In these United States a confusing pack of varying local and state laws govern game hunting with dogs. (Hounds that not only seek out but kill game are taboo in many areas.) In certain states hounds are deliberately used to kill predators such as wolves and coyotes for bounty. Such game hounds are carefully bred for their job, go unrecognized by the AKC, and frequently show a strong dash of European gazehound influences. Braden Finch wrote of an early attempt at predator hunting with Afghans in a 1948 magazine wherein he stated, "But when the Afghan came to the United States a scant score of years ago, it was to work for his living, like any other immigrant. He was imported to rid a Missouri farm of coyotes! And it is recorded that one pair of these powerful speedy

277

hounds within a few months cleaned the coyotes out of one entire Missouri county."

For many years the hounds were used on jackrabbit and coyotes in New Mexico. Miss Amelia White (Kandahar) tells, "My kennel manager, Alex Scott, used to take the dogs out hunting. They had their own system, hunting in couples. One knocked the quarry down. The other went for its throat. Very bloodcurdling and effective."

Today, with the diminishing wild terrain and interfering local customs, gaze hound hunting is a sport indulged by very few owners. Of the hunting sighthounds, Afghans are in the minority because of the hazards to their coats.

To retain and regain the coursing assets of sighthounds in America, there is now organized agitation for the American Kennel Club to provide coursing degrees similar to field trials in other hunting breeds. Mr. and Mrs. Lyle Gillette (under the auspices of the Borzoi Club of America) together with delegates from other sighthound breed clubs, have begun to pursue this ideal. The AKC is not adverse to the suggestion but recommended that coursing rules be developed with all sighthounds in mind (from Whippet to Irish Wolfhound) for the eventual establishment of uniform licensed trials. To this end, a proposed chapter on Sighthound Coursing has been written with a description of rules leading to the possible title of Coursing Champion (C.Ch.). Current trials are run on a practice basis until such time as the AKC endows legal status.

The Pacheco Hunt Club in California (including the Borzoi fanciers who pioneered the coursing degree concept) hold Regular Stakes for Borzoi and Mixed Stakes for all other sighthounds during all but the summer months. The Afghans and owners that have turned out have been highly enthusiastic. The long hairs show a grand natural inclination for the chase. Janet and Gary Gustman's Sheba took the Bronze Medal as winner of the first Grand Course Mixed Stake in 1963 beating a group of Whippets, a Greyhound, and a Saluki.

The New Mexico Canine Breeders Association, a group of Afghan and Greyhound owners, used to train their dogs in a coursing park outside of Albuquerque the year round. Jackrabbits placed in the enclosed coursing park were taught where the escape hatches were when slower dogs, such as Beagles, chased them during the schooling period. During the actual coursing, the rabbits that did not go directly to the holes were caught by the gazehounds or provided a long course until the tiny exits were found. In all coursing trials, the hounds were awarded points on the manner and skill in which they gave chase, counting for as much or more than any kill. The relatively clear coursing park presented less of a coat problem for Afghans than the open fields.

Coursing Greyhounds and Borzoi are frequently active show campaigners, proving that fieldwork improves and tightens their condition rather than being in opposition to show exhibition. But the Afghan must contend with a fur coat that magnetically attracts weeds, burrs, and loose twigs. Retired champs, adolescent stock or non-show Afghans make up the majority of the faithful coursing string found in the fields. The solution of a possible field clip for Afghans has been mentioned, and some attempts at creating a sort of protective suit to cover the fur have been tried but not yet perfected. The best answer was self-discovered by the Afghan who spied a rabbit and, in direct pursuit, plunged through a neck-high mud puddle. The wet earth plastered the dog's fur to his body. After the chase his hair dried in the warm sun, and the loose sand easily brushed out. But this hardly seems to be a permanent answer to the question. It is to be hoped that the coat difficulty will be solved and that the fabulous Afghan will never be denied his full share of glory in any activity open to the Fellowship of Sighthounds. For it is in the fields that owners can best observe and preserve much that is precious to this sighthound extraordinaire in counterweight to what are sometimes artificial show-ring indications.

Rather than using Afghan Hounds for field hunting in America, fanciers have preferred to cling to remnant beliefs in the breed's functional ability through non-professional racing activity. The first recorded Yankee attempt at organized Afghan racing on a Greyhound track over homemade brush hurdles was made in the 1930s by Shaw McKean and Bayard Warren. But the Greyhound owners, soon wary of their vested interest, blocked the plan by making the track unavailable to the long hairs.

In surging battles, generally short-lived, there have been intermittent attempts at setting Afghan racing on a regular footing. Seemingly simple problems of finding permanent track locations and concocting necessary equipment have proved to be considerable.

Among Afghan breeders themselves, some were suspicious that racing could be harmful to show stock causing injuries. Others more reasonably protested the artificiality of racing mountain-bred hounds on flat and generally straight tracks. In match races with Borzoi, Greyhounds or Whippets, the Afghans generally brought up a game but lagging rear on the flat tracks. Farsighted fanciers feared that any undue concentration on developing flatland speed could conceivably bring about breeding practices that unwittingly might sacrifice the Afghan's precious maneuverability. The characteristic differences between the two breeds was amply and accidentally demonstrated in a race with Afghan against Borzoi, in which the Russian hounds not only outran the Afghans but, in their headlong flight, the Borzoi ran right past the lure and smashed into a fence just shortly past the finish line. Obviously the Borzoi were incapable of the quick stops and turnabouts so characteristic of the Afghan. In field hunts, observers quickly noted the manner in which the clever and agile Afghans twist and turn, always staying in line with the darting rabbit, easily overcoming any shortcomings in dead straight speed. It is generally agreed that mixed sighthound races are unfair and undesirable. In some areas experimentation with hurdle racing, better geared to the Afghan's unsurpassed effortless leaping, has been undertaken.

Embryo racing efforts have frequently spawned ridiculous fears among commercial dog and horse racing interests that Afghan racing might become a competitive industry. In California, horse racing groups, apprehensive that the fun races might bring back legalized dog racing in the state, contrive to keep racing dogs off fairground race tracks by subtle influence-wielding tactics. Certainly nothing could be further from the aims of Afghan owners who wish only to race their urban raised hounds, not for prizes or money, but for the stimulation, conditioning effects and joys of watching the flying hounds with fur streaming after them.

The undisputed father of recent Afghan hound racing is Earl Stites who, with the aid of Wendy Howell (of racing, coursing and show Whippet fame) set up makeshift racing equipment in Northern California in 1958. He was quickly joined by other fanciers and his efforts were made a quasi-regular activity of the Northern California Afghan Hound Club. Every race was an experiment with some new piece of lure, wheel, or box. Dogs and owners were enchanted with the new sport and added race events to Sanction Matches. These early tests spawned requests from Afghan groups all over the United States for written words on Mr. Stites' methods and equipment. Later the Stites moved to Southern California to establish the Orange County Racing Association. Previous to this move, another group of race fans, led by Bill and Gini Withington and Dick and Georgianna Guthrie, had formed the Afghan Coursing Associates in the San Fernando Valley area, inspired by movies of the Stites' early races. (The group's use of the word "coursing" rather than "racing" was a deliberate effort to circumvent experienced obstacles against any form of dog racing in the area.) With three semi-regular racing groups in California, show-giving clubs such as Santa Ana and Santa Barbara began to sponsor meets as added attractions at the conformation shows.

Afghan races are also held in greater Chicago, the Mid-West Club area, and Albuquerque, with other regions planning to join the trend when suitable track areas are located. Records of times and wins are not seriously being recorded as yet, nor is there any attempt to handicap the racers.

To the authors' knowledge, the only private circular track for Afghans belongs to Gertrude Curnyn and brothers William and J. E. Curnyn at Devi Baba kennels in Massachusetts. They have built a one-sixteenth mile oval track with turns widened and slightly banked. Six starting boxes are powered electronically. The lure, a stuffed squirrel called "Ignition Up," is mounted on the infield fence in a quarry conveyor. (As the trees in the vicinity are full of chattering squirrels that annoy the dogs, squirrel was chosen for the lure instead of a rabbit.) The dogs are run clockwise one day and then counter-clockwise the next day to develop muscles on both sides of the dog; this track is being used to condition show dogs as well as providing a sport for the owners. On such a circular track the dogs learn to take turns at full speed, a procedure that calls for fine coordination as the dogs must bank, hug the rail, and dig in all at the same time. The Curnyns take 8 MM movies of the races to study the dogs' form.

Almost all Afghan Hounds have a strong instinct to chase any moving prey and automatically love to run. But some respond to the racing lure far stronger than others. Just a few are born runners like Pat Ide's Botar who was practically unbeatable from the first

281

Crown Crest Behapi Goluki, racing in
the first annual races at Santa Barbara
in 1960.

Santa Barbara News-Press photo

Ch. Akaba's Top Brass (l), Ch. Van de
Nicholas (c), and Taj Taert of Mandeville (r).

Gene Daniels photo

Ch. Hullabaloo's Tiger Rag, "blasting
out" of starting box, owned by Betty and
Earl Stites.

J. Barry O'Rourke photo

Devi Baba Schooling and Conditioning
Track in Mass., owned by G. Curnyn.

282

moment he appeared on any track and caught sight of the fur lure. His eagerness was fantastic and he may well have gone down in racing history had he not lost his last race to an automobile, when he slipped unnoticed out the front door of his home. Such natural racers focus only on the moving skin, blind to all else about them and, at the end of the race, they refuse to give up, still fighting to get the lure from the keeper.

Other hounds develop a quick lively interest in the furpiece but lose some of their enthusiasm when they learn it is only a game. Those that thoroughly enjoy a good chase continue to pretend that they are on a mock-hunt. The Afghans that like a good free-for-all are the racing problem children. Many of these rambunctious hounds make fine competitive racers if they ever settle down and run directly for the lure, but too often are disqualified for interfering with other dogs on the track. Such rough tactics can quickly take the racing heart out of timid novice racers, and training classes should be carefully chosen to avoid putting youngsters and bullies together. Many fast Afghans are not real racers, but are followers, adoring the outing but with little incentive to catch the lure. The follower can be quite an aggravation to an ambitious owner when the dog proves that he can keep up with the very fastest as well as with the slower dogs and yet never attempt to gain and hold the leading position. Occasionally such a runner can suddenly be seen to "see the light," and in a flash, focuses directly on the moving lure to become a fine race dog.

Puppies are grand fun to race and are completely unpredictable. There is little need to worry about them overextending themselves, because when they are tired or reluctant, they can see no disgrace in refusing to leave the starting box or may just decide to take a nap in the middle of the race. Older dogs, however, can become carried away with the stimulation of the chase and run until they are seriously exhausted, especially on hot days. Only hounds in the peak of condition should be allowed more than a few widely spaced full speed runs per day.

Equipment needed for Afghan Hound racing includes a race site with straightaway of 450 to 600 feet in length; safe from automobile traffic; parallel a fence; reasonably level turf base; free of weeds and burrs. To utilize such locations, various local ordinances such as leash law, nuisance law and health ordinances may have to

283

be met. Racing muzzles are a must. Each dog should have his own private muzzle to prevent the spread of germs. Large sized Greyhound muzzles can be used. Racing boxes are highly desirable as it is practically impossible to get even starts when slipping dogs by hand. Dimensions of boxes are approximately 28½ to 30 inches high, 30 to 36 inches long, and 9½ to 10½ inches wide. (No wider, please, as some Afghans can turn around inside a 10 inch box.) Sides of box can be made from one quarter inch plywood reinforced at the edges with fir. There should be small holes just large enough for the dog's head at the front of each door to allow the hounds to see the moving lure take off. Both electric and hand devices for opening the doors have been used. Two sets of colored silk racing jackets with numbers in contrasting hues are necessary for identifying winners. (Moving red Afghans all look pretty much alike when muzzled.) Tripod and a lure reeling arrangement must be devised. A surveyor's tripod with a heavy duty hand grinder modified for a large spool can be adapted as a reel. A good grinder has a 12-to-1 turn ratio with 12-inch diameter core on the spool. This can reel in 250 yards of 60 lb. test braided nylon fish line in about 14 seconds. Other miscellaneous equipment that will prove very useful includes 100 ft. reel tape, hammers, rope and posts, stopwatch, binoculars, megaphone or "walkie talkie," starting flag, leather punch, extra muzzles, slip leads, table and entry forms, pencils, and paperweights, unlimited helpers (preferably experienced), and heaping portions of patience for all concerned. Groups who are considering racing would save many hours of experimentation by contacting existing race committees for specific plans and data on successful equipment and race scheduling methods already past the experimental stage.

Obedience trials first became recognized by the AKC back in 1936 after having been held previously in Europe. According to the AKC rules and regulations, "The purpose of Obedience Trials is to demonstrate the usefulness of the purebred as the companion and guardian of man, and not the ability of the dog to acquire facility in the performance of mere tricks . . ." Degrees of Companion Dog (C.D.), Companion Dog Excellent (C.D.X.), and Utility Dog (U.D.) can be won consecutively by all successfully competing purebred dogs.

The gazehounds as a group were rather slow to warm up to the idea of obedience work for formal degrees. Unfortunately the concept of obedience as a competitive sport that a dog with a conformation fault can excel in has never been particularly popular with sighthound fanciers. Among Afghans the list of obedience degree winners is quite short.

Ross Hamilton's Doreborn's Kamu was the first Afghan Hound to hold a C.D. degree. The year was 1939 and by the end of 1940, the dog was a C.D.X. He was followed by Mrs. Hovey's Ch. Harisun, C.D. Late in 1940 Elizabeth Whelan, who had previous successes in gaining obedience degrees for her willing Shelties, determined to put her Afghans through their paces, but found them quite a different breed: "When I started Maharanee on simple heeling and sitting, she was not the least bit interested and absolutely refused to sit— although I am certain she knew what I wanted her to do . . . After several weeks of doing nothing, I decided to try her again. Much to my amazement, she heeled and sat beautifully on the first try. She had discovered that when she did something well, she was praised, and she loved that . . . Afghans never forget a thing they have learned, but one has to be very patient with them in obedience work." Miss Whelan's Maharanee retired as Ch. Maharanee of Arken, C.D.X., and her Ch. Mogul of Arken, C.D., was a famous Best-in-Show hound of his day.

Within the Afghan fancy, obedience training is too seldom considered. Wild tales of the breed's stupidity, or its super-intelligence, have been circulated by the fringe. Other owners believe that like oil and water, showing and conformation do not mix. The record easily disproves the latter point as a large number of obedience degree holders are also champions of record, including the modern Best-in-Show hound Ch. Desert Chieftain of Mikai, C.D., and the group winning Ch. Khyber Kim, C.D., of the 1950s.

Concerning the Afghan's temperament and intelligence, there is much that needs saying. Trainers that want a high-scoring dog that performs like an automatic machine are certain to come away disappointed and oftimes resentful of the Afghan. These hounds are highly individualistic, but most of them retain a great sensitivity and stubborn sense of independence, being determined to make the final decisions. In other words, they must come to accept and to want to do the things that are asked of them. This insistence is a perfectly natural attitude for any hound whose function in life was to use *his own wits* in tracking down and overcoming treacherous wild game. Unlike many other breeds, at no time has the Afghan been bred for any form of mental subservience. For this reason they can be most exasperating to train, but a constant and fascinating challenge to the understanding owner. These breed characteristics are also noted by the professional dog trainers. Mrs. Frank Burger, who has a group of Afghans in her famous circus act, has this to say: "At present we use about 20 dogs in our act, 8 of which are Afghan Hounds. They are very difficult to work with as they are strong-headed and will only learn a trick when they are good and ready . . . However, once they learn a certain trick, we never have any trouble with them. It takes about two months to train a Terrier or Poodle, but the Afghan about one year. They are intelligent and independent and bribery will get you nowhere with Afghans . . . They are trained to skip double rope, a three round boxing match, cake-walk dance and about a dozen other tricks. They attract a lot of attention wherever they have been shown and we're very proud of them." Mrs. Burger has also confessed to having rather disliked the stubborn hounds on first acquaintance, but once she understood them they became her favorites.

Each Afghan has its own idiosyncrasy on what tricks it rebels against, but as an overall breed characteristic in the C.D. training, it is the "recall" that is the most troublesome; the Afghan by nature being a bit resentful of having to be told just when to come and when not to. Away from obedience areas, the fact that the Afghan hates to come when called is common knowledge. This command is best learned at a very early age, before the dog ever learns the meaning of unadulterated freedom.

Among C.D.X. Afghans, the most challenging phase is certainly the Retrieving, an act evidently alien to the Afghan's nature. Teaching this requires a saint's patience until the day when the Afghan finally accepts what seems to him a highly ridiculous act. You can practically hear them say, "You can put that thing in your mouth if you like, but I am certainly not going to put it in mine." From Betty Whelan's time until today, trainers wail about the vexation of convincing the Afghan that he should take and hold a dumbbell in his mouth. But all say that once the hounds accept this basic idea, teaching them the remainder of the retrieve is easy. All Afghans adore the hurdle work. In C.D.X. training, Virginia Withington found the long sit one of the toughest tricks for her dogs, and finally concocted a pulley tied-to-a-tree technique to prevent a dog from always lying down the moment she went out of sight. Afghan trainers become highly resourceful in pitting their wits against their clever Afghans.

Neither the age of a dog nor of its owner is a necessary deterrent to obedience training. Charlotte Gilbert when just 13 years old trained her Afghan, Valair Ditto of Dido, obtaining the dog's C.D. in three straight shows. And while it is true that most young Afghans are far too unsettled to take formal training seriously, Jean Givens (15 years old) set a new record for precocious learning in the breed when her personally-trained Firishta of Kubera gained a C.D. when just seven months and one day old. Among the older hounds one of the authors' own bitches, Ch. Sultan's Cuttingadido, C.D., began her formal obedience training as a five-year-old granddam, to dispute the "you can't teach an old dog new tricks" theory.

The first steps to the successful training of Afghans is to understand the breed nature and then to properly assess the temperament of the specific dog under training. The big brash hound takes far firmer handling than the over-sensitive hound who panics at the sound of a cross word or a strong jerk. It is certainly advisable to take the dog to formal training classes if possible, but several Afghans have won degrees based on training hints found in books. The texts written by Blanche Saunders or W. R. Koehler are the most popular. Afghan owners should avoid any obedience classes run by rigid teachers whose methods are inflexible and not geared to the individual dog. Cruel force will not work with Afghans. These sensitive hounds respond only to kindness, understanding firmness and great patience. They will turn sullen, mean, or hopelessly frightened if bullied in any way. Trainers must realize that the Afghan often goes through periods of vacillation as he accepts and then rejects training dogma before finally becoming a reliable worker. He is only making up his own mind about the worth of these things, and testing his owner's reactions rather than witlessly accepting commands. Very few Afghans are ready to compete for their degrees in any reliable manner at the end of a ten-week course.

A sensitive insight to the nature of the Afghan is provided in *Challenge for Angel* by Francis Priddy. This book is a teen-ager's story but is for both those who have and those who have not had the joy of training the unpredictable Afghan Hound. Miss Priddy has trained both her Afghans in obedience: Shah, a clown; Satin, a

San-Dhi's Kuza Nama of San-Dhihi, C.D.X. (dog), earned C.D.X. in three consecutive shows, average score 193 plus; owned and trained by Mrs. B. V. Houtsma.

Tut and Rajhah, the world's only boxing dogs.

Suzon, skipping rope in Burger's Performing Animal Revue.

High jump with Farouk, nine months.

good worker. Shah's counterpart in the book is Shazam or "The Abominable Snowman."

The best working Afghans are the ones which enjoy obedience work and associate it with praise and fun. The breed does have a weakness for tom foolery while working. This should be ignored rather than actually squelched to retain a certain amount of gaiety in the dog's work.

To date, just three Afghans have achieved Utility degrees. The first of these and probably the best known, having appeared in films, was Virginia Withington's Koh-i-Baba who became a U.D. dog in 1953. His degree was hard won. Baba, always a favorite with the ringside, was a terrible ham, considering the audience's reaction as his personal cue to ad lib. His favorite joke was an unorthodox method of coming to heel in which he insisted in hurling himself sky-high, spinning around in mid-air with fur flying every way, to land slightly out of kilter in a sedate sitting position next to his embarrassed mistress with a "Well, what's everyone laughing about?" expression on his smug muzzle. Some people accused Virginia of teaching him to do this deliberately, but the truth of the matter is that she would have much preferred that he confined his coming to heel with ordinary motions as the stuffy judges were often unamused, and points lost by this act often meant the difference between winning a leg and having to try again on another day.

In 1959 two other dogs crashed the tough U.D. barrier, those being Tazi Jini Mabat and Ivardon Tufon Khan. Dr. W. H. Ivans, Jr., was co-owner of Ivardon Tufon Khan which was trained and shown by Rose Thompson.

The long years of the breed in America have only served to prove the astute observations of Mary Amps who repeatedly stated that Afghan Hounds must live as partners with their loved humans, as when relegated to the kennel they become disobedient or half-developed. There are many cases of insecure or difficult hounds who were duds in the show ring until their self-confidence was bolstered by the proof of love and attention gained from obedience training. The only conflict between the two trainings is the temporary confusion that can be caused by expecting the dog to sit when brought to a halt in obedience work. But patient owners find that these intelligent dogs quickly differentiate between the demands of the chokechain collar and the light leather show lead. All other phases of obedience training are assets to a show dog, especially the "stand for examination." Owners who do not wish to chance confusion may prefer to concentrate on one form of training at a time and schedule obedience and then conformation aims accordingly.

Whether formal obedience is attempted or not, all owners would do well to remember the words of Lt. J. T. Sharkey who trained Afghans successfully in the service, when he wisely pointed out, "There is no such thing in civilized life as an untrained dog. That idea is a fallacy. Every domestic animal is a trained animal whether he has acquired good habits or bad; and whether he has come from the alley or from a fine home. Every dog is either trained or he is a wild beast . . . The habits he has formed alone from puppyhood, plus those he has been helped to establish, have been his training up to date."

The following list of Afghan Hound Obedience Titled Dogs places the dog by the year that the Companion Dog (C.D.) degree was awarded. This list has been compiled as carefully as possible. Some dogs on this list may have made their Champion title after they completed their obedience degree; their championship status is not necessarily reflected here. Any omissions should be brought to the attention of the publisher for inclusion in future editions.

Afghan Hound Obedience Titled Dogs

1939	Doreborn's Kamu, C.D.X. (C.D.X. 1940)
1940	Ch. Harisun, C.D.
	Ch. Maharanee of Arken, C.D.X. (C.D.X. 1941)
1942	Far Away Kuh-i-Dom, C.D.
1943	Ch. Mogul of Arken, C.D.
	Kerrin Fachamoson, C.D.
1944	Ch. Anubis, C.D.
	Kymor of Allsworth, C.D.X. (C.D.X. 1946)
	Laineux Baksheesh, C.D.
	Ch. Maharanee Kohibaba, C.D.
1946	Ch. Kush Omar Kaf, C.D.
	Ch. Yusseff, C.D.
	Far Away Ab-i-Diz, C.D.X. (C.D.X. 1949)
1947	Ch. Zevadne of Elcoza, C.D.

1948	Sushila of Kingway, C.D.
	Frosty, C.D. (Not registered)
1949	Kurki of Jofran, C.D.
	Tarza of Shalimar, C.D.
	Jinniyeh of Long Meadow, C.D.
	Shira Dar of Lakoya, C.D.
1950	Koh-i-Baba, U.D. (C.D.X. 1952; U.D. 1953)
1951	Ch. Azib Beg of Lazy T, C.D.X. (C.D.X. 1952)
	Tab Begum of Lazeetee, C.D.
	Ch. Khyber Kim, C.D.
	Durrani of Khym, C.D.
1952	Nekha el Khani, C.D.
	Jamna of Jebul Musa, C.D.
1953	Ch. Laineux Jaba Jinh, C.D.
	Safiya Al Baal Hamon, C.D.
	Ch. Windtryst's Ba-Liki, C.D.
	Jan Siyah Ru, C.D.
	Tazi Jini Mabat, U.D. (C.D.X. 1955; U.D. 1959)
1954	Ch. Rozeclyde's Jasmin Khalik, C.D.
	Sahib Ali Shan, C.D.
	Ch. Little Fir Cyrano, C.D.
	Taj Kallidassi of Bur-Mur Farm, C.D.
	Sambala El Myia, C.D.
1955	Ch. Crown Crest Kob I Baba, C.D.
	Ivardon Tufan Khan, U.D. (C.D.X. 1957; U.D. 1959)
	She, Daughter of the Nile, C.D.
	Valentino, C.D.
	Ch. Zarif of Hu-Ed, C.D.
	Ch. Suki of Bur-Mur Farm, C.D.
	Ch. Kisu Khan of Crown Crest, C.D.
1956	Little Fir Damon, C.D.X. (C.D.X. 1956)
	Su-Ric's Safar, C.D.X. (C.D.X. 1958)
	Ch. Desert Chieftain of Mikai, C.D.
	Ch. Taj Gin of Grandeur, C.D.
1957	Cyrano De Bergerac De Concert, C.D.
	Hassan Bey of Bur-Mur Farm, C.D.
	Hughcliff Theiz Macan, C.D.
	Badkash Rana of Wooten, C.D.
	Soraya of Sunset Hill, C.D.

	Ch. Faith, C.D.
	Ch. Fairlawn's Pasha, C.D.
	Ch. Taej-A-Belle, C.D.
	Turkia of Grandeur, C. D.
	Crown Crest Subhi Sadik, C.D.
1958	Ch. Crown Crest Jasmine, C.D.
	Raspoutin of Puhari, C.D.
	Mystery Minx of Granada, C.D.
	Little Fir Hazard, C.D.
	Caballero De Desierto, C.D.
	Ch. Crown Crest Khittiku, C.D.
1959	Sultan's Omar of Anaheim, C.D.
	Aladdin of Hu-Ed, C.D.
	Ghomoi's Ehmilhe, C.D.
	Ch. Crown Crest Rain Willow, C.D.
	Ch. Dezi Fury of Mikai, C.D.
	Hughcliff Beau Akiba, C.D.
	Sultan's Hareem of Shady Lane, C.D.
	Khan Yun's Sheena Deloro, C.D.
	Majara Midas, C.D.
	Mikai Tim Tam Tai, C.D.
1960	Princess Azymandia, C.D.
	Tasha Rana of Kabu, C.D.
	Lynbil's Buddakha, C.D.
	Ch. Jester of Longlesson, C.D.
	Sardar of Grandeur, C.D.
	Ch. Sardar's Sarlana, C.D.
	Ch. Shamask's Taj Alif, C.D.
1961	Alladdin's Zoro, C.D.
	Ch. Hurrah, C.D.
	Patrician's Dakari, C.D.
	Ch. High Ho's Khyber Khyaam, C.D.
	Mikai Tai First Love, C.D.X. (C.D.X. 1964)
	Bakira of Bachelor's Acre, C.D.
	Sultan's Capriccio, C.D.
	Bombay's Ebony Escapade, C.D.
	To Kalon's Aph-Phable Respons, C.D.

| 1962 | San-Dhi's Kuza Nama of San-Dhihi, C.D.X. (C.D.X. 1963) |

1962   San-Dhi's Kuza Nama of San-Dhihi, C.D.X. (C.D.X. 1963)

Ch. Sultan's Cuttingadido, C.D.

Ch. Tajmir Bhijhupiter, C.D.

Zarah Al-Yarrum, C.D.

Ch. Alif's Naveh El Kandahar, C.D.X. (C.D.X. 1963)

Ay-Rab of Amberlea, C.D. (C.D.X. 1965)

Charikar Sarabande, C.D.

Kopperwood's Sinbad, C.D.

Rhaffia, C.D.

Ch. San-Dhi's Hatim Tai of San-Dhihi, C.D.

1963   Shahmirs Saturna, C.D.

Ch. Pharaoh Taj Khan Khyyam, C.D.

Shahmir's Gayla Lady, C.D.

La Angel Del Desierto, C.D.X. (C.D.X. 1964)

Valair Ditto of Dido, C.D.

Pascha D'Orlando Peti, C.D.

Alif's Kalat El Kandahar, C.D.

El Mari Pasha of Khandu, C.D.

Ch. Taralane Jinah Lala Brijida, C.D.

Ch. Taralane's El Karubah, C.D.

Little Fir Mercury, C.D.

Ch. Charaj El Jasmine, C.D.

Shahmir's Pogo, C.D.

1964   Ch. Firishta of Kubera, C.D.

Little Fir Nebuchadnezzar, C.D.

Shahmir's Fiffie, C.D.

Shaadar's Lady Nathyia, C.D.

Taz Mahal Allah's Kamala Om, C.D.

Thunder Bay's Sonata, C.D.

Ch. Coronado's Miamana-I-Saki, C.D.

Longlesson Ben-Hur, C.D.

Rhyna Tayl Lynx, C.D.

Crown Crest Red Rock Luv, C.D.X. (C.D.X. 1968)

Kushkin of Thames, C.D.X. (C.D.X. 1966)

El Mari Khyyam of Khandu, C.D.

Ch. High Life Zareef of Camri, C.D.

H. M. Wells Silk of Shashmir, C.D.

Ramachandar, C.D.

Satin Selfada, C.D.
Ch. Yiil-Yiin Rampart, C.D.
Akbar El Kandahar, C.D.
Etaoin Shrdlu, C.D.
Winmarleigh Shadrack, C.D.
Valair Brazen Image, C.D.
Indrani, C.D.X. (C.D.X. 1966)
Benzaad of Grandeur, C.D.

1965   Ronanjo Storm Yogi of Samar, C.D.X. (C.D.X. 1966)
King Tutan Khamen, C.D.
El Sabok R Amadi, C.D.
Patterson's Achilles, C.D.
Ter Veen's Golden Babylon, C.D.
Farashee Kismet, C.D.
Nefertiti of Memphis, C.D.
Ch. Vishtah Jon-Cyn, C.D.
Ter Veen's Bijou, C.D.X. (C.D.X. 1967)
Saluda, C.D.
Ch. Concert's Firebird, U.D. (C.D.X. 1966) (U.D. 1969)
Kymer Kym Khan of Heritage, C.D.
Dragon Lady Darci of Swan Song, C.D.
Saakym of the Empire, C.D.
Ch. Winmarleigh Meshach, C.D.

1966   Akaba's Brass N'Soot of Camri, C.D.
Marway's Kassi Rama, C.D.
Tajmir Tangerine, C.D.
Continental Farah E Shastre, C.D.
Karosal's Bandar, C.D.
Ch. Valair Brass Knuckles, C.D.
Sir Willow Azerbaijan, C.D.
Bluemarc's Tameo of High Ho, U.D. (C.D.X. 1966) (U.D. 1967)
Ceylan, C.D.
Dingo, C.D.
Makarabi's Shana, C.D.
Prince Ahmed Khan, C.D.
Tamora's Sheeq, C.D.
Berrot's Vigilante, C.D.

Shadowlawn's Chinah Barai, C.D.
Syrahk Honey Bear, C.D.
Ch. Sunny Day Zibia, C.D.
Kahandii Ariana Pamir, C.D.
Ch. Serram's Kopper Kahn, C.D.
Shaadar's Jewyl of Tarika, C.D.
Shazar's Bomarc of Tasha, C.D.
Ch. Valair Circe El Sayyad, C.D.
The Sultan of Sarka, C.D.

1967   Taj's Ebony Wind of Grandeur, C.D.
Thunder Bay's Heather, C.D.X. (C.D.X. 1968)
Lac-Dar Ziva, C.D.
Pashto of Ghazni, C.D.
Omar Scent of Sandlewood, C.D.
Tomashah of Naej, C.D.
Red Rock Duhst, C.D.
Sebastian Idol of Shamalan, C.D.
Hi-Lu's Koh-I-Baba of Keva, C.D.
Ch. Kopperwood's Tartan of Camri, C.D.
Silver Cloud of Deer Run, C.D.
Erin's Singe Chien Al Bonn, C.D.
Marhjo's Hora Staccato, C.D.
Belinda of Ellis Farm, C.D.
Cheri's Apricot Sharif, C.D.
Jalalabad Kayan, C.D.X. (C.D.X. 1968)
Taha Kebir of Yhenn, C.D.
Cyndu's Suki, C.D.
Excalibur Black Narcissus, C.D.
Gay Alura Shesta Sprite, C.D.
Pati's Princess Alyoshka, C.D.
Rajah, C.D.
Sultan of Sarai, C.D.
Berrot's Scimitar, C.D.
Kamir's Greybriar, C.D.

1968   Ch. Ali Baba of Scheherezade, C.D.
Ch. Barbe Bleue El Sae-Zaan, C.D.
Blu-Kale Cinnamon Khyam, C.D.
Idyl-Dell Muztagh of Tajmir, C.D.
Samuel MG Vahja, C.D.

Ch. Concert's Firebird, U.D. (Ch. Rujha's Rigoletto De Concert ex Rujha's Susahra), bitch, owned by Dr. and Mrs. Franklin, trained and handled by Mrs. Joycelyn (Joy) E. Franklin. First champion with a Utility title in Afghan Hounds.

Pepper Howes, C.D.X.T. (C.D.X. 1971) (T.D. 1969)
Excalibur Desert Sand, C.D.
Mts Al Nary, C.D.
Ravenwood Cascading Champane, C.D.
Kasul Kif Saiyad of Peshawer, C.D.
Shalamar of Baala Hissar, C.D.X. (C.D.X. 1969)
Tanya fo Patrician, C.D.
Ch. Donna-Smain El Sayyad, C.D.
Durani Thunderball of Kalizma, C.D.
Motara of Pajarito, C.D.
Zaheda of Anadara, C.D.
Lady Bath Sheba of Kashmiri, C.D.
Lady Shavon, C.D.
Su-Saada of Province, C.D.
Samar Czar Tane, C.D.
Dahnkar Shammah, C.D.
Bowman's Jhaz Beau, C.D.X. (C.D.X. 1970)
Desert Beauty, C.D.X. (C.D.X. 1972)
Ch. Vinroc's Country Girl, C.D.X. (C.D.X. 1970)
1969   Ch. Kopperwood's Echo of Kismet, C.D.
Starlight Blue Gypsy, C.D.
Ch. Balkhwood's Maho-Gany Sher-San, C.D.
Gemini Aghanaut Bhavana, C.D.
Karlyle's Ninevah of Ijon, C.D.
Valair Brutus of Akaba, C.D.
Lynncrest Kurili of Andarab, C.D.
Shoreview Princess Kasima, C.D.
Marhjo's Valkazar, C.D.
Afsham's Photo Finish, C.D.
Churondola's Queen of Sheba, C.D.
Javalin of Scheherezade, C.D.
Idyl-Dells Mohammed, C.D.X. (C.D.X. 1971)
Princess Tanja of Pamon, U.D. (C.D.X. 1971) (U.D. 1974)
Shiek Mahmud Kandahar, C.D.
Halcar's Zsa Zsa, C.D.X. (C.D.X. 1971)
1970   Drum Hill Lyra Lisa, C.D.
Grand Lady of Diway, C.D.
Ch. Sheik Khyber of Antonio, C.D.
Kalizma El Hombre, U.D. (C.D.X. 1972) (U.D. 1973)

Drum Hill Amanda, C.D.
Fizabad's Rebel of Jericho, C.D.
Aradok's Balalaika Robin, C.D.
Sahara's Desert of Kandulla, C.D.
Zereda of Kandulla, C.D.
Ch. Crown Crest Texas Lone Star, C.D.
Ta Ala's Kahmi Darrah, C.D.
Ch. Longlesson Summer Sun, C.D.
Ch. Najla Sacher of Sherlistan, C.D.
Nattie, C.D.
Shandar Monki, C.D.
Sharif, C.D.X. (C.D.X. 1973)
Zandik Ahsand, C.D.X. (C.D.X. 1972)

1971   Abashagh Renaissance Fair, C.D.X. (C.D.X. 1972)
Ahmad, C.D.
Aisha Sultana, C.D.X. (C.D.X. 1973)
Alpha Dal Desierto, C.D.
Amber Lane's Kirsta, C.D.
Arbarre's Shaik, C.D.
Crown Crest Camelot's Classic, C.D.
Divels Kohizata, C.D.
Green Hills Bryce Cardinal, C.D.X. (C.D.X. 1972)
Jamna's Serenade, C.D.
Kaufman's Sir Charlemagne, C.D.
Khali's El Shem-Shi-Da, C.D.
Ch. Khan Dar Khan of Scheherezade, C.D.
Lohn-Dels Abigale of Aradok, C.D.
Loki's Ali Baba, C.D.
Ninth Turn Harvest Moon, C.D.
Peggy's Dream Serenade, U.D. (C.D.X. 1972) (U.D. 1973)
Sha's Harem Glow of Gemini, C.D.X. (C.D.X. 1972)
Ch. Shakar Zahrah of Kubera, C.D.
Sharame's Golden Temptation, C.D.
Sheba Mehsu, C.D.
Sheikha Mehsu, U.D. (C.D.X. 1972) (U.D. 1973)
Skol, C.D.X. (C.D.X. 1972)
Stardust Golden Girl of Akaba, C.D.
Tar-Zhan's Trina Tiara, C.D.
Tasha, C.D.

298

Two views of Indrani, C.D.X., bitch, eleven years old and still working in Obedience. Indrani is a Canadian champion. Owned by Natalie Waznys.

Photos by Jimmie.

The Doodoopukid of Durmaj, C.D.
Tsaru's Serendipity, C.D.
Yours Truly Gabrielle, C.D.

1972 Abi Ibrakim Pasha, C.D.
Angels' Sassy Brass, C.D.
Blackmor's Rameses, C.D.
Calahorra Isfandiyar, C.D.
Dureigh's Prince Stevie, C.D.
Ghahyl Temujhin, C.D.
Heatherleys Huckle-Beri, C.D.X. (C.D.X. 1974)
Ch. Holly Hill Mata Hari, C.D.
Honiego's Spirit of Apollo, C.D.
Ch. Jomad's Shiro Hime, C.D.
Khadine Faidhra, C.D.
Ch. Kismet's Jaccala, C.D.X. (C.D.X. 1974)
Ch. Kleopatra of Scheherezade, C.D.
Kyandra Moon Mist of Kashmiri, C.D.
La Rouge's Kings Gold, C.D.
Lynncrest Little Bit of Honey, C.D.
Mahirajah of Index, C.D.
Mehsu's Sharif Ben Cini, C.D.
Omar Sharif II, C.D.
Phaedra of Province, C.D.
Princess Saaj's Sa Mur, C.D.X. (C.D.X. 1973)
Rani Ari Pashami, C.D.
Samar El Cazador, C.D.
Scharlau Tazi of Sari, C.D.
Sforzy Feisal, C.D.
Shah Ben Khiva, C.D.
Scharlau Windy Khiri, C.D.
Shtaala's Buff Pride of Khafik, C.D.
Storybook's Desdemona, C.D.
Suzuki's South End Dhumble, C.D.
Tamora' Starlet, C.D.
Windsor Way's Special Edition, C.D.

1973 A-Dar Zulinde, C.D.
Alfique D'Amour, C.D.
Ch. Andarab Aida of Lynncrest, C.D.
Aryana of Rojan, C.D.

Sheikha Mehsu, U.D. (Shah Ben Cini ex Sheba Mehsu), bitch, owned by Leslie and Joel D. Nelson. Between her first and second U.D. legs, she took time out to have a litter of nine.

Ch. Belden Medina, C.D.
Ch. Big Poona, C.D.
Cleopatra of the Highlands, C.D.
Dic Mar's Moonlight Sonata, C.D.
El Tazzi Kisagotami, C.D.
Eshahan Mark of Love, C.D.
Ch. Grandeurs Little Miss Love, C.D.
Highhate's Blue Shayne of Jari, C.D.
Moniego's Image of Athena, C.D.
Kalizama Maharani of Antonia, C.D.
Kennelot's Thoughts of Gibran, C.D.
Keva's Sahara Sultan, C.D.
Ch. Kings Royal Lucinda, C.D.
Kings Royal Shadrack, C.D.
Loki's Promise, C.D.
Lord Merlin Tully of Asgard, C.D.
Lovely Lady Shasta, C.D.
Moonraker's Mystic Kadallah, C.D.
Nazrullah of Rojan, C.D.
Pasha IV, C.D.
Pat-Y-Bil's Kompatible of Camri, C.D.
Pla Vog's Black Orchid, C.D.
Princess Tiko of La Sonie, C.D.
Rakassa Jamal, C.D.
Sahaba's Mistress of Grandeur, C.D.

301

Saladin of Sacacen, C.D.X. (C.D.X. 1973)
Samarkahn of Scheherezade, C.D.
Ch. Santana's Maximillian Hunter, C.D.
Shikari's Ghiva, C.D.
Starlanes Standing Ovation, C.D.
Sweet Tczara of Fox Run, C.D.
Tarah Zael-Sheba, C.D.
Titan's Montezuma of Zareth, C.D.
Vantage Rinki Right On, C.D.
Wazir's Mood Indigo, C.D.
Westwind's Kuvi of Kuhsan, C.D.
Yoko Zackular of Mordor, C.D.X. (C.D.X. 1974)

1974   Apache's Apache Streak, C.D.
Beema Sena of Chales, C.D.
Belishaba of Shadsil, C.D.
Chaparral Chuka of Dureigh, C.D.
Chaparral Pagan of Dureigh, C.D.
Charisma Alpha Centauri, C.D.
Dhandi Musa Shafiq, C.D.
Eden's Lady Brandywine, C.D.
El Sultan Tabare, C.D.
Fizabad Alexia Nefertiti, C.D.
Hi-Lu's North Star Beau, C.D.
Jaduli's Alhambra Karim, C.D.
Ch. Jeffrey of Dea Zenga, C.D.
Kalahmere's Miroku, C.D.
Karebare Kharefree Karacter, C.D.
Kashmir Khan, C.D.
Ladenia of Rhaman Khan, C.D.
Majas That's Who of Fox Run, C.D.
Ch. Mandith Pericles, C.D.
Marrakesh Bachelor Button, C.D.
Ms Bombadil of Elrond, C.D.
Ch. Pla-Vog's Silver Peppercorn, C.D.
Pla-Vog's Thunderboltz, C.D.
Rob-Jo's Pandora of Altz, C.D.
Rokada's Rhaven, C.D.
Sabaca's Trillium, C.D.X. (C.D.X. 1974)
Sammi Raja's Somthin' Special, C.D.
Sappho of Serses, C.D.

Suzy, C.D.
Tajmir Bacchus of Kilnamona, C.D.
Tallee-Jolis-Noire, C.D.
Tamora's Black Knight, C.D.
Tasha Autumn Wind of Wildwood, C.D.
Tethys Tahr Tiki Tikura Topaz, C.D.
Thakur Orel of Seasu, C.D.
The Chase Gadabout, C.D.
Titan's Roohullah Scherazade, C.D.
Trail of the Cove, C.D.
Tully's Bu-T-Phal Delilah D'Naro, C.D.
Valair Taurus of Aswan, C.D.
Whiski's Black Windrose, C.D.
Schalazar's Hassan Ibn Sabah, C.D.
Schernova Tiara of Pierce, C.D.
Shah Alfredo De Kharisma, C.D.
Shah Jahann of Maya, C.D.
Shasta Sheimajr Mekim, C.D.
Sheimar's Harvest Gold, C.D.
Sherwyns Suzuki Bean, C.D.
Silk Hound's Marmaduke, C.D.
Sistin Angel of Scheherezade, C.D.
Sorkness Khristell Star, C.D.
Summyr Mist's Chamois, C.D.
Sundara Star Sapphire, C.D.

BIBLIOGRAPHY

ALL OWNERS of pure-bred dogs will benefit themselves and their dogs by enriching their knowledge of breeds and of canine care, training, breeding, psychology and other important aspects of dog management. The following list of books covers further reading recommended by judges, veterinarians, breeders, trainers and other authorities. Books may be obtained at the finer book stores and pet shops, or through Howell Book House Inc., publishers, New York, N.Y.

Breed Books

AFGHAN HOUND, Complete   *Miller & Gilbert*
AIREDALE, Complete   *Edwards*
ALASKAN MALAMUTE, Complete   *Riddle & Seely*
BASSET HOUND, Complete   *Braun*
BEAGLE, Complete   *Noted Authorities*
BOSTON TERRIER, Complete
Denlinger and Braunstein
BOXER, Complete   *Denlinger*
BRITTANY SPANIEL, Complete   *Riddle*
BULLDOG, New Complete   *Hanes*
BULL TERRIER, New Complete   *Eberhard*
CAIRN TERRIER, Complete   *Marvin*
CHIHUAHUA, Complete   *Noted Authorities*
COLLIE, Complete   *Official Publication of the*
Collie Club of America
DACHSHUND, The New   *Meistrell*
DOBERMAN PINSCHER, Complete
Noted Authorities
ENGLISH SETTER, New Complete   *Tuck & Howell*
ENGLISH SPRINGER SPANIEL, New
Goodall & Gasow
FOX TERRIER, New Complete   *Silvernail*
GERMAN SHEPHERD DOG, Complete   *Bennett*
GERMAN SHORTHAIRED POINTER, New   *Maxwell*
GOLDEN RETRIEVER, Complete   *Fischer*
GREAT DANE, New Complete   *Noted Authorities*
IRISH SETTER, New   *Thompson*
IRISH WOLFHOUND, Complete   *Starbuck*
KEESHOND, Complete   *Peterson*
LABRADOR RETRIEVER, Complete   *Warwick*
MINIATURE SCHNAUZER, Complete   *Eskrigge*
NEWFOUNDLAND, New Complete   *Chern*
NORWEGIAN ELKHOUND, New Complete   *Wallo*
OLD ENGLISH SHEEPDOG, Complete   *Mandeville*
PEKINGESE, Quigley Book of   *Quigley*
POMERANIAN, New Complete   *Ricketts*
POODLE, New Complete   *Hopkins & Irick*
POODLES IN PARTICULAR   *Rogers*
POODLE CLIPPING AND GROOMING BOOK,
Complete   *Kalstone*
PUG, Complete   *Trullinger*
PULI, Complete   *Owen*
ST. BERNARD, New Complete
Noted Authorities, rev. Raulston
SAMOYED, Complete   *Ward*
SCHIPPERKE, Offical Book of   *Root, Martin, Kent*
SCOTTISH TERRIER, Complete   *Marvin*
SHETLAND SHEEPDOG, New   *Riddle*
SHIH TZU, The (English)   *Dadds*
TERRIERS, The Book of All   *Marvin*
TOY DOGS, Kalstone Guide to Grooming All
Kalstone
TOY DOGS, All About   *Ricketts*
WEST HIGHLAND WHITE TERRIER,
Complete   *Marvin*
WHIPPET, Complete   *Pegram*
YORKSHIRE TERRIER, Complete
Gordon & Bennett

Care and Training

DOG OBEDIENCE, Complete Book of
Saunders
NOVICE, OPEN AND UTILITY COURSES   *Saunders*
DOG CARE AND TRAINING, Howell
Book of   *Howell, Denlinger, Merrick*
DOG CARE AND TRAINING FOR BOYS
AND GIRLS   *Saunders*
DOG TRAINING FOR KIDS   *Benjamin*
DOG TRAINING, Koehler Method of
Koehler
GO FIND! Training Your Dog to Track
Davis
GUARD DOG TRAINING, Koehler Method of
Koehler
OPEN OBEDIENCE FOR RING, HOME
AND FIELD, Koehler Method of   *Koehler*
SPANIELS FOR SPORT (English)   *Radcliffe*
STORY OF DOG OBEDIENCE   *Saunders*
SUCCESSFUL DOG TRAINING, The
Pearsall Guide to   *Pearsall*
TRAINING THE RETRIEVER   *Kersley*
TRAINING YOUR DOG TO WIN
OBEDIENCE TITLES   *Morsell*

Breeding

ART OF BREEDING BETTER DOGS, New
Onstott
HOW TO BREED DOGS   *Whitney*
HOW PUPPIES ARE BORN   *Prine*
INHERITANCE OF COAT COLOR
IN DOGS   *Little*

General

COMPLETE DOG BOOK, The
Official Pub. of American Kennel Club
DOG IN ACTION, The   *Lyon*
DOG BEHAVIOR, New Knowledge of
Pfaffenberger
DOG JUDGING, Nicholas Guide To
Nicholas
DOG NUTRITION, Collins Guide to
Collins
DOG OWNER'S HANDBOOK, The New
Hajas & Sarkany
DOG PSYCHOLOGY   *Whitney*
DOG STANDARDS ILLUSTRATED
DOGSTEPS, Illustrated Gait at a
Glance   *Elliott*
ENCYCLOPEDIA OF DOGS, International
Dangerfield, Howell & Riddle
JUNIOR SHOWMANSHIP HANDBOOK
Brown & Mason
SUCCESSFUL DOG SHOWING, Forsyth Guide to
Forsyth
TRIM, GROOM AND SHOW YOUR DOG,
How to   *Saunders*
WHY DOES YOUR DOG DO THAT?
Bergman
WORLD OF SLED DOGS, From Siberia to
Sport Racing   *Coppinger*
OUR PUPPY'S BABY BOOK (blue or pink)